AN INTRODUCTION TO
ECONOMIC REASONING

THE BROOKINGS INSTITUTION is an independent organization devoted to nonpartisan research, education, and publication in economics, government, foreign policy, and the social sciences generally. Its principal purposes are to aid in the development of sound public policies and to promote public understanding of issues of national importance.

The Institution was founded December 8, 1927, to merge the activities of the Institute for Government Research, founded in 1916, the Institute of Economics, founded in 1922, and the Robert Brookings Graduate School of Economics and Government, founded in 1924.

The general administration of the Institution is the responsibility of a self-perpetuating Board of Trustees. The Trustees are likewise charged with maintaining the independence of the staff and fostering the most favorable conditions for creative research and education. The immediate direction of the policies, program, and staff of the Institution is vested in the President, assisted by an advisory council, chosen from the staff of the Institution.

In publishing a study, the Institution presents it as a competent treatment of a subject worthy of public consideration. The interpretations and conclusions in such publications are those of the author or authors and do not purport to represent the views of the other staff members, officers, or trustees of The Brookings Institution.

An Introduction to
ECONOMIC REASONING

BY

MARSHALL A. ROBINSON
HERBERT C. MORTON
JAMES D. CALDERWOOD

FOURTH REVISED EDITION

Originally published by
THE BROOKINGS INSTITUTION

Anchor Books
Doubleday & Company, Inc.
Garden City, New York

FOREWORD

This book on economic reasoning is an introduction to economics for laymen. It is for adults who have a fragmentary knowledge of economic affairs and who seek a framework for more systematic thinking about economic issues. Its purpose is to help the reader explore the meaning of economic events and acquire skills for thinking economic issues through to some conclusion. It is hoped that this treatment will show that economic analysis can assist those who wish to reason for themselves and can help them reach independent judgments respecting economic matters.

The book was originally prepared for the use of adult discussion groups. The topics covered and the length of the volume were dictated by the needs of these groups. In an effort to help them, the authors have attempted to strip economic analysis to its bare essentials. They do not wish to make economic analysis appear easier than it is. But they do believe that laymen with varied backgrounds and experience, who are far removed from college courses and have many demands on their time, need a way to get started on the subject—a way to get into it. They hope that this book will serve to encourage further study. Because of the growing public interest in economic affairs in recent years, the audience for the book has exceeded expectations, not only in the United States but abroad as well. Translations have appeared in eleven languages: Arabic, Bengali, Dutch, Farsi, Gujarati, Hindi, Japanese, Korean, Marathi, Portuguese, and Spanish. A special edition incorporating a supplement on the Australian economy was published by the Tudor Press.

For the Anchor edition, new information has been added throughout the text to bring the statistics up to date and to reflect new developments. Essentially, however, the book follows its original plan: It is a *way of thinking* about economic issues rather than a full review of economics that is introduced here. The purpose is to show how to examine an economic question, rather than to display the warehouse of economic knowledge that experts might apply. Thus the approach is to present the essentials of fact and formal definition, and to hurry the reader on to a consideration of selected problems on which he may exercise his powers of analysis.

With each chapter there are suggestions for additional reading. The materials selected have been chosen for the purpose of helping the reader expand his general background. Therefore those interested in detailed analysis of specific problems will want to look beyond the selections listed. In the belief that an extensive bibliography frequently tends to discourage beginners by forcing them to make premature choices of what to read, these lists have been kept to a minimum. It is hoped, however, that with this beginning, readers will obtain the skill needed to select and read additional economic literature.

Three books that are especially recommended are listed below. References from them are given in most chapters.

1. *Economics—An Introductory Analysis,* by Paul A. Samuelson (New York: McGraw-Hill Book Co., Seventh edition, 1967). This is one of the most widely used books in the beginning college course in economics. The author has an easy style of writing. Technical sections that may be difficult have frequently been put in separate appendixes.

2. *Economics—An Introduction to Analysis and Policy,* by George L. Bach (Englewood Cliffs, N.J.: Prentice-Hall, Inc., Fifth edition, 1966). This book covers most of the same fields as the preceding one. It also presents an inter-

esting section entitled "Straight Thinking in Economics," which will be helpful in examining economic issues.

3. *Readings in Economics,* edited by Paul A. Samuelson, John R. Coleman, and Felicity Skidmore (New York: McGraw-Hill Book Co., Fifth edition, 1967). This book contains a large number of short readings on a variety of economic subjects. Some of the selections are designed to present the views of different organizations on highly controversial topics. To get the full benefit of these selections, they should be read after developing some familiarity with the subject.

These books have been chosen as representative samples of introductory materials in economics. As most introductory books in economics tend to be rather long and cover considerable ground, an attempt has been made to select those that do not have to be read from cover to cover. Generally, the authors of these books notify the readers when certain sections must be read in sequence.

This volume, *An Introduction to Economic Reasoning,* has been prepared under the direction of Dr. Marshall A. Robinson, Officer in Charge of Higher Education and Research of the Ford Foundation, formerly Dean of the Graduate School of Business, University of Pittsburgh, and a member of the Senior Staff of The Brookings Institution. Co-authors were Dr. Herbert C. Morton, formerly of the Amos Tuck School, Dartmouth College, and now Director of Publications at Brookings, and Dr. James D. Calderwood, formerly of the Claremont Graduate School and now professor, School of Business Administration, University of Southern California.

The authors and The Brookings Institution are grateful to many members of the economics profession and to the leaders and participants of test groups who generously provided suggestions for the improvement of the book. A special debt is owed to the following people who read and criticized an early draft of the volume: Sumner H. Slichter, G. L. Bach, Horace Taylor, R. A. Gordon, Arthur Upgren, Walter Salant, John G. Gurley, L. H. Kimmel, and Sylvia

Stone. The authors' view of the requirements of this type of book prevented them from accepting some of the suggestions that were offered; thus the authors alone are responsible for the final result. The authors are indebted to Edna Birkel, who prepared the manuscript, to Evelyn Breck, who edited the manuscript, and to Ynid Robinson, who indexed the volume.

The suggestion that a volume of this sort be written came originally from Mr. C. Scott Fletcher of the Fund for Adult Education. Mr. Robert D. Calkins, President of The Brookings Institution, proposed the approach followed in this treatment. The Institution is indebted to the Fund for Adult Education for providing financial support for this project. To the authors who have labored to prepare successive editions of this introduction to economic reasoning, the Institution is especially grateful.

Kermit Gordon
President

The Brookings Institution
1775 Massachusetts Avenue, N.W.
Washington, D.C. 20036
July, 1967

CONTENTS

CONTENTS

AN INTRODUCTION TO
ECONOMIC REASONING

Chapter 1

PROBLEMS AND GOALS

Economic problems are everybody's business because they are part of everybody's life. We read in our newspapers about taxes, foreign aid, strikes, farm price-support programs, poverty and unemployment, inflation, urban renewal, the impact of technological advances, the balance of payments, Medicare, the national debt, and many other things. We read of economic problems confronting the community, the state, the nation, and the world. We are urged to vote, to serve on committees, and to be for or against particular proposals that affect economic life. In fact, we are overwhelmed by information, interpretations, appeals, arguments, and advice.

To form opinions on current issues and to make judgments on public problems under these conditions, we all need the help of economic analysis. We need methods by which explanations may be found and alternative courses of action may be evaluated. This is what a study of economics can provide. Economics does not offer explanations and solutions ready-made. Instead, it offers the tools and methods for the analysis of economic problems. It leaves to the individual the task of applying these tools and methods to the problems he wishes to solve.

This book concerns a method of analyzing economic problems. It does not cover the entire subject of economics, but deals only with certain aspects of our own economy. It stresses problems of economic policy and explores them from the standpoint of (1) their effects on the growth and

1

stability of our national income and (2) their effects on the structure of our economic system. It concentrates on such problems and their background in order to illustrate the way that economic analysis can help the citizen.

WHAT IS ECONOMICS ABOUT?

Economics is generally described as the study of how society produces and distributes the goods and services it wants. More specifically, it examines the activities that people carry on—producing, saving, spending, paying taxes, and so on—for the purpose of satisfying their basic wants for food and shelter, their added wants for modern conveniences and comforts, and their collective wants for such things as national defense and education.

Economics also includes the study of various systems that people organize in order to satisfy their wants. These systems include not only the American system but also communism, socialism, the peasant village system of rural India, and the tribal arrangements of the Amazonian Indians.

Every society needs a system of production and distribution because the things people want are not provided free by nature. Goods and services must be produced, and the means of production—natural resources, human labor, machines and other forms of capital—are scarce in relation to the demand for them. Therefore, people cannot have everything they want. They have to make *choices*. They have to decide what to produce now and what to produce later, how to use their scarce resources most efficiently, and how to distribute goods and services among the people. They must also consider whether these choices are to be made by the government, by a free price system, or by a mixture of both.

As a first step to understanding how these choices are made in our society, let us look at our objectives. What do we want our economy to do? What do we want it to be?

THE GOALS OF OUR ECONOMY

The goals of a free society are the goals of its people.
The American citizen is free, within wide limits, to direct
his economic affairs so as to serve his personal and social
interests. He may save, join a union, buy a car, run a store,
and make a variety of other voluntary decisions. Political
democracy also gives him a voice in determining the role
that government shall play. He may vote directly for new
schools or highways. Indirectly, he may influence governmental policies by electing representatives who pass
legislation on taxes, foreign aid, control of utilities, the
size of the public debt, or other governmental activities.
Thus a predominantly free economy and a democratic
government give the American citizen freedom to determine his personal economic goals and the broader goals
that society shall pursue.

Some of these goals are objectives of certain groups;
some are objectives for the whole society; and some are
objectives that conflict with others. Some are transitory
objectives designed to deal with particular problems without reference to the long-run goals of the public.

A few of the more familiar economic objectives are
shown in the following list.

Stable prices
High wages
A better return on investments

Free trade among nations
Protection from the competition of foreign producers
Closer economic ties with our allies

Conservation of natural resources
Freedom from government restrictions
Increased consumption of goods and services

Increased leisure
Stability of income and employment
Technological advancement

3

Co-operation among economic groups
Increased competition
Government aids for various economic groups

The full meaning of these objectives may not be clear at this point, but the list will give an indication of the diverse, and often conflicting, objectives of the American people. How do we go about reconciling such divergent interests? This is not an easy task, and we shall offer only a tentative answer at this point. We may begin by looking for a common goal that seems to underlie all the individual and group objectives stated above. What is the broadest economic goal on which we can all agree?

The broad economic objective of the American people appears to be the achievement of high and rising levels of income and consumption under conditions that afford opportunity for individual advancement and free choice. Of course, we could debate whether having more goods and services will bring greater happiness or greater welfare, but in economics the amount of goods and services produced and consumed is generally regarded as one suitable measure of economic welfare. This does not mean that economists believe that material goals are more important than other—moral, spiritual, or cultural—goals. But they usually proceed on the assumption that each of us is the best judge of what will best serve his own welfare. They assume that our actions indicate how we seek our goals.

In general, therefore, the economist assumes that income and consumption can be used as one measure of human welfare because man has shown that he is usually willing to use his effort and ingenuity to produce things for his material satisfaction. But in every society there are economic, cultural, and moral limits to man's desire for more income and consumption. In this book, we shall concentrate on the economic conditions of welfare, leaving to others the larger task of defining what constitutes "the good life."

4

Greater income and consumption are only the first in-gredients of "economic welfare." A number of other re-quirements must eventually be added to arrive at a full definition of this goal.

How are goods and services to be shared by the people in the society? Should everyone receive an equal share or should 1 per cent of the people get 1 per cent, 50 per cent, or 95 per cent of the goods?

A complete definition of economic welfare must also include some concept of how much people should work. Should people have to work 6 or 8 or 14 hours a day? And who should make that effort? Should everyone, in-cluding children and the aged, have to work or should certain groups receive income without working?

The definition of economic welfare must also include some notion of what kinds of goods should be produced. Should production be limited to munitions and nutritious food or should a variety of things be produced? If so, what? Should some production be prohibited? If so, what?

The decisions involved in defining "economic welfare" are the basic economic decisions confronting every society. What goods and services should we produce and how should we produce and distribute them so that we will get the maximum yield from our efforts? In the Soviet Union and in France (or any other country), these decisions are made differently than in the United States. And in the United States, they are made differently today than they were made a century ago or even several years ago. The reasons for these differences will be explored in subsequent chapters, but now it will be useful to obtain a general idea of how these decisions are made in the United States.

HOW DOES OUR ECONOMY PURSUE ITS GOALS?

One of the important characteristics of the American economy is its strong reliance on individual economic de-cisions. For this reason, it is frequently given the name "private enterprise system." This term implies that an individual can usually choose his way of earning a living; he can save or consume as he sees fit; and he can pursue his personal goals even when they do not conform with those of society as a whole—as long as they do not unduly hinder important social goals or the freedom of others.

How this unplanned and unregulated economy might function successfully was first explored systematically more than 150 years ago by a Scottish philosopher, Adam Smith. In his *Wealth of Nations*, Smith argued that most people are primarily concerned with their own interests (that is, they want things for themselves, their families, or their communities). He also noted that if people will specialize in their work and exchange the fruits of their labor with one another, everyone will be better off. He argued that the individual could best help himself by producing the things that other people want. Thus with individuals free to show what they want by the prices they are willing to pay, producers would tend to supply the things demanded by the public. Free competition, together with a price system that reflected the desires of consumers and the capabilities of producers, would, he argued, bring order and efficiency to an economic system.

Smith recognized that a free economy needs "rules of the game"—and the government must be the umpire. When individuals combine forces to get the better of someone else, or when other private restraints are put on individual competition, the self-interest of one individual may actually harm the rest of society. Hence he argued that one of the necessary functions of the government in a private enterprise system is to control restraints on competition. With the passage of time, these and other "rules" have multiplied; they have multiplied because the economy today is much more complicated than it was in the time of Adam Smith.

As the American economy has grown, each part has become more dependent on the functioning of the other parts. Consider, for instance, the number of people and the variety of occupations that are required to keep the average city worker at his job. He is far more dependent than his forefathers on a smoothly functioning economic system; indeed, his life depends on it.

Understandably, then, additional "rules" have been developed to meet the needs of this interdependent society. For example, government now attempts to moderate the business cycles that throw men out of work in depression or destroy their savings in a price inflation. It also tries to reduce the insecurity of individuals by such devices as insuring depositors against bank failures, providing unemployment benefits for jobless workers, and paying old-age benefits to retired workers. In all these activities, the American people have used the government as a means of improving the behavior of their economic system.

Governmental intervention is also frequently necessary because certain types of economic activity cannot be carried out by individuals operating on their own initiative. A military force, for instance, cannot be operated as an individual enterprise. Highways, postal systems, water supplies, sanitation, police protection, and many other economic services have been found to require the intervention of "government enterprise." All of these services reflect essential collective wants that for one reason or another cannot readily be satisfied by "private enterprise."

The powers of the government are used to modify the workings of a private enterprise system in many ways. By tariffs the government tries to protect certain producers and workers from the effects of competition from abroad; by subsidies it encourages the production of a variety of minerals and farm and industrial products. It taxes the rich more heavily than the poor; and it even passes laws that help prevent one firm from selling a product at a lower price than another.

In view of all this governmental activity, the American economy can hardly be called a wholly "private enterprise system." Perhaps a better term is "a mixed economy"— a system based on a combination of private and govern-

7

mental economic decisions. Individual decisions in the free market still play a major role in determining what things will be produced and how they will be produced and distributed, but the effects of individual actions are modified in a number of ways by the government.

Thus the American people pursue their economic goals by both individual and collective action. Their personal decisions, the decisions of their "special interest" groups, and the decisions of their government have an impact on the welfare of everyone. To prepare the way for increased understanding of the importance of these economic decisions, the rest of this chapter will explore some of the problems involved in economic reasoning.

REQUIREMENTS IN ECONOMIC REASONING

In analyzing economic problems, we need to keep three basic requirements in mind. It is important (1) to use language carefully; (2) to abide by the ordinary rules of logic; and (3) to understand the tools of the economist and to use them as they are intended to be used.

Effective communication requires that words should convey the meaning intended. They should mean the same thing to the speaker and to the listener, to the writer and to the reader. Such abstractions as democracy, capitalism, and welfare are especially open to misinterpretation. Obviously, such abstractions are occasionally necessary (this chapter, for instance, has many more than the others), but they should be discussed and defined when they are used.

In economics a good deal of confusion also arises because many everyday terms are used in a technical sense. Thus in common usage, "production" means growing or making something tangible, such as potatoes or automobiles. But to the economist, production has a broader meaning. It means rendering satisfaction to others. The manager of an automobile factory, the assembly-line worker, the writer of automobile ads, the salesman—all are producers. Those who provide a service that commands a price and fulfills a need, such as the physician and the teacher, are also engaged in production.

Two other terms that cause confusion are "capital" and "investment." To the layman, "capital" usually means the funds awaiting investment or the stocks, bonds, and real estate a person owns. But to the economist, "capital" also denotes the tools, machines, factories, and other goods used to produce commodities. It is even used at times to include holdings of consumer goods such as automobiles and washing machines. "Investment" is popularly used to mean the purchase of stocks, bonds, and real estate or other property yielding an income. But to the economist, it generally means the expenditure of funds on new equipment and other goods used in production. It is, in other words, part of the process of creating "capital."

Other economic terms have several meanings. For instance, it is unusual to find a group of people (even economists) who define "money" in the same manner. All of them may offer reasonable definitions but, because each is stressing certain aspects, the definitions differ. "Competition," "depression," "demand," and "income" are additional words that will need to be defined when they are to be used in careful analysis.

The solution of economic problems requires adherence to principles of logical thinking. These rules cannot be reviewed here in detail as they would be in a book on logic. But warnings can be stated against several types of error that frequently creep into ordinary discussion.

First is the fallacy that if one thing precedes another (or always precedes it), the first is the cause of the second. The error is clearly illustrated in the sequence of day following night. Day does not cause night, or vice versa. Both result from the workings of the solar system.

Second is the error of thinking that a single factor causes a given result, when, in fact, a combination of factors may be responsible. For example, many people have

9

had the mistaken idea that wage increases were the sole cause of the inflation that followed the Second World War. In fact, a variety of influences were involved: the backlog of demand caused by wartime production controls, large savings balances, and easy availability of bank credit, to mention a few.

Third is the fallacy of supposing the whole to be like the parts with which one is familiar. For example, it is a common error to suppose that government finance operates on the same principles as household finance whereas government finance is really quite different. The government generally has substantially more ability to fit its income to its expenditures and substantially more power to borrow.

Fourth is the fallacy that if things have happened in a given sequence in the past, they will happen that way again. This notion led many people to expect a collapse in prices shortly after the Second World War.

Fifth is the error of wishful thinking—seeing what one wants to see and believing what one wants to believe. This was the prevailing mood before the great stock market crash of 1929.

Another fallacy, which is not limited to discussions of economics by any means, may be called "personification" of a problem; that is, identifying a very complicated situation with a prominent person. The identification of former President Hoover with the depression of the thirties and of former President Truman with the postwar inflation are examples of personification. This form of oversimplifying complex economic and political forces is a way of expressing emotions, but it adds little to the understanding of the issues involved.

A reasoned solution of problems also requires an attitude of detachment and objectivity. We must be able to accept logical results and not blind ourselves to them because we dislike them. "The first active deed of thinking," said Albert Schweitzer, "is resignation—acquiescence in what happens."[1] Objectivity, of course, is a term that is universally approved but only rarely defined. It implies that we are able to free ourselves from preconceptions that would otherwise prejudice our analysis and our conclusions. It is important that we understand the nature of some of the most common types of preconceptions.

Many preconceptions stem from personal interest and from environment. For example, a businessman who fears foreign competition naturally finds it difficult to think objectively about tariff reduction. He may have to struggle to be objective about a revision of trade regulations and to view the problem in terms of larger foreign policy objectives. Similarly, workers who want higher wages find it difficult to be objective about the possible inflationary consequences of a wage increase.

Other preconceptions arise out of past experience. Once we have adjusted our thinking to the times, we are inclined to continue thinking the same way long after the circumstances have changed and new patterns of thought are required. For example, we can neither understand nor deal with government today by employing the accepted views of a generation ago. Instead of bringing our ideas up to date, too often we attempt to escape from the problems of the present by seeking refuge in an idealized past.

Reasoning about economic problems frequently requires the use and understanding of statistics. Many problems can be more accurately appraised by reference to figures on wages, prices, employment, production, and a host of other economic factors. But statistical evidence must be used with care. It is useful only if we know what the statistics measure. For instance, what does it mean to say that the "average" family income in 1965 was about $8,400? It certainly means something different from the "median" income, which was about $7,000. The average merely divides the total income by the total number of

[1] "Religion and Modern Civilization," *The Christian Century*, Vol. 51 (1934), p. 1520.

families. Thus a few very large incomes can pull the average up quite a bit. The median (or half-way) figure shows that half the families got more and half got less than $7,000. The difference is important and must be understood if the figures are to be used correctly.

This book cannot examine all the danger points in statistics, nor can it provide a list of "acceptable" sources of statistics. It can only urge the beginning student to make sure he knows what his statistics mean. If he does not, he would do better to avoid them.

Another tool of economic analysis is sometimes called "model building." It involves the use of assumptions to simplify the analysis of a complicated situation. Rather than attempt to consider all factors at once, the analyst may set up a hypothetical "model" that enables him to consider various possibilities, one at a time. To take a simple model, let us consider the question: Will the sales of a particular make of new car increase if its price is reduced by $200?

Offhand, most people would say yes; but their answer is based on a "model"—even though they do not say so explicitly. In other words, their conclusion probably rests on the assumption that other things do not offset the effect of the price cut. It assumes, for example, that the incomes of potential buyers do not decline. If wages and salaries fall, sales may stay the same or even decline. It also assumes that sellers of other automobiles do not reduce the prices of their cars. Again it assumes that tastes do not change. If tastes change, consumers may prefer to use public rather than private transportation and have the extra income to buy television sets or some other product.

In other words, in order to state the effect of a price cut on sales, we have to consider the possible changes in various other factors that can influence sales. "Model building" is simply the procedure of thinking through the effects of such influences in various combinations.

Some of the more intricate forms of model building depend on a number of assumptions. These assumptions are chosen either to approximate the conditions actually expected in a given problem, or to see what the consequences might be in a special situation. As a great deal of economic analysis utilizes such models, let us attempt to clarify the procedure.

The use of models in economic analysis is similar to the sort of thinking we do all the time. For example, a man may decide to go to the beach on Sunday *assuming* four things work out the way he expects: (1) the weather is sunny; (2) the car is running properly; (3) his wife wants to go; and (4) he does not have to work at home over the weekend. There are other assumptions he has not put into his model because they seem less likely or less important; however, he is aware of them. For example, on the chance that his relatives may come for a visit that day, he tells his wife to have refreshments on hand. Thus he prepares for other possibilities, including the possibility that his assumptions will not be borne out.

It is also worth noting that in this illustration the man will probably not only announce the conclusion of his theoretical analysis ("we go to the beach Sunday") but he will also *state his assumptions.* If he fails to do so, he may be misunderstood. In other words, the "model builder" must explain both his conclusions and his assumptions.

The dangers in using models as aids to thinking are that some important conditions may be left out, or that a simplified "model" may be inappropriately applied to a complex situation. There is a familiar comment that "it is all right in theory but it won't work in practice." Yet if the theory follows sound logic and is applied where the model fits, it *will* work in practice. If it is logical, but is misapplied and therefore does not work in practice, the theory can still be valid for other occasions.

When economic theory is used in a changing world, a number of alternative "models" must be considered to fit the conditions that may occur. If, for example, we want to estimate the consequence of an increase in income taxes, it will be advisable to explore the results under several possible conditions. Three such conditions are (1) gradual economic growth, (2) rising unemployment, and (3) price inflation. Each condition, or assumption, will lead to different results because the effects of a tax increase are contingent on whether economic stability, depression, or inflation actually prevails. The analyst, therefore, justifiably says that the result will be one thing if one condition prevails and another if another condition prevails. His answers specify that *if* so and so occurs, *then* such and such will probably result.

Allowance must also be made for different results at different times. Because there are several stages of action and reaction in economic conditions, the economist must reckon with time in his analysis. A decline in milk production may lead first to higher prices for dairy products, then to higher prices for substitute products, later to an increase in milk production, and perhaps ultimately to a return of prices to their earlier level. Thus we must distinguish between the immediate—the "short-run"—and the "long-run" consequences of an event.

Clear and logical thinking helps us to make better decisions. The ability to apply the rules for clear thinking and the ability to use relevant information are basic requirements. Only if we master the use of simplified assumptions and learn to follow economic changes through to their many possible consequences can we arrive at useful conclusions for the conduct of economic affairs.

One of the major obstacles to economic understanding is the difficulty of sifting the volume of economic facts for those that will aid in the solution of a problem. It is important, therefore, to develop a systematic approach to the analysis of problems. Accordingly, the following sections illustrate an approach that may be used to analyze the two principal types of problems that confront the economist. The first is a problem that requires explanation, and the second is a problem that requires a decision.

EXPLAINING AN ECONOMIC EVENT

To explain an economic event is to answer the questions: What is it? Why is it? What of it? Suppose we try to explain a 5 per cent rise in prices as shown by the consumer price index. We want to know what happened, why, and what consequences may be expected.[2]

First, we try to *identify* the type of price increase that has occurred. Have all prices risen or only a few? Was the rise rapid or gradual? Did wages also rise? In other words, we try to determine the distinguishing characteristics of the price increase.

Second, we *look for causes,* by drawing on available information and economic theory for clues. If we observe that only the price of foodstuffs has increased, we look for changes in conditions that may have influenced the supply and demand for foodstuffs. We do so because experience tells us that a decrease in supply or an increase in demand, or both, tends to increase prices. Thus we might look for the causes in a possible crop failure, interruptions in food processing, changes in consumer demand, or comparable factors.

If, however, we observe that prices of clothing, furniture, and most consumer goods are also rising, we look for changes in conditions that affect the whole price structure: an increase in government spending or an increase in the money supply, for example. We do so because economic analysis tells us that an increase in total spending in the economy without a comparable increase in the supply of goods tends to increase prices. These, of course, are but a few of the possible causal factors. Many alternatives

---

[2] This price index is an average of the prices of many items, expressed as a percentage of some "base period." For instance, if we decide that the average of the prices consumers paid in the "base period" 1957–59 will be labeled 100, then a 5 per cent rise from that period will cause the index to rise to 105.

must be examined to attempt to discover why the event occurred.

Third, we *explore the possible implications* of the event. Although we can never know definitely what will occur in the future, it is important to figure out what is possible, and what is probable; a bare description of an economic event is seldom useful. Are prices likely to continue rising, to level off, or to decline? Will the price increase result in fewer sales and decreased production? The implications for future prices, production, and employment are what give the price increase its greatest significance. We try to determine the implications or potentialities of an event by reasoning out what could follow from it under various conditions. We look for historical precedents. Does past experience with inflation suggest any clues? We also make assumptions for purposes of analysis that certain conditions may or may not prevail—that the economy will be in a boom or a depression, that war or peace will prevail, that production will expand or shrink with rising prices. Under each of these sets of assumptions about future conditions, we reason through the possible consequences of the price rise under study.

There are therefore three steps in explaining an economic event:

1. *Identify the event by describing it and by comparing it with other events that are similar and familiar.*

2. *Explore the factors that may have caused the event.*

3. *Try to discover the implications of the event by considering what the consequences might be under various circumstances.*

MAKING ECONOMIC DECISIONS

Problems of decision require the consideration of alternatives. Personal problems of decision (such as buying a car or home), business problems (such as setting production levels or sales policies), and public policy problems confronting citizens all require the same basic methods of analysis. They require an examination of *alternative* policies or courses of action for achieving goals and a *choice*.

We can illustrate in simplified form the main steps involved in the analysis of an economic problem by continuing the example of the 5 per cent increase in the consumer price index. An increase of about this size occurred between June 1950 and December 1950—the first six months of the Korean War.

1. *Identify the problem and define the issues.* The first step in dealing with any problem is to make sure the problem is understood. A problem that has not been identified cannot be solved. In the foregoing illustration, a problem was created by the increase in consumer prices (as well as other prices), which was harming certain consumer and business groups. Rising prices also threatened to lead to labor strikes, further hoarding of goods, and other disruptions in the war program.

The background for this problem was also identifiable: a gradual inflation since the close of the Second World War, interrupted briefly during the recession of 1949, and a wave of panic buying after the Korean War began. Complicating factors were also identified: the growing drain of men and materials from the civilian economy into military production; the growth of credit purchases by consumers; the tendency for consumers to cut down on savings in order to purchase scarce goods; and the uncertainty about the possible severity and duration of the war, to mention a few.

2. *Identify the objectives.* The objectives or goals that are to be served are often vague and require specific identification. In the foregoing illustration, the immediate goal seemed quite clear: to restore stability to the general price level. But in striving for any goal, a host of related conditions must also be met. These requirements must also be identified.

Following the invasion of Korea, the nation wanted price stability, but it also wanted an enlarged defense pro-

17

gram. Moreover, it did not seem to want price stability at the cost of destroying the prevailing economic system.

Therefore, any price stabilization program would have to allow, among other things, for large governmental purchases of goods and services and continuation of private enterprise in production and distribution and as few direct controls over the use of our resources as were necessary. Obviously, there were some conflicts in these objectives, and the conflicts had to be identified so that a choice might be made.

3. *Pose and analyze the alternative courses of action.* Seldom is there only one way to deal with a problem. It is important to seek a number of alternatives and to consider the probable consequences of each one. In the foregoing illustration, a federal tax on consumption spending was not considered to be a feasible alternative because of the belief that such a tax works an unfair hardship on lower-income groups. (Does this imply another goal?)

Public policy makers studied the alternative ways by which the government could encourage consumer saving. They studied alternative types of taxation—"luxury" taxes, income taxes, manufacturers' taxes, and corporation taxes. They explored the feasibility of various types of legal price and wage ceilings. They evaluated the possible effects of increasing interest rates, rationing materials, restricting speculation, and so on.

4. *Appraise the alternatives and decide.* The choice of one or of a combination of different courses of action rests upon an evaluation of the possible consequences of these alternatives. How far will each advance the nation toward its objectives, and at what cost? It may also involve a restudy of the goals. In this instance, the government was persuaded to adopt the several measures it thought would be most productive. The program that gradually emerged included, among other measures, a variety of credit restraints, tax increases, a new savings bond program, increases in interest rates, and limited price and wage ceilings. The government did not at that time prohibit all

price or wage increases, draft labor, or ration consumer goods.

Thus a number of policies were adopted or rejected in dealing with this complicated problem. Some of the policies aided price stability without conflicting with other goals, but some, such as price and wage controls and the control of scarce metals, were imposed even though they directly restricted economic freedom. Such conflicts in goals must generally be faced time and again in exploring the consequences of various measures. The problem therefore is not merely a process of choosing alternative ways to reach a given goal—it also involves a *choice* among goals.

To summarize, the foregoing steps are:

1. *Identify the problem and clarify the issues by studying their background and origin.*

2. *Identify the objectives and requirements that must be met in treating the problem.*

3. *Pose the alternative courses of action and analyze their consequences.*

4. *Appraise the alternatives and decide by determining how well each alternative fulfills the objectives and requirements.*

This chapter has stressed the following ideas:

1. Every society contains a variety of individuals and groups with divergent goals. Because economic resources are scarce in relation to wants, each society must, therefore, devise a way to select the goals it will pursue. In the American economy this selection is made by a combination of individual and group decisions. The study of economics is largely devoted to the implications of these decisions.

2. The beginning study of economics does not require an extensive vocabulary as long as the student will make sure the terms he is using are clear to him and to others. Poor use of logic and the careless use of assumptions are by far the greatest handicaps to an understanding of economic affairs. Because our economy is a complex, inter-

dependent system, it is important to go beyond superficial or fragmentary information to get a complete answer to an economic question.

3. In dealing with questions of economic policy (deciding what to do) it is important to take the time to decide what we *want* to accomplish. Then, by analyzing the consequences of various plans of action, we can make a reasoned decision on what we should do. Skill in "analyzing the consequences" is, for the most part, the major benefit of studying economics.

Suggested Reading

Paul A. Samuelson, *Economics—An Introductory Analysis* (Seventh edition, 1967), Chaps. 1 and 2, pp. 1–38. George L. Bach, *Economics—An Introduction to Analysis and Policy* (Fifth edition, 1966), Chaps. 1 and 2, pp. 1–21. These readings discuss the ways in which economic affairs influence our lives, the topics included in economics, and some of the problems involved in thinking about economic affairs. Further references to these two volumes appear in most of the chapters that follow; additional comments about them are located in the Foreword of this book.

Chapter 2

THE ECONOMY AND ITS INCOME

No Jack-of-all-trades could possibly produce for himself the extraordinary assortment of goods and services that a modern industrial economy puts within his reach. We know this well enough from our own experience. Virtually no one today is entirely self-sufficient. Division of labor and technological progress have made all of us dependent on the energy, skill, and creativity of others.

What may be less apparent is the way all the specialized tasks and diverse economic institutions are co-ordinated. If we have thought about the matter at all, we have probably been puzzled about how things get done in a predominantly free economy. For example, more than 70 million Americans are at work producing goods and services for the nation. They are operating over 4 million farms, over 4 million business establishments, and over 100,000 governmental units that have an economic as well as governmental role to fulfill. By the end of 1965, they were producing goods and services at the rate of more than $700 billion per year.

But if we look to see who is calling signals, or who has the master plan, we look in vain. No central authority has told workers where to work or what occupations to choose. No blueprint decreed that movies should be made in Hollywood and steel in Pittsburgh, or that many people should start to consume oleomargarine instead of butter. The 8.8 million cars and trucks that rolled off the assembly lines in 1965 were not produced as part of any grand national design. Nevertheless, these things have happened.

21

How, then, are things co-ordinated in the American economy? This is one of the first questions we must explore if we are to prepare ourselves for analyzing economic problems and policies. Therefore, in this chapter we shall try to see how our economy manages to get things produced and distributed. Then we shall look at the national income statistics that help keep us informed about how the economy is working. Finally, we shall examine the way in which income is distributed, and the controversial and troublesome problems associated with this distribution.

THE "MARKET SYSTEM"

Chapter 1 stated that every economic system must answer three basic questions: What will be produced? How will things be produced? Who will receive what is produced? In the United States, the "market system" provides most of the answers to these basic questions.

A "market" permits goods and services to be bought and sold. Some markets are geographically small, covering only one town or a few city blocks; others are national or international in scope. For instance, a local restaurant typically draws its customers from a limited area, while a leading chemical manufacturing concern may draw its customers from all over the world. Some markets have a large number of buyers and sellers, and some have only a few. Some markets are tightly controlled by the government, and some are wholly private. Some involve transactions in only one specified product, and others include a wide assortment of products. Buyers and sellers in some markets make careful and rational decisions, and in others they act on the basis of habit, custom, or spur-of-the-moment impulses. In spite of these differences, all markets have certain common characteristics—they provide a link between consumers and producers, and they permit the exchange of goods and services.

The term "market system" has a more explicit meaning than mere exchange. Generally, it refers to the economic relationships in a society in which the physical means of production are privately owned, and in which private individuals respond to opportunities for greater income. In a market system prices for goods and services are the basic signals that direct production and distribution. Prices in a market system are determined largely by impersonal relations between buyers and sellers rather than by government order.

Deciding What Will Be Produced

In a sense, consumers "vote" for what they want by spending their incomes on the things they most desire. Producers tend to respond to these "votes" in order to earn income. The producer tries, by advertising and other means, to make consumers want his product, but in the last analysis, his output reflects "the election returns." When consumers are willing to pay enough to cover the costs of production and a profit to the producer, a commodity will tend to be produced. If consumers will not pay enough for a commodity, that item will generally be dropped and other commodities will be produced.

The market system also helps indicate how much to provide for investment in the improvement of our productive capacity. When people save, they reduce the number of votes cast for consumption goods. By making their savings available to business firms, they enable business to "vote" for the production of tools, machines, and other capital goods. Thus if producers are willing to pay an adequate reward to lenders, they may induce people to use their income for investment rather than consumption.

The market system is impersonal; it does not supply a moral judgment of the pattern of consumer demand. If the pattern of consumer demand were to give preference to submachine guns or opium instead of typewriters and flowers, the market system would tend to deliver a corresponding pattern of production. As producers in a market system only respond to consumer desires that are backed up with money, the system will supply a whipped cream

23

dessert for a fashionable party even though some poor children are going without milk.

The market mechanism does not have complete control over what we produce. In this country, laws control the production and sale of submachine guns and opium, and public funds provide free milk for poor children. In other words, buyers and sellers in the market do not give all the answers to the question what will be produced; society, operating through the government, also exerts some control. By taxation, the government reduces our power to "vote" for goods we want, and by passing and enforcing laws, it bans or regulates some production and exchange.

Deciding How Things Are to Be Produced

Once the market has indicated what to produce, a choice must be made of the mode of production. Should it be produced with many workers and little capital equipment, or should it be produced with a lot of equipment and few workers? What firms should produce what items? What persons should work on what jobs? Broadly speaking, the market tends to indicate the method, the firm, or the person that can produce things most efficiently. Because consumers generally attempt to get the most for their money, they tend to purchase from producers who give them more per dollar. As long as businessmen and workers are interested in greater earnings from their effort, they tend to move into the forms of production that consumers prefer.

The market system does not always establish the most efficient mode of production. Supposedly, the market can show producers or workers whether they are producing the right thing in the right way. If they are not, profits and wages may fall. If the people involved have a strong income motive, they will move to another business where they can earn a better return for their efforts—where they are more efficient. But often other motives are more important than the desire for income. Farmers may enjoy being "close to the soil." Teachers may receive personal

THE FLOW OF SPENDING AND PRODUCTION

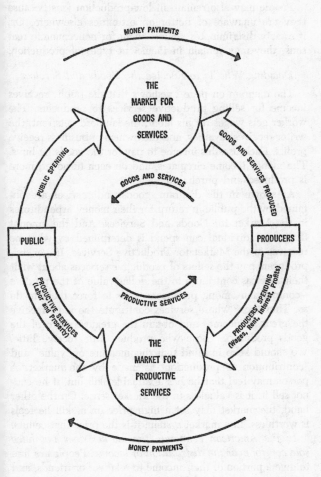

satisfaction from working with young people. Older people may be unwilling to leave their neighborhood and move on to other jobs. Thus people may not respond to the main driving force in the market system.

People may also remain in low-production jobs because they are unaware of better opportunities elsewhere. Or, if society discriminates against them for noneconomic reasons, they may remain in inefficient types of production.

Deciding Who Is to Receive the Goods and Services

The diagram on page 25 shows that the public receives income for selling productive services to producers. The worker gets wages for his labor, the landlord gets rent, the writer receives royalties, and the owners of business receive profits. Each uses his income to pay for the goods he buys. The money income circulates, and on each turnover, more is produced and purchased.

As shown in the diagram, goods and services are obtained by the public in return for their money expenditures in the Market for Goods and Services. And the amount that any individual can spend is determined by what he receives in the Market for Productive Services. In general, producers pay the sellers of productive services about what their services contribute to the dollar value of the product —competition among producers tends to force them to do so. Thus those whose services contribute the most receive the greatest incomes and obtain the greatest share of the goods produced. Those who produce little receive little. We should keep in mind that this measure of "value" and "contribution to production" is made by the market. A person may feel that he has a valuable skill but, if he cannot sell it, it is valueless in the market sense. On the other hand, the market may set a high price on a skill he feels is worthless. In a market system, it is the price that counts.

In the American economy, the market does not have sole control over the distribution of income. People are free to give a portion of their income to relatives or friends, and charities are supported by private donations. Furthermore, society as a whole has decided to compensate some groups beyond their reward from the market. Veterans are given bonuses and pensions; old people receive government subsidies; schools are provided for children, and many governmental services are provided for people without regard to their ability to pay. The American people, in other words, feel that the market method of deciding who will receive the things produced is not always adequate.

The government also changes the distribution of income by measures that work within the price system. It supports the price of certain agricultural commodities so that farmers will be able to receive a higher income. It imposes tariff regulations and fosters "fair trade" practices that boost prices of some products above the competitive level. By a variety of such policies, the government affects the prices of goods and services and therefore influences the distribution of income and production.

WHAT IS THE OUTPUT OF THE AMERICAN ECONOMY?

Having examined briefly how the market and government co-ordinate our economic activity, let us now try to observe what our whole economy actually has produced. We shall make this a bird's-eye glimpse of the whole economy—the part controlled by the free market as well as the part controlled by government. We shall begin by "looking at the books." Just as a businessman may examine his accounting records to check on how he is doing, so can the citizen find out how the economy is doing by looking at the gross national product and national income accounts. Familiarity with these statistics will help us understand news reports and interpretative articles on economics published regularly in newspapers and magazines. Later we shall see how these figures help us evaluate the desirability of different economic activities and the effectiveness of past policies.

The total value of goods and services produced in the

economy during the year is called the "gross national product" (*GNP*). This is the most comprehensive measure of *what* we produce. It measures the output of all economic activity at prevailing market prices. The price measure provides a common denominator that enables us to add up all the dissimilar things we produce. Movies, dishwashers, wheat combines, ditch digging, police protection, toys, locomotives, and thousands of other goods and services can all be added by using their prices as a measure. However, as we shall see later, we must be sure we understand what these prices mean.

The goods and services included in the gross national product are sold to four major groups: consumers, producers, governments, and foreign buyers. In 1965, these groups purchased the following amounts of goods and services:[1]

Consumers	$431 billion
Producers	107 billion
Governments	136 billion
Foreign buyers (net)[2]	7 billion
Gross National Product	$681 billion

[1] These figures are based on statistics compiled by the U. S. Department of Commerce. For simplicity, the figures in this chapter have been rounded and some categories have been combined with others. The basic source of these and the other figures used in this section of the chapter is *Survey of Current Business*, a monthly publication of the U. S. Department of Commerce. The same figures may also be found in the *Federal Reserve Bulletin*, a monthly publication of the Board of Governors of the Federal Reserve System, and the Appendix to the *Economic Report of the President*, transmitted to the Congress annually in January.

[2] Usually labeled "net export of goods and services," this item involves some accounting complexities that will not be discussed here. An explanation is provided in U. S. Department of Commerce, *National Income, 1954*, A Supplement to the Survey of Current Business. Chapter 9 (below) contains an extensive discussion of the foreign trade of the United States.

Purchases by consumers—officially labeled *Personal Consumption Expenditures*—include three types of goods and services: *durables* (such as automobiles and television sets), *nondurables* (such as food and clothing), and *services* (such as house rent, movies, and medical and legal advice). In 1965 consumers spent $431 billion for these purposes, as follows:

Durables	$ 66 billion
Nondurables	190 billion
Services	175 billion
Total	$431 billion

Purchases by producers—labeled *Gross Private Domestic Investment*—are subdivided into *Fixed Investment* and *Change in Business Inventories.* *Fixed Investment* includes *nonresidential construction,* such as offices, plants, warehouses, pipelines, and gas and oil wells; it also includes *producers' durable equipment*—the machines, tools, and other equipment used in business enterprises, as well as the tractors and machinery purchased for use on farms. (Purchases to replace "worn out" equipment as well as expenditures for additional equipment are included.) *New housing* and farm structures, whether for rental or personal use, are also treated as fixed investment.

The other type of investment—*Change in Business Inventories*—measures the increase or decrease in the stocks of goods and materials held by business. An increase in inventories is considered to be a form of investment because it represents goods being processed or awaiting sale for *future* demand. For accounting purposes, these "unsold" goods are considered to be purchased by producers. Sometimes, as happened in 1958, the change in business inventories will be negative. This means that by the end of 1958 businesses had sold more goods than they produced during the year. That is, they sold some of the goods that were produced in an earlier period. Thus in order to determine what was actually produced during 1958, we have to *subtract* the inventory sales from the total sales. If we did not subtract them, the GNP—total spending on goods and services in 1958—would not be an accurate measure of production in that year.

Expenditures for these components of *Gross Private Domestic Investment* in 1965 totaled $107 billion, broken down as follows:

Fixed Investment		$ 98 billion
Nonresidential structures	$25 billion	
Producers' durables	45 billion	
Residential structures	28 billion	
Change in business inventories		9 billion
Total		$107 billion

The third major type of purchases—*Government Purchases of Goods and Services*—includes expenditures by state and local governments throughout the country as well as those by the federal government. Federal expenditures are broken down into two main categories:

National security, which includes purchases of munitions and payments to members of the armed services, and *Other*, which covers all additional outlays for such things as the services of government employees and the purchases of goods from business. State and local expenditures involve outlays for roads, schools, public works, and all the other services provided by city, county, and state governments. These governmental expenditures in 1965, totaling $136 billion, may be broken down as follows:

Federal		$ 67 billion
National Security	$50 billion	
Other	17 billion	
State and local		69 billion
Total		$136 billion

A breakdown of GNP according to expenditures by the major groups of buyers helps us to see the variety of things our national economy produces. For instance, the

$431 billion that consumers spent in 1965 was spent for the purposes shown in the following table:[3]

Food, beverages, and tobacco	$106.8
Clothing, accessories, jewelry	43.4
Personal care	7.5
Housing	63.2
Household operation	61.9
Medical and death expenses	28.1
Personal business (legal and financial service)	22.1
Transportation	57.8
Recreation	26.3
Private education and research	5.6
Religious and welfare activities	5.6
Foreign travel and payments abroad	3.2
Total	$431.5

To be even more specific, the *Survey of Current Business* shows that in 1965 consumers spent $8.4 billion for tobacco; $3.2 billion for haircuts and beauty parlor services; $7.8 billion for physicians; $1.8 billion for burial expenses; $2 billion for books, and $1 billion for radio and television repairs. In 1965, people spent more money for toilet articles ($4.3 billion) than they spent for dentists ($2.7 billion). But the most significant aspect of this breakdown is that it shows that our economic system responds to a wide variety of consumer interests. In 1965, the economy produced $431.5 billion of goods and services that were wanted by consumers. In 1965, it also produced another $250 billion of goods and services wanted by producers, governments, and foreign buyers.

The figures for gross national product also give some indication of how fully the nation is using its economic resources. For example, a decline of $10 billion in GNP generally indicates a slowdown in economic activity; it suggests that some workers or firms are idle or for some reason are producing less. As we shall see in Chapter 7, the

[3] *Survey of Current Business* (July 1966), p. 20. The figures have been rounded.

policies the government adopts to combat such a decline will depend partly on whether the decline has occurred in investment spending, consumer purchases, or government spending, or some combination of all three. In other words, the figures for gross national product can help show when trouble is developing, and they can also give some clues for dealing with the problem. However, as we shall see, such changes in GNP must be examined carefully.

The gross national product may rise or fall without a change in physical production. An increase may only mean, for example, that prices have risen. As all GNP figures are based on market prices, an increase in the price level may result in a higher gross national product even though real production of goods and services has remained the same or has fallen. Thus if we want to use GNP figures for comparative purposes or as a measure of *real* production, we must adjust the figures for changing prices. The following table shows how much difference changes in the price level can make over a period of a few years:[4]

Year	GNP in prices prevailing at the time (In billions)	GNP in prices prevailing in 1965 (In billions)
1929	$103	$226
1933	56	158
1940	100	252
1944	210	400
1954	365	452
1965	681	681

Without the correction for falling prices, the first column indicates about a 50 per cent decline in production between 1929 and 1933; the second column, in which GNP is expressed in constant prices, indicates a decline of 30 per cent. The same type of contrast is shown for the

[4] *Economic Report of the President* (January 1966), p. 209. The price index used is given on p. 214.

period 1954 to 1965; the increase in production looks much greater until we take the price changes out of it. The increase, expressed in market prices, is nearly 90 per cent; in constant prices it is about 50 per cent. This price adjustment is important if we want to use GNP figures to compare output for two different periods; if we do not take it into account, we are measuring both production changes and price changes.

Figures for gross national product tell us *what* we produce, but they do not tell us *how* we produce it. We can get some idea about this by looking at our national income.

NATIONAL INCOME

The national income is the total income earned by those contributing to current production. The United States Department of Commerce has developed a method for counting the incomes of laborers, executives, firemen, artists, and everyone else engaged in production, and it provides us with official estimates of the total. In 1965, for example, our national income was estimated to be $559 billion.

National income figures exclude payments that do not arise from productive effort. They exclude, for example, the allowances that fathers pay their children, the pensions or bonuses paid to veterans, and the interest on the public debt. Regardless how essential we may feel these payments are, they are excluded from the national income because they are not payments for "current production." Interestingly, compensation of housewives for their services is also excluded. Few people would deny that housewives perform a large volume of useful service—cleaning, washing, baby-tending, and so on—but their contribution is not included in GNP or in national income. If a man has a servant do all the house work, the servant's income is included, but if he marries his housekeeper (and gives her an allowance equal to her former wages), it is no longer a part of the national income figures. Why? Primarily because it would be too difficult for the Department of Commerce to make an accurate estimate of the value of housewives' services.[5]

In 1965, the national income was $559 billion and the gross national product was $681 billion. How do we account for the difference in totals? National income is the total income received by those contributing to current production, and gross national product is the total amount spent for goods and services currently produced—and both are stated in terms of current prices. But GNP is bigger because it includes some spending that is not considered income. The Department of Commerce can check its figure for national income by subtracting these non-income items from GNP.

The first deduction is an allowance for using of capital equipment. This deduction is necessary so as not to overstate the income produced during a calendar year. The example given below illustrates the role of capital in the economic process and shows why the allowance for the cost of replacing plant and machinery is not considered a part of national income.

Suppose Mr. A agrees to dig a ditch for $200. To dig the ditch he must supply the labor and the capital equipment—in this case a new shovel, which he buys for $10. By the time the job is completed, the shovel is worn out. Thus his product (the $200 ditch) is produced by combining $190 worth of labor and $10 worth of capital. Mr. A's net income is $190 and the other $10 represents expenditure of capital. If Mr. A treats the whole $200 as income and spends it—without making an allowance of $10 to replace his shovel—he will reduce his ability to produce

[5] It may come as a shock to some men to find out that the market value of all the services their wives perform may exceed the income of their husbands. A discussion of the many problems of measuring national income can be found in U. S. Department of Commerce, *National Income*, A Supplement to the Survey of Current Business.

as efficiently in the future. In other words, in order to determine what he produces by his own labor he has to deduct the cost of his worn-out ("depreciated") capital. Similar allowances are made in calculating the income of a whole society.

GNP also includes another cost that is not considered income—the cost of some business taxes. These taxes, such as manufacturers' sales or excise taxes, are added to the cost of the product before it is sold. They increase the market price (the basis for measuring GNP) but do not represent a reward to one of the productive units. They are a transfer of funds from consumers to the tax collector and are not a payment for current production. Thus a package of cigarettes costing 30 cents may include only 19 or 20 cents for the services of the grower, manufacturer, and dealer; all the rest goes to the federal and state tax collectors. Of course, the other 10 or 11 cents will eventually be used by the government to pay for "current production"— but it is counted when the government spends it, not when it is collected.

To summarize, the gross national product less capital consumption and business taxes equals national income. This relationship is shown by the following diagram. Together national income and gross national product measure the flow of income and the flow of goods and services. By looking at how the national income was earned, we can get some idea of how the goods and services were produced.

GROSS NATIONAL PRODUCT AND NATIONAL INCOME, 1965

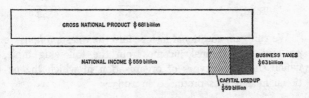

The table below, showing which industries produced

the National Income in 1965, gives some indication of how we produce our goods and services.[6]

Manufacturing clearly accounts for more employment and income than any other industry. A century ago this was the position held by agriculture. Retail and wholesale trade is our second largest source of income, producing more income than finance, insurance, real estate, and mining combined; and the transportation, communication, public utilities group produces more income than agriculture—with about the same number of workers.

Industries	Persons engaged in production in 1965 (In millions)	Income produced in 1965 (In billions)
Private industries		
Agriculture, forestry, and fisheries	4.0	$ 21.0
Mining	.7	6.4
Construction	4.0	28.3
Manufacturing	18.4	170.4
Transportation, communication, public utilities	4.0	45.8
Wholesale and retail trade	13.1	83.6
Finance, insurance, real estate	3.0	61.0
Services and other	11.8	63.0
Government		
Federal	5.3	33.5
State and local	6.9	41.8
Rest of the world	—	4.2
Total	71.2	$559.0

We can gain additional insight into the question *how* we produce our national income from the following table, which shows the types of organization in which the national income was produced in 1965.[7]

[6] *Survey of Current Business* (July 1966), pp. 15 and 31.
[7] *Survey of Current Business* (July 1966), p. 15.

Type of organization	Amount of income produced in 1965 (In billions)
Corporations	$317.5
Partnerships and proprietorships	106.3
Other private business	44.8
Government	67.8
Households and institutions	18.3
Rest of the world	4.3
Total National Income	$559.0

Corporations are clearly the dominating form of economic enterprise in our society; they permit the development of large pools of capital, and for a variety of reasons, they seem to be popular among investors and workers. Although the table does not show a separate classification for the single-owner form of business, it does indicate that the so-called "individual enterprise" is not nearly as important to total national income as we might think. Corporations and government are both "collective enterprise" so, even if all the rest were single-owner firms (which they are not), "individual enterprise" would account for only one third of national income.

Further information on *how* we produce our national income can be obtained from the following table showing the manner in which the national income was distributed in 1965 among what might be called "the services of labor and property."[8]

Compensation of employees	$393 billion
Business, farm, and professional income	56 billion
Corporate profits	74 billion
Rental income	18 billion
Interest income	18 billion
National income	$559 billion

Let us further examine the components of this breakdown of national income in 1965.

[8] *Survey of Current Business* (July 1966), p. 14.

Compensation of employees, totaling $393 billion, is income earned by hired labor. It includes the wages paid to workers in all types of productive activity, the salaries paid to white collar workers and the executives of businesses. It includes the payments made by employers for pensions and welfare programs for employees.

Business, farm, and professional income, totaling $56 billion, includes the income (or profit) of unincorporated businesses and farms, and of doctors, lawyers, and other professional people. It is therefore a mixture of independent labor income (about two thirds) and property income (about one third).

Corporate profits, totaling $74 billion, include all the profits of the corporate businesses in the country. As such, it is the income earned by corporate property. When combined with the payments to businesses, farms, and professional people, it includes all the earnings of owners and operators of producing organizations.

Rental and interest income, totaling $36 billion, includes housing and commercial rents and interest payments on bonds, savings accounts, and insurance policies. These are payments made to persons for the use of their real or financial property.

Thus the national income of $559 billion in 1965 was earned by labor, operating a business, and owning or renting productive property. Inasmuch as operating a business is considered a form of labor, about three fourths of our national income may be said to be earned by labor services and one fourth by the services of property.

The above figures showing the industries, the types of producing units, and the types of services involved in creating our national income help us to see how the national income is produced, and they also give us some clues regarding how the national income is distributed. In order to obtain a clearer idea of *who* receives the goods and services produced, we must examine the figures more closely.

Not all of the national income is distributed to individuals. Some of it is held by business, and some is transferred to the government. Thus national income is not the same as the total of all individual incomes—or what is called *personal income.*

Some examples will help show why personal income is less than national income. In 1965, corporations distributed only about $19 billion of their income in dividends; they paid almost half of their income—$31 billion—in corporation income taxes, and they retained $24 billion to plow back into investment. So only about $19 billion of corporate profits was actually paid to people in 1965.

Moreover, not all of the payments for wages and salaries were actually received by employees. Business paid over $29 billion directly to the government for social security programs. Thus retained earnings of corporations, the corporation income tax, and the payments for social welfare programs are all parts of national income that are not included in personal income.

The fact, shown graphically in the accompanying chart, that not all national income is available to individuals is sometimes interpreted to mean that some income is "taken out of the economy" by corporations or government. But this is like saying that corporations and the government are not a part of our economy. Actually, the funds retained by business are used to purchase such things as capital equipment and inventory, and the funds taken by government are used to purchase the wide variety of goods and services needed for governmental operations.

But there are also some extra payments to persons that were not included in national income. National income, it will be recalled, is the total of payments for productive services in our society. Some individuals, however, receive income payments that do not result from their current production. These payments are called *transfer payments.* A large volume of transfer payments arise from government and are included in personal income. Government transfer

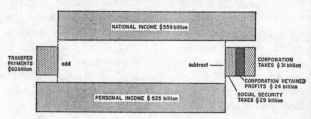

NATIONAL INCOME AND PERSONAL INCOME, 1965

payments are of three broad types: (1) payments to recipients of various relief and social programs; (2) payments to veterans; (3) payments of interest on the national debt. These governmental and business transfer payments amounted to $48 billion in 1965. Personal transfer payments for interest on consumer debt and to foreigners amounted to an additional $12 billion.

Finally, we should note that not all of the income paid to individuals (personal income) is available for personal use. There is a difference between what we quote as our wage or salary and what we get "after taxes." Income taxes, property taxes, and other taxes on individuals reduce the income we have for our own use. The deduction of these taxes from personal income leaves what is called *disposable personal income*—the income that individuals may use as they wish. In 1965, the figures were as follows:

Personal income	$535 billion
Less personal taxes	66 billion
Disposable Personal income	$469 billion

Of this sum, the people saved $26 billion and spent the rest, $443 billion, for consumption.

Before inquiring how this personal income was divided among our population, let us bring all these parts of the flow of income and production together. The diagram on page 41 shows how all these concepts are related. Because the concepts used in this diagram will be used later in this volume, it will be helpful to study this picture of the flow of income carefully.[9]

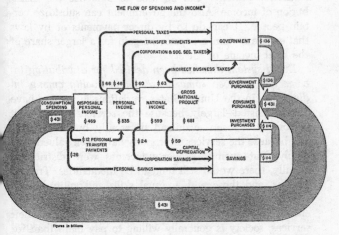

THE FLOW OF SPENDING AND INCOME[a]

[a] Data based on *Survey of Current Business* (July 1966). Foreign buyers (net) are included with investment purchasers.

HOW IS PERSONAL INCOME DISTRIBUTED?

In general, the income of our economy is distributed according to the market value of the individual's contribution to production. The determination of the individual's contribution is made, in principle, in the market where the actions of buyers and sellers rule. The linkage of income with productive contributions of individuals supplies much of our incentive to produce.

But productivity is not the only factor in our scheme of income distribution. Under a market system, it is possible for some persons to get a larger share by controlling the

[9] How could investment total $114 billion when private saving totaled $109? Government savings of $5 billion provided the difference (government tax receipts less transfer payments were $141 billion and government expenditures over $136 billion).

supply of things being sold, as price reflects not only the usefulness of a good but also its scarcity. Thus a variety of restrictive practices can be used to influence the distribution of income. Also the government can subsidize certain people. It can do so by direct payments or by laws that enable certain groups to bargain for a larger share of the total income of society.

Every system that has been devised for distributing income has involved some degree of inequality among individuals. In the United States, variations in income have always existed—largely because the services of different persons have been evaluated differently by the market and because the services of property have been valued very highly. But even if property incomes were distributed equally, there would still tend to be inequalities. Trained persons, and those with unusual skills and aptitudes are considered more productive than those who are inexperienced, untrained, or lacking in special abilities. For their services, society is generally willing to pay more than for the more easily available services of unskilled workers.

In recent years, the inequalities in distribution of money income have been reduced. Early data are not wholly reliable, but it appears that near the turn of the century, about half of our income receivers had near-subsistence incomes. Fifty years later only a quarter of our income receivers were in this category. A more specific indication of the change is given by the declining share of personal income after taxes going to the top income bracket.[10] The top 5 per cent of the income receivers obtained about:

34 per cent of the total disposable personal income in 1929
27 per cent of the total disposable personal income in 1939
18 per cent of the total disposable personal income in 1946

[10] Arthur F. Burns, *"Looking Forward,"* National Bureau of Economic Research, 31st Annual Report (1951), p. 4. See also *Survey of Current Business* (April 1964), p. 4. Note that this tabulation refers to income only. It does not indicate distribution of wealth.

Recent data indicate that the share of the top 5 per cent is probably about the same as in 1946.

Regardless of the changes that have occurred in the distribution of income, there is still an observable concentration in income payments. Looking at the following chart we see that in 1963 at the low end of the income scale, 11 per cent of the spending units of the nation earned less than $2,000 and shared only 2 per cent of the personal income of the nation. At the upper end of the scale, 8 per cent of the spending units earned more than $15,000 and shared 26 per cent of the personal income.

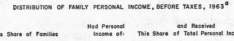

DISTRIBUTION OF FAMILY PERSONAL INCOME, BEFORE TAXES, 1963[a]

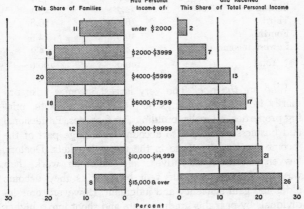

a Source: *Survey of Current Business* (April 1964), p. 4. Other valuable sources of information on income distribution are: U. S. Department of Commerce, *Income Distribution in the United States* (1953); Selma Goldsmith, "Income Distribution in the United States, 1950–53." Families are defined to include unattached individuals.

Personal income is defined slightly differently in this section from the Department of Commerce definition used earlier.

This picture of the distribution of income is changed only slightly by the federal income tax. Although the impact of the income tax on incomes over $50,000 is very great, there are so few people in this income bracket that taxes have only a slight effect on the over-all distribution. In 1962, for example, the share of income received by the top fifth of income receivers was cut only from 45.5 to 43.7 per cent by the federal personal income tax. The following table shows for 1962 how the distribution is changed by the income tax.[11]

Income bracket (Each group includes one-fifth of the spending units)	Percentage share of: Total family income before tax	Total family income after tax
Highest income group	45.5	43.7
Second	22.7	23.1
Third	16.3	16.8
Fourth	10.9	11.5
Lowest income group	4.6	4.9
Total	100.0	100.0

Who are the rich? The very largest incomes arise primarily from large holdings of property—real estate, mining properties, oil wells, buildings, or factories. Professional and business earnings also account for a large part of the income received by those in the upper brackets. Doctors, lawyers, business executives, and salesmen work their way up the income scale year by year as they become older and gain efficiency and judgment. However, some individuals by-pass this gradual route and shoot into a higher income level in a short period of time. Successful speculators, actors, writers, and salesmen, for example, may "get rich quick." A change of luck, a shift in consumers' tastes, a brilliant idea, or a change in the weather can move people into and out of the high income class in a short time.

Who are the poor? Aged people, broken families, or those supported by a wage earner who is sick or handicapped are often among the poor. So are part-time work-

[11] *Survey of Current Business* (April 1964), p. 8.

ers, lazy individuals, and those who refuse to move out of low-value production (for instance, farming on low-grade land) and into occupations where their efforts would be worth more. Some are kept from seeking better opportunities by racial and other types of discrimination. Geographical location may also play a part; education, job opportunities, and the over-all standard of living are lower in some sections than in others.

One of the continuing challenges to the American economy is to find ways to improve the economic status of the low-income groups. For example, in his *Economic Report to Congress,* in 1966, the President of the United States said: ". . . 32 million Americans remain in poverty and millions more are unable to realize their full economic potential." The President was supporting a "War on Poverty," designed to develop the earning capacity of these people.

Generally, the living standards of our lowest-income groups can be improved in two ways: first, by increasing the output of the American economy so that more goods are available for everyone; and second, by changing the distribution of what is available so that the poor get a bigger share. The first method will be discussed in Chapter 8 on Economic Growth and the second method might be explored as follows:

The Problems and the Issues

We have seen that the unequal distribution of incomes is the result of two influences: decisions in the market, and decisions by the government.

When the market decides how income shall be distributed, it does so on the basis of economic criteria—supply, demand, and bargaining. Generally, it gives more income to those considered more productive. But individuals are not helpless in the market. In addition to increasing their actual output of goods and services, they can also use various devices to increase the dollar value of what they produce. They can join with others to hold up the price of what they sell, and they can attempt to persuade consumers that they should want (and pay more for) their product. Individuals can also enlist the aid of the government to control the supply or the prices of the things they are selling.

When the government (society) decides how income will be distributed, it may use noneconomic standards for distributing income. The humanitarian goal that no one should be allowed to starve may guide policy. Or policy makers may decide that society owes a moral obligation to some groups. Government may provide more income for some groups as a part of a political bargain, or because it feels that our social customs result in an unfair treatment of these people. In other words, when the government intervenes directly, it views the distribution of income not only as an economic problem but as a social, moral, or political problem as well.

If we are concerned about inequality, then the basic issue may be to decide how much the distribution of income should be based on the economic rules of the market system and how much it should be based on the other rules that government can impose. More specifically, the issue may be how much the powers of the government should be used to reduce the degree of inequality of income distribution.

The Objectives

First of all, we want to improve living conditions for low-income groups. In addition, we may want to create more economic equality to correspond with our concept of political equality. We may want to curtail what seems to be wasteful consumption by those in the upper-income brackets. We may want to eliminate the advantages or disadvantages that arise from an inherited economic status. Or we may want to make the economic system seem more "fair" to some people in order to avert political unrest.

At the same time, we may want our economic system to produce a growing volume of goods and services. We may want to preserve incentives so that people will want to improve themselves, economically and culturally. We may also require that our system be free from rapid fluctuations between prosperity and depression.

Some of these objectives and requirements may be in conflict. For instance, we may find that large fortunes are needed to finance the continued growth of our productive capacity. If we do, we shall either have to change our objective or find a substitute way to provide capital. In thinking through such problems, it is vitally important to define these objectives and requirements so that such conflicts can be identified. We must be sure that the things we want can be obtained.

The Alternatives and Consequences

We might consider three principal courses of action: (1) allowing the forces of the market to drive individuals to whatever economic status their initiative and surrounding conditions will permit; (2) redistributing some of the income received by the rich by giving it to the poor; and (3) dealing with the physical and social causes of low productivity. Each of these approaches may involve a variety of specific proposals, each of which should be explored to determine its consequences.

Those who would rely exclusively on the market system say that economic pressure will induce people to improve their productivity. Critics claim that this approach has only limited possibilities. Greater effort will hardly help the income earner who is handicapped. It will do little good for those persons who, because of race or national origin, are excluded from various occupations. In general, unless people in the low-income groups have access to adequate educational and training opportunities, they may be thwarted in their desire to improve their economic status, regardless how much harder they work.

A second approach to the problem is to transfer some income from the rich to the poor. A progressive income tax, together with relief payments and other subsidies for low-income groups, is one way in which inequalities of income have been reduced. The obvious limitation of this approach is that it may reduce the incentive of the recipients to improve their status, and it may have a harmful effect on the incentives of those who are paying the costs.

A third approach to the problem involves a variety of specific programs designed to attack the different causes of poverty. Crop insurance and training in farming techniques may help the farmer; vocational rehabilitation may help the handicapped; legal and educational programs may reduce arbitrary restraints caused by racial and other types of discrimination; social security and unemployment insurance may help sustain the flow of income after retirement or lay-offs; vocational high schools and on-the-job training may improve the skills of youths. Altogether, it is argued, such programs would open up greater opportunities for economic advancement—opportunities that it is hoped low-income groups would accept. But here also, the proposal has limitations: Someone must pay for such programs; and since the low-income groups have a limited ability to pay, the costs must be borne by the rest of society.

In some cases, it is difficult to clearly identify the consequences of a program. For instance, what would be the consequences of expanding our program of low-cost federal housing? It might eliminate some slums and improve the health of many people. It might channel some income to other purposes—education, recreation, or even savings. This, in turn, might induce receivers of low incomes to seek ways to earn more. On the other hand, after obtaining new housing at low cost, they might feel less inclined to work hard. Moreover, the taxpayers who are subsidizing such projects may feel less inclined to work for the support of others. The net effect may therefore be uncertain without more precise information.

Perhaps there are other programs the consequences of which can be more clearly defined; for example, soil conservation, free school lunches, veterans' bonuses. It is beyond the scope of this book to explore the variety of such programs, but even the beginning student of economics can make some reasonably informed guesses about the possible consequences of some proposals.

The Decision

We have illustrated some of the reasoning involved in an economic problem—but this is as far as we can go in this volume. We all have different goals, hence each person must make the final decisions for himself.

This chapter has stressed these basic ideas:

1. We indicate through the market and through the government what we want produced, how we want it produced, and who is to get it. Because each of us is a producer, an income receiver, and a spender, these decisions are linked to one another.

2. The economic process may be viewed as a circular flow of income and production. Income arises from production. In the last analysis, our income *is* what we produce. Broadly speaking, we are concerned with two aspects of this circular flow: (1) the total amount of income and production available for society, and (2) the way that the total flow is distributed and used. The national income and gross national product accounts are comprehensive measures of the sources and uses of this flow of income.

3. Proposals for changing the distribution of income must be judged with an understanding of their effects on the operation of the entire economic system. There may be moral or political grounds for proposing changes, but, before accepting or rejecting such proposals, they should be explored for their economic consequences. Proposals that are economically desirable may be found to be politically or morally inadequate, or vice versa.

Suggested Reading

Paul A. Samuelson, *Economics—An Introductory Analysis*, Chaps. 3 and 4, pp. 39–75, Chap. 6, pp. 105–22, Chap.

10, pp. 170–92. George L. Bach, *Economics—An Introduction to Analysis and Policy*, Chap. 5, pp. 44–66. These readings give further information on how our economy operates, how the national income is created, and how the national income is distributed. See also "Free Private Enterprise" by Sumner Slichter in *Readings in Economics* (Samuelson et al., eds.), pp. 23–31. This is one of the best short statements of the theory and practice of a free enterprise system. Some of the issues it discusses will be especially helpful in preparation for Chapter 3.

Chapter 3

COMPETITION IN OUR ECONOMY

One of the satisfactions of shopping is to encounter rival retailers who are vigorously competing for our business. A chain store advertises lower prices; an independent retailer offers better service. Sometimes it is a heady experience to find many sellers vying for our favor, and we conclude that the consumer is a rather important individual after all.

Of course, we can't choose between rival electric power companies or among several different water suppliers. We cannot haggle over our telephone bill as we might haggle over the price of a used car. But at the same time we know that usually where we have no choice in the matter, the seller is not free to exploit us. If a single utility firm serves the community, a regulatory commission is likely to be on the job to see that the community is properly served and that the firm makes no more than a reasonable profit.

Most of us know from experience that competition and monopoly exist side by side. We have been taught to believe that competition is desirable and monopoly undesirable. Somehow competition is supposed to provide, at favorable terms, the goods and services most wanted by the public, while monopoly must be regulated to ensure the same result. Thus competition is supposed to foster the efficient use of the nation's resources and to discourage the inefficient use of these resources. In brief, we support competition because we believe it to be a means to greater economic welfare. But how does competition work? How does it promote economic welfare? Why is it self-regulating? And why is monopoly considered less dependable for serving the welfare of the general public? What is the justification for regulating monopoly?

THE FUNCTION OF COMPETITION IN AN ECONOMIC SYSTEM

A first step in understanding competition is to recognize that there are differences in markets. At one extreme is the broad "American Market." It includes all the things bought and sold in this country. In this "market," all sellers compete vigorously for their shares of the consumer's dollar. At the other extreme, the market for Tiffany diamonds is extremely narrow; as the product is defined, there is only one seller. In the first case, everything can be considered in some measure a substitute for everything else in the consumer's living standard; and in the second case, there is no substitute at all. In defining such markets, the concept used by the economist is the "degree of product substitutability." Sellers tend to be more competitive when their products can be readily substituted for one another.

Some firms compete almost exclusively with rivals that produce the same or nearly identical products. Tool makers, for instance, compete primarily with one another—on the basis of their ability to design and produce tools to meet various specifications. There may be alternative tool makers—and thus competition within the industry—but there is no alternative industry to which a buyer can turn to meet his needs. The degree of substitutability is low between the tool industry and any other.

On the other hand, movie theaters compete not only with other movie theaters but also with stage shows, television, and, less closely, with night clubs. Similarly, steel competes directly with steel, less directly with aluminum, and more remotely with wood. In other words, the breadth of the market depends on the degree to which goods can be substituted for one another, and this in turn influences the range of competition.

In general, competition exists when there are a number of sellers of a product or a service and no single seller can exercise control over the market price. In a sense, this means the individual seller is "controlled" by the market. Competition means that in the search for income new firms are free to enter into any kind of production, and workers are free to shift from job to job. Ultimately, it means that the distribution of workers, capital, and other resources is determined by the "votes" in the market.

Competition also implies freedom of choice for consumers; and it helps to guide production in accordance with consumer desires. Each consumer is free to allocate his income in a way he believes will yield him the greatest satisfaction. This spending pattern tends to direct production into a pattern that reflects the wishes of consumers.

The price system is the prime mover. A simple illustration will show in theory how a competitive price system works.

A company producing nails must pay its workers as much as they could get by working elsewhere. (Competition means there are alternative places for them to work.) Similarly, the company must pay the going price for all the other materials and services it uses in producing nails. In other words, competition determines what the firm pays for productive resources. That is, competition determines the price of labor (the wage rate) and the price of all the other things the firm buys.

Competition also determines how much the seller can charge for his nails. If the price consumers are willing to pay for nails is not high enough to cover all these costs, the company will lose money, and ultimately it will have to stop producing nails. The workers and the other productive resources that have been used by the firm will then tend to move to other firms where consumer demand for the product is great enough to cover all the costs. The resources move to firms where the prospects of earnings are greater.

On the other hand, if the demand for nails increases,

the price of them will tend to rise, permitting nail producers to earn larger profits. These larger profits will attract new producers and induce the original producers to expand production and to bid for more labor and other productive resources. These resources will be diverted from other production where demand is weaker. As a result, the supply of nails will increase, and this will tend to bring the price down to the point where the nail producers are "in equilibrium"—they are covering their costs and earning a normal profit.

Price competition also helps to weed out the less efficient producers. The successful firms will be those nail producers who, through efficient operation, can sell nails at the lowest price. Those who cannot pay the "going wage" (the competitive wage) or earn the normal profit at the prevailing price for nails will eventually have to give up production.

Clearly, the role of prices is important in a competitive system. A rise in prices, for example, will accomplish two things. First, as noted above, it will offer producers an opportunity to bid workers and other resources away from other activities and into the production of nails. Second, a price increase will eliminate some buyers from the market; only those who can afford the higher price will continue to buy nails. In brief, there will be high prices to match the limited supply, but there will be no "shortage" (just as there is usually no "shortage" of Cadillac automobiles today, even though a lot of people cannot buy them). Falling prices would, of course, tend to bring the opposite results—less incentive to produce and more buyers. Thus flexible prices can help bring about the necessary adjustments in purchases and production.

However, if competition is restrained so that prices cannot move up, an increase in consumers' demand for a certain quality of nails may only result in "shortages"; people may be willing to buy them at the fixed price, but the supply will not be adequate. In such circumstances, the nails will go to those buyers who get to the store early and buy while the supply lasts. On the other hand, if the price cannot move down, a decrease in consumer demand may merely mean unsold goods on sellers' shelves.

The price system, even in highly competitive markets, seldom works perfectly. Its operation is sometimes impaired by the presence of too few buyers or sellers, lack of knowledge of alternative opportunities, and too many restrictions on competitive practices. Because real markets seldom operate with perfect smoothness, the economist has developed the concepts of "perfect competition" and "pure competition" to describe an "ideal" market in which adjustments in production and distribution would work out as smoothly as our nail illustration. This type of perfect market never exists, but the concept is a useful theoretical tool with which to compare the actual performance in a market.

Monopolistic firms may perform like competitive firms, but there is no assurance that they will. Monopoly is at the other end of the scale from competition; it means literally "one seller," but the term is commonly used to mean any producer who has substantial control over prices in the market.

The monopolist, as sole or dominant supplier of a product, occupies a sheltered position. If his product is a necessity, and if no good substitutes are immediately available, the monopolist may restrict his output and increase his profits by charging high prices. He will not be obliged to heed the desires of consumers or the pressures of competition. In his sheltered position, he can operate in a settled way, without modernizing his equipment and without keeping abreast of new technology.

Monopoly distorts the workings of the free market. It does not yield the checks and incentives that are provided by competition. Nor does it always provide an automatic stimulus to innovation and economic growth. In order to perpetuate itself, it must regularly prevent rivals from developing. In other words, monopoly may not only permit resources to be used in an inefficient manner but it may also obstruct or prevent the entry of firms that would correct the situation.

The monopolist, however, may not take advantage of his sheltered position; he may never try to exploit the public. But the fact that he has the power to act contrary to the best interests of society is often considered justification for curbing that power. For these reasons, whenever it is more practical to serve the public by means of a monopoly, such enterprises usually are regulated to prevent the abuse of monopoly power.

These general comments about the theory of competition and monopoly give us some indication why our people have a tendency to prefer competition. However, our preference for competition is not absolute. As we shall see, there are a number of instances in which governmental restraints or private restraints on competition have been judged to be preferable to free competition.

AMERICAN EXPERIENCE WITH COMPETITION AND MONOPOLY

Laissez faire, the philosophy of minimum governmental interference in economic affairs, guided our economy during its first century. A growing population and an open frontier fostered the competitive notion of "every man for himself." With abundant resources to develop, there were widespread economic opportunities—and those who accepted these opportunities were not likely to be controlled by government. Competition for expanding markets was heightened by the richness of the rewards for success. Competition in the market helped direct production, and in doing so probably speeded the economic development of the nation.

However, a laissez faire policy did not create a wholly competitive economy. Monopolies existed in nearly every town and city. As a small community could support only one "general store" or blacksmith, many a tradesman was spared any competitive challenge in his locality. We have no way of knowing how much of the work of the economy was done under such conditions, but we do know that improved transportation and the growth of markets spelled the end of many of these local monopolies. In other words, as the economy grew, competition often became more vigorous.

Economic expansion also fostered the development of the so-called "natural" monopoly. This is a firm that can provide service at lower cost than two or more competing firms. The railroads were early "natural" monopolies. Because wagon trains were comparatively slow and inconvenient, and because it was too costly or risky to build a competing railroad alongside an existing one, the first railroad in operation was generally able to maintain its market advantage.

Some of the railroads used their monopoly power to exploit the public. As a result, some state governments attempted to control railroad activities, but the laws were often ineffective. As public resentment against the monopolistic practices of railroads grew, and as more railroads crossed state lines, there was a growing demand for federal regulation.

The establishment of the Interstate Commerce Commission in 1887 was one of the earliest efforts of the federal government to regulate monopolistic activities. It had been the practice of many railroads to cut their rates for preferred customers and to raise rates for others; as usually there was no competing railroad for "short hauls" along the area between large cities, they charged what the traffic would bear; and on "long hauls" they occasionally embarked on "rate wars", which were designed to destroy rivals so that rates could subsequently be increased. The ICC was formed to prevent these and related practices and to require the railroads to perform more in the public interest.

The rise of cities led to the growth of additional "natural" monopolies. Water, sewage disposal, urban transportation, and later, electricity and gas became necessary for the community. Because competitive services were generally inferior or wasteful, the community usually gave one firm an exclusive franchise. In return, the firm accepted some municipal or state regulation. More recently, the federal government has also regulated public utilities that cross state lines. Telephone service, electric power, and gas pipelines are but a few of the industries in which federal regulation has supplemented state and local regulation.

The intent of regulation was seldom to impose competitive conditions, for in most instances competition would have been costly and wasteful. Rather, regulation attempted to cause the monopolist to operate in the public interest as well as his own interest. Government regulation of "legal monopolies" was a substitute for control by the competitive market.

As business expanded, a new challenge to competition arose. Many producers began to combine with competing firms or to destroy other competing firms by a variety of cut-throat practices. The formation of the Standard Oil Trust in 1881 is a familiar illustration.

John D. Rockefeller engaged in price wars to smash rivals and experimented with various kinds of pooling agreements and rebates from railways to tighten control of supply in the richest markets. His most effective innovation was the voting trust, by which stockholders of competing companies gave their voting rights to a central group of trustees who thereby were able to manage production and prices of all the participating companies as though they were one large firm. The success of the trust movement in the oil industry led quickly to similar devices in the sugar, whiskey, match, steel, tobacco, and other industries.

The development of these trusts provoked widespread public resentment and eventually led to restrictive federal legislation. In 1890, a decade after the organization of Standard Oil, the Sherman Antitrust Act was passed. It sought to prohibit all kinds of agreements, contracts, and voting trusts that restrained trade. But the law was written in general terms, and enforcement was difficult. Hence, despite the publicized "trust-busting" activities of President Theodore Roosevelt's administration, business sought and found new ways to diminish competition—by establishing holding companies, buying up assets of other firms, and engaging in many discriminatory trade practices.

In 1914, new legislation—the Federal Trade Commission Act and the Clayton Act—was passed in an effort to control practices that were not clearly subject to regulation under the Sherman Act. Price discrimination among different buyers, tie-in sales that required the buyer of a given product also to buy other products from the same seller, and purchasing the stock of competing firms were some of the practices attacked under the Clayton Act. The Robinson-Patman Act was passed in 1936 to further regulate the pricing policies of firms, and in 1950, the Clayton Act was strengthened by the passage of the Antimerger Act which made it unlawful for one firm to acquire the assets of another where the effect may be to substantially lessen competition or tend to create a monopoly.

Apart from the regulation of natural monopolies, governmental policy has thus attempted to prevent practices that tend to restrain competition. By enacting the antitrust laws (more accurately, the "antimonopoly" laws) and establishing the machinery to enforce them, Congress has worked toward some "rules of the game" designed to maintain an effective market system. These laws, primarily the Sherman Act and the Clayton Act, do not catalogue all the things that business can and cannot do—that would be impossible. They cite some general practices that can lead to monopoly, and give the courts wide discretion in deciding what constitutes illegal "restraint of trade" or what practices "substantially lessen" competition.

Over the years, the interpretation of these laws has changed as circumstances have changed. The enforcement agencies, the United States Department of Justice and the Federal Trade Commission, and the courts have changed their views a number of times about what business firms can and cannot do. The process of judicial review, whereby cases or rulings are decided in the federal courts, has enabled the changing ideas of the members of the judiciary to play a crucial role in the changing interpretation of the laws.

In general, the antitrust laws do not punish the mere size of firms. On the issue of large firms that seemingly had the power to control the level of prices and determine the degree of competition, the courts said in two cases:

1. A firm that produced 95 per cent of the shoe machinery output—

> The company, indeed, has magnitude, but it is at once the result and cause of efficiency, and the charge that it has been oppressively used is not sustained.[1]

2. A firm that controlled about 50 per cent of the output of steel products—

> The Corporation is undoubtedly of impressive size and it takes an effort of resolution not to be affected by it or to exaggerate its influence. But we must adhere to the law and the law does not make mere size an offense or the existence of unexerted power an offense.[2]

Later, however, the Aluminum Company of America, which produced about 90 per cent of the aluminum ingots, was held to have acquired a monopoly in violation of the law. "Nothing compelled it to keep doubling and redoubling its capacity before others entered the field,"[3] said the court. Other decisions involving the tobacco and taxicab industries also implied that the magnitude of market domi-

---

[1] U. S. v. *United Shoe Machinery Company*, 247 U. S. 56 (1918).

[2] U. S. v. *United States Steel Corporation*, 251 U. S. 451 (1920).

[3] U. S. v. *Aluminum Corporation of America, et al.*, 148 Fed. (2d) 431 (1945).

nation should be considered in antitrust cases. But even this view has been modified by subsequent decisions so that the prevailing stress seems to be less on the share of the market held by a firm and more on the particular practices a firm may use to restrain trade and control prices.

In deciding what constitutes illegal restraint of trade, the court has maintained a flexible attitude. In 1911, the court said it was guided by the "rule of reason"—that it did not condemn all restraints of trade but only those that appeared to exert an *unreasonable* restraint on competition and trade. Of course, some such statement was necessary as the Sherman Act prohibited "every contract, conspiracy or combination in restraint of trade." This broad terminology seemed to conflict with established rights of contract. The "rule of reason" was simply a statement that the legality of the behavior of any firm must be judged in terms of the particular facts of the case; absolute standards simply could not be applied in a complex economic system.

As the American economy has encountered new problems, it has frequently modified its policy on free competition. In the period before the Civil War, for instance, competition in the banking field led to a number of abuses that harmed the operation of the monetary and banking system. The National Banking Act of 1863 was passed partly in order to control some of these abusive practices. Pure food laws, child labor laws, "truth in advertising" laws, are all results of the attempt of society to make competition conform to certain standards—they are attempts to restrict competitive practices in order that the market mechanism will yield results that conform with the desires of the community.

Various amendments to the antitrust laws have also been made, permitting certain groups of producers to work together in combination. The Webb-Pomerene Act (1918) permits firms engaged in selling goods abroad to combine in their export operations. The act was designed primarily to enable American firms to compete with similar combinations in other countries. The Miller-Tydings Act (1937), and the McGuire Act (1952) permit manufacturers to restrict competition among retailers by setting "fair trade" prices. The Clayton Act, one of the basic antimonopoly laws, specifically excludes agriculture and labor associations from the provisions of the law, and subsequent legislation has also been passed to strengthen this position. Both of these groups were apparently felt to be at a competitive disadvantage in the developing industrial economy and, therefore, were given special opportunities to combine.

The biggest departure from the policy of free competition was the National Industrial Recovery Act (1933). This act, which encouraged business, labor, agriculture, and professional groups to work together to determine price and output policies, was designed to combat the depression. In words that are similar to those of many present-day supporters of "fair trade" laws, President Franklin D. Roosevelt said about the act:

> Its goal is the assurance of a reasonable profit to industry and living wages for labor with the elimination of the piratical methods and practices which have not only harassed honest business but also contributed to the ills of labor.[4]

The NRA "codes," which were the government-approved restrictions on competition drawn up by each industry, lasted only two years, but in that time they became the nation's guides for competitive behavior. They were a product of the depression and a reflection of the hope that by stabilizing prices and competitive practices, the nation could find the way to recovery.

How do we account for the enactment of these laws that seem to contradict the general principles of our antitrust legislation? Some people think they merely reflect the

[4] *The Public Papers and Addresses of Franklin D. Roosevelt,* Vol. II (1933), p. 246.

power of small, self-seeking pressure groups. Others consider them to reflect the defects in the competitive system. There is some truth in both of these views, but there is more to the problem than that.

Competition needs rules, and society uses these rules to achieve a variety of objectives. For example, the American people have generally been sympathetic to the underprivileged. Therefore, some laws are designed to strengthen the position of those who appear to be in a relatively weak bargaining position. This is clearly an important reason for the legislation permitting workers to combine into labor unions and farmers into co-operatives. It is interesting to note that, unless such combinations are thought to be "abusing" their power, they are seldom even called "monopolistic."

Public opinion today also seems sensitive to the adverse effects of vigorous price competition. It is also sensitive to the needs of small businesses. Thus even though the independent retailer may charge more for a product than a chain store or a "discount house," he is protected by "fair trade" laws. The public has not always been sensitive to these issues—nor should it always be expected to be sensitive to them in the future.

Clearly, the American public is not concerned with the preservation of competition merely for the sake of competition. It desires competition because in most circumstances the competitive market provides an efficient means of allocating the productive resources of the nation. But there is no measure to show how much a given deviation from competition harms this allocation mechanism.

When the practices of a particular firm clearly violate our loosely defined ideals of competition, the government makes an effort to stop them. But governmental action may also have an undesirable effect on other objectives such as the increased productivity of large-scale enterprises, the incomes of farmers, workers, or other groups, the continued existence of small business, or the growth of research and technology.

If these other goals appear to require the use of monopoly powers, the government obviously cannot make a flat commitment to destroy all monopolistic elements in the economy. All it may do is to seek out and destroy those particular practices that seem, all things considered, harmful to the performance of the economy. To many people, this seems to result in a weak and ineffectual public policy toward monopoly; but the government must consider a variety of goals, some of which cannot be attained in a perfectly competitive society.

KINDS OF MONOPOLY IN EXISTENCE TODAY

Many practices that seem competitive are also in some degree monopolistic. For instance, branding and product differentiation are attempts by a given seller to distinguish his product and to acquire a special advantage for it. They are competitive efforts to attract consumers. At the same time, they provide some protection from the actions of rival producers. The difference, in other words, between what is called competition and what is called monopoly is to some extent a matter of degree—the degree of control the seller has over the market price.

Collusive activities among sellers are clearly monopolistic. Competitors who get together to decide on a uniform pricing policy or a division of the market, or to impose restrictions on the area of competition, violate the law. Such agreements between competitors are illegal in themselves. The government does not need to prove that the effect of these agreements will be to lessen competition. It only has to prove that the agreement was made.

But it is often difficult to find out whether agreements have been made. A casual conversation during a game of golf or a trade association meeting may accomplish the same uniformity of practice that the "Gary Dinners" did when they brought steel producers together to agree on competitive practices in the steel industry. There is no way of knowing how prevalent such collusion is, but the conviction of several executives in 1961 for price-fixing in the electrical industry was a reminder that agreements to limit competition still pose a problem.

Mergers, consolidations, and holding companies can also restrain competition. These legal combinations are subject to review and prosecution by government, but in each case the government must show that competition has been restrained or will be substantially lessened by the combination. However, the very elusiveness of the concept of competition frequently makes it difficult for the government to prove its case.

Many people regard the growth of big business as an indication that our economy is highly monopolistic. Much of the production of the nation comes from giant firms that dominate an industry. The Federal Trade Commission has estimated that in 1962—out of 420,000 manufacturing firms—assets of the five largest companies accounted for 13 per cent of all assets of manufacturing firms (measured in dollars). The 50 largest companies had 35.7 per cent of the total, the 100 largest companies 46.1 per cent of the total, and the 200 largest had 55.9 per cent of the total.[5] In other words, less than 1 per cent of the manufacturing companies do over half of all the manufacturing business.

Some industries with a handful of dominating firms are listed on the following page. Figures from a study made by the Bureau of the Census show how the value of shipments in each industry is concentrated in the four largest companies. Of course, these figures tell only part of the story about market power; cane sugar still competes with beet sugar, and synthetic fibers compete with natural fibers. The figures indicate only that production in some manufacturing industries is highly concentrated. Clearly, a number of such industries exist in the modern economy—automobiles, chemicals, and typewriters, to mention a few

[5] *Economic Concentration,* Hearings Before the Subcommittee on Antitrust and Monopoly, Senate Committee on the Judiciary (1964), pp. 113, 115.

others. But it is dangerous to generalize about the effectiveness of competition from statistics about concentration.

Industry	Percentage of value of shipments by 4 largest companies[a]
Locomotives and parts	97
Flat glass	94
Electric lamps	92
Electron tubes, receiving type	87
Cigarettes	80
Metal cans	74
Tires and tubes	70
Computing and related machines	67
Photographic equipment	63
Blast furnaces	50

[a] *Concentration Ratios in Manufacturing Industry, 1963,* Report prepared by the Bureau of the Census for the Subcommittee on Antitrust and Monopoly of the Senate Committee on the Judiciary (1966), Part 1, Table 2, pp. 5–41.

It should be pointed out that these figures are for *manufacturing* industries, and manufacturing accounts for slightly less than a third of our national income. In other industries, such as retail and wholesale trade, construction, and the service industries, production is far less concentrated. It is important to remember, therefore, that the 4 million non-farm businesses of the nation operate under a variety of market conditions, and that despite the concentration of assets among large firms in the economy, competition has not declined. The number of firms has, in fact, grown along with our population; in both 1950 and 1960 there were 26 firms per 1,000 people in the United States compared to 25 in 1940 and 21 in 1900.

Some economists contend that monopolistic behavior is fostered when one or a few sellers are much more powerful than all the rest in the market. Others argue that competition can be more vigorous. Most economists would probably agree that competition can exist in industries in which oligopoly (a few sellers) exists, but that it will be very different from the competition among a large number of sellers of similar size. For example, in a market where there are many small firms, each producer tends to operate on the assumption that if he cuts prices, other sellers will not promptly retaliate. He supplies too small a part of the total market to seriously injure his rivals. But if there are only a few producers, each firm must consider the possible reactions of the other firms. Thus if a large producer is contemplating a price cut that might increase his share of the market from, say, 25 to 30 per cent of the total sales, he must expect the other large producers to retaliate. Seemingly, this fact limits price competition—without any collusion on the part of the sellers.

The view has been expressed that large enterprises are held in check by "countervailing power." Bigness in one sector of the economy appears to beget bigness in another, and a new set of checks and balances may result. It is argued that these centers of power offset each other, and perform a function similar to the role played by competition among many small producers. In addition to giant manufacturing corporations, there are large labor unions and large farm organizations that also wield tremendous economic power. The government itself is one of the strongest bargaining forces. When these groups bargain with each other, the power of one limits the power of the other.

This display of power against power is apparent when government deals with industry in public housing and hydroelectric power development, when professional men face the government on compulsory health insurance, when labor bargains with management and so on. But it is also more specific. The giant buyer confronts the giant seller within an industry. The giant steel companies are confronted by giant automobile manufacturers as buyers of sheet steel, and by giant can manufacturers as buyers of tin plate. And the giant steel companies must compete against giant aluminum or other metal producers in order to hold their markets. Large electrical manufacturers buy from large copper producers, and large food processors must bargain with large chain store distributors. Thus it is suggested that however remote this system of power versus power seems from the ideal of perfect competition, its results may be somewhat similar. Countervailing power may, in other words, be a way in which prices may be kept within bounds and the abuse of economic power may be checked.

But these powerful units do not always compete with each other. They may find it advantageous to pool their interests or combine their power. For example, building contractors and trade unions have occasionally formed collusive agreements designed to close local markets to new workers and new builders and thereby to control prices. The fact that big firms frequently merge with competitors or integrate their operations to avoid bargaining with suppliers or distributors suggests that countervailing power cannot be considered an adequate regulator of economic power.

It is sometimes argued that large firms will operate in the public interest because big business has bred a new type of leader who has a greater sense of social responsibility. The "robber baron" seems to be passé. "Industrial statesmen" may be more typical of the American scene at mid-century. Certainly impressive evidence can be gathered to show that businessmen today are far more aware of their public responsibilities. Either because they are sensitive to the needs of the public or because they fear the consequences of public criticism, more businessmen appear to be responsive to public opinion.

A faith in "good leadership" as a substitute for public enforcement of a competitive society assumes that private interests and public interests are the same, or that executives can always wisely compromise conflicting private and public claims. But these are questionable assumptions. Although the rise of better qualified executives with a broader vision of their private and public responsibilities is to be applauded, this development does not in itself seem to provide a satisfactory regulating mechanism for economic life. A system of checks and balances provided by competition or governmental policy has generally proved to be safer for the American economy.

The monopolistic features of our economy are not always easy to identify, nor are the best measures for coping with them easily determined. As we have seen, agreements among sellers, mergers, and consolidations may be used to eliminate rivalry between competing firms. Some forms of rivalry may also be diminished if a few firms become considerably stronger than all the rest. If this happens as a result of greater efficiency or more vigorous competition, the economist must generally evaluate the specific performance of the industry. But as the following section shows, there are different types of competition, and we cannot always be sure which types are best for the American economy.

HOW DO FIRMS COMPETE TODAY?

Product variation, advertising and promotional activities, and price cutting are the major competitive weapons. However, the use of these weapons varies from industry to industry. Price cutting is the principal form of competition in farm commodities. Automobile manufacturers ordinarily put less emphasis on price competition, but maintain a vigorous rivalry in terms of the style and quality of cars. Many retail firms compete primarily by the services they supply with the product, or the credit terms on which the product is sold. In some, such as the cigarette industry, competition appears to be largely a matter of advertising with relatively little rivalry in either the product or the prices charged by competing firms.

Product improvement is a widespread form of competition in the American economy. Creating new products and improving old products has frequently taken the place of price competition as the principal basis for economic rivalry. Accordingly, over the years the range of products and the opportunities for the exercise of consumer choice has steadily broadened. For example, wool suits now compete not only with other wool suits but also with rayon, dacron, and cotton suits. Continued multiplication of grades and varieties of products has increased the range of substitution and inter-product rivalry.

Product variation implies that each producer will sell a product that is partially different from that sold by any other producer. Thus the market consists of a number of partial monopolies in which each producer has more control over his price policy than he would if a number of producers were selling an identical product. In the fabled mouse-trap market, the man who "built a better mouse trap" was somewhat free of the check of competition—and, accordingly, he could behave in some degree like a monopolist (until someone built one that was even better).

An increasing degree of product variation is clearly one way to meet the variety of wants of the public. It is also a way to improve the quality of the things we consume. But the problem of choosing the right product has become a more complicated task for consumers; for sellers the cost of stocking all grades and varieties has become greater and greater. These and the costs of product research and experiments are the price we pay for variety and improvement; they are the price we pay for this form of competition.

Promotional activity is the most familiar form of competition. Advertising, branding of products, and the services of salesmen and dealers supplied with products, are well known to consumers today. It is sometimes claimed that these activities impose unnecessary costs on the public, but in general, promotional activities perform an important function. They bring information about products to the attention of consumers, and as a consequence the degree of competition may be heightened. If they expand markets, they may result in lower costs through mass production.

In some respects, promotional activities come close to being variations in product. Many selling campaigns are designed to make the consumer feel that one product is different from all others when in fact it may be quite similar. For example, a brand name is designed to make the consumer think specifically of a given product: "Don't ask for a widget; ask for an Acme Widget with a super-horizontal-platidone—just ask your dealer for S-H-P." The services of the dealer combine with the advertising and brand name to make the product appear, in the mind of the consumer, as a complex package of services for which he may have a slight preference. The creation of this preference is the objective of the promotional activities.

When the product cannot be distinguished from its near-substitutes either by its own characteristics or by the services and promotion of its seller, price variation is the main basis of competition. This was the basis of competition in our earlier illustration of the nail producer. But price competition can also operate alongside the other forms of competition. The television industry is a familiar example. Since the first television sets were produced for large commercial sales over a decade ago, they have undergone major changes. Quality has improved, and costs of production have declined. These cost savings have led to greater price competition. At the same time, television manufacturers have expanded promotional activities in an effort to increase consumer preference for a particular make or model.

However, price competition has diminished in a number of industries where a "live and let live" policy prevails. Druggists, jewelers, and a number of other retailing groups have supported laws to prevent unrestricted price competition. Automobile dealers have tried to stop what they call "bootlegging" cars—selling them at reduced prices. Manufacturers' groups have established a variety of pricing schemes to control price competition. Labor unions have exerted a high degree of control over wage competition among individual workers. Agricultural groups have limited competition by participating in production quotas and marketing agreements.

Understanding of the long-run effect of these limitations on price competition requires individual market studies. Broad generalization cannot be applied to so diverse and complex an economy as that of modern America. Most economists, on principle, would urge that price competition should be expanded, but many recommend exceptions to meet the special circumstances of today's economy. It is on the specific exceptions that economists mostly disagree; for example, labor, agriculture, steel, banks, to mention a few. Some indication of the complexity of the problem can be seen if now we take a further look at our policy toward mergers. We shall use the framework outlined in Chapter 1.

The Problem and the Issues

Fifteen years after passage of the Antimerger Act of 1950, mergers were at an all time high in the United States. Vigorous enforcement programs by the Department of Justice and the Federal Trade Commission had not stemmed the tide of industrial combinations.

Some observers saw in the continuation of this trend into the 1960's evidence that the laws governing mergers needed to be strengthened. Others said that the laws had already gone too far in inhibiting industrial growth, and they argued that the amount of merger activity is not a very helpful indicator of the state of competition.

To evaluate the rival points of view and the underlying issues requires some understanding of the dimensions of the current merger movement, the reasons why firms seek to combine, and the difficulties in trying to preserve competition through antitrust action.

The merger movement that has developed since the Second World War is the third major one since the passage of the Sherman Act in 1890. At the turn of the century, huge combines were built up to dominate such industries as sugar, tobacco, steel, and petroleum. In the 1920's the automotive, farm machinery, motion picture, chemical, and electrical industries were the focal points of merger activity. At the end of the Second World War the number of mergers began to rise, though they dipped momentarily during the 1949 recession. But the trend seemed ominous to some observers who found the implications of one particular case especially troubling. It was the acquisition of a West Coast steel plant by a subsidiary of U.S. Steel (then controlling 32 per cent of the nation's steel output). When the court upheld the merger, congressional action to enact stricter laws gained momentum. The drive for legislative action centered on a loophole in Section 7 of the Clayton Act which prohibited the acquisition of stock where the effect would be to lessen competition substantially, but said nothing about the acquisition of assets. This loophole was closed by congressional action in 1950.

But meanwhile managements were finding many attractive reasons for acquiring other firms. Mergers enabled them to acquire new technology quickly and economically, to achieve diversification that would lead to larger and more stable earnings and employment, and to secure additional outlets or more assured sources of supply.

Given the incentives to merge and historical evidence that indicated that mergers tend to increase during periods of high economic activity, it was not surprising that by the mid-1960's merger activity, as estimated by the FTC, had reached a record high of nearly 2,000 mergers a year.

But this is only one side of the story. The period since 1950 has also seen more vigorous application of antimerger laws. More mergers were halted than during the previous 35-year period.

For example, in 1956 the Department of Justice was successful in its effort to block the proposed merger of Bethlehem Steel, the nation's largest producer, and Youngstown Sheet and Tube, the sixth largest. The court rejected the company argument that the merger would increase the ability of Bethlehem to compete with U.S. Steel. It was more concerned with the fact that Bethlehem's share of the market would be increased from 15 to 20 per cent, and this might give impetus to further mergers in the industry as other firms sought to strengthen their capacity to compete against the Big Two.

In 1962, in the first case under the Antimerger Act to reach the Supreme Court, the Brown Shoe Company was ordered to divest itself of the Kinney Shoe Company. The court said that this merger between the eighth and third largest shoe distributors would accelerate a trend toward concentration in the shoe industry.

Cases such as these made it clear that the government would probably attack mergers by competitors in the same line of commerce (horizontal mergers) when one or both of the firms involved held a substantial share of the market.

Acquisition of suppliers or outlets (vertical mergers) have presented issues of greater complexity for the government since economic evidence on the competitive effects of a vertical merger are more debatable. But vertical mergers have also been challenged. The Brown Shoe case had vertical as well as horizontal aspects. Brown was a manufacturer as well as a distributor, and the court feared that Brown might require Kinney stores to carry Brown shoes, thereby closing part of the market to Brown's rivals.

The most dramatic and controversial vertical merger decision (based on the original Clayton Act) was the 1957 order that required DuPont to dispose of its holdings of General Motors stock acquired forty years earlier.

Consequences of acquiring quite unrelated firms (conglomerate mergers) are especially difficult to assess since the firms are neither rivals in the same market nor customers for one another.

Nevertheless, they do result in the disappearance of some firms as distinctive, individual enterprises. The question has been asked whether an enterprise will be as effective a competitor when it is a division of a huge firm as it had been as an independent. Another aspect of conglomerate mergers was raised in the FTC order requiring

Procter & Gamble to divest itself of the Clorox Chemical Company, a manufacturer of bleaches. The FTC argued that although P&G neither bought nor sold bleaches the huge Procter & Gamble resources, particularly in marketing of P&G products, could be put at the disposal of Clorox, giving it a great advantage over its rivals.

The wisdom of several recent antimerger prosecutions has been heatedly debated, and the objectives of the government have been challenged by critics who charge that the increase in antimerger cases is designed to protect specific competitors, rather than competition.

A particularly troublesome issue for all concerned with antitrust has been the problem of defining the market. To conclude that a merger will give a firm too large a share of the market requires first that the market be defined. The general criterion, as indicated in this chapter, is that firms are considered to be in the same market if the products they produce are substitutes for one another.

But are glass containers and metal cans in the same market? The court held that they were in blocking the merger of the Continental Can Company, second largest producer of metal cans, and Hazel-Atlas Glass Company, the third largest producer of glass containers. The company argued in vain that the markets were separate, and a minority of the court accused the majority of inventing a single market by joining glass and metal containers—but not including plastic or other kinds of containers in that market.

The definition of the market was the crux of the famous cellophane case. Here a broad definition worked to the advantage of the company. The court cleared DuPont of monopolizing cellophane because it interpreted the market broadly to include all flexible wrapping materials—aluminum, waxed papers, glassine, and others—rather than cellophane alone.

But in a more recent case, a merger was struck down because the FTC defined the market narrowly to include only steel wool pads instead of all kinds of scouring pads.

The arguments that go into determining the boundaries of a market are very complex and are not easily understood without a close examination of the evidence, and the standards being used appear to be in flux.

The Objectives

The broad purpose of antitrust policy is to help keep the economy vigorously competitive so that production will be efficient, prices low, and innovation encouraged. Merger policy is aimed more specifically at blocking or breaking up combinations that impair competition or are likely to impair it. Mergers may reduce the number of effective rivals, for example, or make it more difficult for new firms to enter the market. Some observers assert, in addition, that the growth of the giant firm should be deterred for social and political reasons; they fear the concentration of economic power in private hands.

At the same time, there appears to be no disposition among policy makers to prohibit all mergers. Thus, a requirement of policy may be to keep the merger route open as a useful way of achieving business expansion and reorganization.

The Alternatives

One alternative is to accept the existing legislation as adequate. The 1950 Act, it is said, closed an important loophole, and the government is now able to attack mergers that would have been immune under the original Clayton Act. The government should, therefore, concentrate on the maintenance of vigorous enforcement efforts and on the development of better tools for determining which mergers should be halted.

Another alternative, based on the assumption that merger activity is unduly high, is to seek a solution through modification of governmental policies other than antitrust policies. An antitrust program, it is argued, cannot by itself maintain a competitive economy if governmental policies on taxation, defense purchases, international trade, and so on undermine competition by continually favoring one or another group of firms.

Another alternative is to enact tougher antimerger laws. One proposed legislative change would require firms that are planning a merger to notify the Department of Justice of their intentions so that enforcement officials will not have to rely on the trade press as a source of information on pending or completed mergers. Another possibility would be to outlaw horizontal mergers that involve firms controlling a 20 per cent or larger share of the market.

Still another alternative would be to eliminate all antimerger legislation and confine antitrust prosecution to instances of monopolizing or collusive behavior.

Appraise the Alternatives

Choices among such alternatives as these may be related to three different approaches to antitrust problems.

One is the market structure approach. Some observers argue that there is a very close relationship between the number of firms in a market and their relative size, on the one hand, and the behavior of firms on the other. They give great weight to data about the level of concentration in any industry—the proportion of assets, sales, or employment that are accounted for by the four largest or twenty largest firms in the industry. The antitrust program should strike at possession of undue market power, irrespective of a firm's conduct.

A second approach is to put major stress on conduct. While structural evidence is relevant, some experts argue that in the type of economy we have today, with its many monopolistic elements, it is futile, if not harmful, to insist on any particular structure. The essential issue is the firm's conduct—its pricing practices, the quality of its products. Is it engaged in collusive activities or monopolistic practices in which mergers form one aspect of a broad effort aimed at obtaining and maintaining undue market power?

A third approach is to stress performance. After all, say proponents of this view, if our objective is maximum growth consistent with price stability and full employment, we should judge firms by their contribution to these goals. If the firm is an innovator, if it is efficient, and so on, questions of structure, and perhaps even of conduct, are secondary.

In examining the alternatives and the various approaches to them, each of us must try to be specific about the meaning of "proper" structure, conduct, or performance and to test these specific meanings against the facts of individual cases.

This chapter has stressed the following ideas:

1. Competition, especially price competition, is a basic characteristic of a free market system. It can perform the function of a regulator of production and consumption and provide a framework of incentives for the achievement of greater economic efficiency.

2. Unrestrained competition, however, does not always yield results that agree with our social objectives. First, competition may actually destroy itself as some firms destroy others. Second, competition may harm certain groups that are weak in bargaining power. Third, in some instances competition may be more wasteful than monopoly. Therefore, in order to obtain socially desirable results the government has imposed certain "rules of the game."

3. Rivalry by product improvement and advertising is not the same as price competition. Economists differ in their views of which provides better service to consumers, but most economists would urge the maximum degree of price competition consistent with developing technology and an expansion of production.

4. In evaluating the desirability of restrictions on price competition, we must consider not only the interests of the persons directly affected, but also the long-run interests of the American people as a whole. We are able to do

this only if we make an effort to trace the consequences of the restrictions and then see how well they serve our objectives.

Suggested Reading

Paul A. Samuelson, *Economics: An Introductory Analysis*, Chap. 26, pp. 483–506. This illustrates some of the price policies of business firms. It also shows some of the issues we meet in linking public welfare with various types of competition or monopoly. George L. Bach, *Economics: An Introduction to Analysis and Policy*, Chap. 29, pp. 461–78. See also "The Case for Competition," by John Maurice Clark, in *Readings in Economics* (Samuelson et al., ed.), pp. 183–86, and "Communication and Collusion: The Case of the Electrical Industry," by John Brooks, in the same volume, pp. 217–29.

A comprehensive view of competitive and regulatory issues is presented by Clair Wilcox in *Public Policies Toward Business* (Third edition, 1966). Two Brookings books deal with competitive problems in greater detail: *Competition and Monopoly: Legal and Economic Issues*, by Mark S. Massel (1962), and *Pricing in Big Business: A Case Approach*, by A. D. H. Kaplan, Robert F. Lanzillotti, and Joel B. Dirlam (1958).

For an interesting collection of readings, see *Monopoly Power and Economic Performance*, edited by Edwin Mansfield (1964).

Chapter 4

LABOR AND UNIONS

One of the continuing questions in any economy is: Who gets how much? In an economy of competitive markets, this question is answered by a stream of decisions in the market place. But in the American economy impersonal relations among buyers and sellers do not rule alone. The government helps decide who gets how much when it taxes one group more heavily than it taxes another, or makes payments to one group and not another. When farmers organize co-operatives, they too are trying to do the same thing—alter the distribution of income. Doctors, businessmen, and other groups have used various devices from time to time in attempts to enlarge their share of the output of the nation. So have labor unions.

Labor union activity is of particular interest because over one fifth of our employed population belongs to labor unions—about 16 millions of a total civilian employment of 72 millions. Unions are also important because they can exert substantial pressure on wages and working conditions, not only for themselves but for all workers. They sometimes create pressures on prices and employment. They exert political power, they occasionally fight among themselves, and they sometimes challenge or sometimes defend basic aspects of a free market economy.

In this chapter we shall explore some of the effects of labor union action. We shall also examine one of the pressing problems of governmental policy—what to do about work stoppages in vital industries. Some people believe that such stoppages should be strictly controlled, others believe that these stoppages must be tolerated as a necessary cost of our kind of economic system. In a broad sense, the discussion that follows illustrates the way we might examine other economic groups—farmers, electric power producers, or any other group. We want to find out what they are, what they want, how they try to get it, and the consequences of their behavior.

OBJECTIVES AND GROWTH OF UNIONISM

The avowed objective of American labor unions has been to obtain higher wages and better working conditions for their members. In contrast to the more politically minded labor movements in foreign countries, American unions have been predominantly business-minded. They have sought to get "more" without overturning the economic system. During the past thirty years, labor unions have been far more active politically than they had been for the preceding half-century. They have sought to gain more of their goals through legislation. Yet the biggest job of the union is still its direct dealings with management.

Labor organizations of some sort—fraternal orders and unions of craftsmen—date back to colonial times. They existed in isolated local communities, frequently as secret societies in order to avoid retaliation by employers. The era of industrial strife following the Civil War brought an increase in union activity and in attempts to form national organizations.

In 1869, the formation of the Knights of Labor brought many unions together in a loose federation. The Knights of Labor was predominantly utopian and politically motivated, although it pursued some immediate economic objectives and engaged in strikes for better working conditions. Its influence declined, however, after the organization of the American Federation of Labor in 1886. The AFL, which was composed mostly of skilled workers, espoused the cause of business unionism and opposed intervention in political affairs, and it was this philosophy of unionism that triumphed.

The immediate goal of the early union was to sign up members and win recognition as the bargaining agent for the workers it represented. This was the essential preliminary to bargaining for higher wages and better working conditions. The battle for union recognition progressed slowly against the opposition of employers, the apathy of workers, and the distrust of the public.

Union membership grew slowly and irregularly from 1890 until the First World War. Then came an increased demand for labor, and wartime government officials recognized union leaders as spokesmen for the workers. As a result, the prestige—and the membership—of unions increased. By 1920, 5 million workers were organized. A large proportion of them were skilled craftsmen, and only a few industries, such as the coal mines, were unionized on an industry basis. The mass production industries were virtually unorganized.

Union strength waned during the twelve-year period following the depression of 1920–21. The decline was a result of several factors: competition from nonunion workers and labor-saving devices, public and governmental antagonism to unions, complacency of many union leaders, and aggressive antiunion policies pursued by business firms. The law and its interpretation by the courts also generally favored employers. Many employers maintained peaceful relations with their employees, but others fought the rise of unionism by suing union workers for damages or obtaining injunctions prohibiting unions from organizing or striking to enforce their demands. Some employers used spies to check on employees who were spreading the doctrine of unionism. At times they imported strikebreakers to take the jobs of striking workers and to fight them if necessary. Workers who joined unions were not only fired, but they were also "blacklisted"—that is, their names were circulated among other employers who would refuse to give them jobs. Sometimes, in order to get employment,

83

workers were required to sign "yellow dog" contracts, which bound them not to join a union if hired. These practices contributed to the shrinkage in union membership during the twenties.

The long history of conflict between unions and management, together with the violent and often bloody strikes, gradually awakened the public to the need for a constructive policy to govern industrial relations. One of the first positive steps by government was the Railway Labor Act of 1926, which guaranteed railroad employees the right to organize and bargain collectively. The act also set up machinery for the mediation and arbitration of disputes between the workers and the employers. Another step was the Norris-La Guardia Act of 1932, which limited the use of injunctions in labor disputes and outlawed the yellow dog contract. With these laws, the government was again making some "rules of the game"—only this time they applied to the rivalry between labor and employers.

The passage of the National Industrial Recovery Act in 1933 marked the beginning of a new spurt in union growth. The act provided for a number of changes in the economic structure of the nation; one of these was that "employees shall have the right to organize and bargain collectively through representatives of their own choosing." This right of labor was declared a parallel to the power given to employers to control competition, and it had an immediate impact. The new stature given to unions brought a sharp increase in membership. The act was later declared unconstitutional, but the provision that applied to the newly-won rights of labor was re-enacted in another law—the National Labor Relations Act of 1935 (the Wagner Act).

The Wagner Act declared that peaceful collective bargaining is an objective of federal public policy. It defined unfair labor practices on the part of employers. It created the National Labor Relations Board to supervise union elections, to certify newly organized unions, and to ensure good faith in collective bargaining. Given this legal stimulus, trade union membership jumped from about 3.5 millions in 1935 to almost 9 millions in 1940. This was a period of bitter organizing drives and vigorous employer opposition to unions, but gradually more and more unions won recognition.

This period also saw the formation of the Congress of Industrial Organizations (CIO) after the American Federation of Labor (AFL) could not decide how to organize workers in mass production industries. The AFL was basically a federation of unions organized along craft lines—carpenters, plumbers, and so on. In organizing an entire industry, such as steel or automobile manufacturing, these AFL unions wanted workers to join the established craft unions. But the supporters of industrial unions wanted to organize workers by industries—one union for steel workers, another for auto workers, and so on. As a result of this conflict, some of the unions broke away from the AFL and formed the CIO. For 20 years these two organizations competed and grew and then, in 1955, they merged into a single confederation which embraced five out of six organized workers. The membership of major unions—AFL-CIO affiliates and independents—is given in the accompanying table.

NATIONAL AND INTERNATIONAL UNIONS
REPORTING 100,000 OR MORE MEMBERS, 1964[a]

Union[b]	Members
Teamsters (IND.)	1,506,769
Automobile Workers	1,168,067
Steelworkers	965,000
Machinists	808,065
Electrical (IBEW)	806,000
Carpenters	760,000
Hotel and Restaurant	444,581
Garment, Ladies'	442,318
Laborers'	432,073
Retail Clerks	427,555
Clothing Workers	377,000
Meat Cutters	341,366
Building Service	320,000

Union[b]	Members
Engineers, Operating	310,942
Communications Workers	293,900
Musicians	275,254
Electrical (IUE)	270,842
Railway and Steamship Clerks	270,000
Plumbers	255,765
State, County	234,839
Mine, District 50 (IND.)	210,000
Painters	199,465
Railroad Trainmen	185,463
Textile Workers	177,000
Pulp, Sulphite	176,048
Letter Carriers	167,913
Retail, Wholesale	167,000
Electrical (UE) (IND.)	165,000
Rubber	164,661
Oil, Chemical	162,000
Packinghouse	145,000
Ironworkers	142,676
Postal Clerks	139,000
Government (AFGE)	138,642
Bricklayers	135,168
Transport Workers	135,000
Transit Union	133,357
Papermakers	133,000
Boilermakers	125,000
Maintenance of Way	121,151
Railway Carmen	121,000
Sheet Metal Workers	116,989
Printing Pressmen	115,589
Fire Fighters	115,358
Typographical Union	113,453
Teachers	100,000

[a] Source: U. S. Bureau of Labor Statistics, *Directory of National and International Labor Unions in the United States, 1965*, Bulletin No. 1493 (April 1966), p. 53. Based on union reports to the Bureau of Labor Statistics.

[b] All unions not identified as independent (IND.) are affiliated with the AFL-CIO.

After the Second World War, unions began to lose public support. The labor shortage and sympathetic aid of the

government to the labor movement contributed to the
growth of unions during the war. But strikes in vital industries, jurisdictional disputes between rival unions, and
defiance of the government by some union leaders caused
a reaction that resulted in the passage of the Taft-Hartley
Act in 1947. This law, which amended the Wagner Act,
reaffirmed the principle of collective bargaining, but placed
a variety of restraints on the powers of the unions. The
closed shop was outlawed, the union shop came under
regulation, as did the check-off, welfare funds, and certain
other union programs.[1] Some "unfair labor practices" were
listed, employers were given more freedom to move
against unions, and restrictions were imposed on certain
strikes. All in all, the law changed the "rules of the game"
by restricting union practices.

Dissatisfaction with portions of the Taft-Hartley Act and
evidence of corruption in some unions led to the passage of
the Labor-Management Reporting and Disclosure Act of
1959 (Landrum-Griffin Act), which permitted federal intervention into internal union affairs. The act put restrictions on the use of union funds by union officers and sought
to protect certain rights of individual union members. It
required unions to file annual financial statements and required employers to report nonwage payments to union
officials and payments to consultants. Amendments to the
Taft-Hartley Act included outlawing secondary boycott
agreements, limiting organization picketing, giving strikers
on economic issues the right to vote in representation
elections under certain conditions, and exempting the
building trades from the prohibition on the closed shop.

*While seeking to improve working conditions and wages
by collective bargaining, unions have also used political
action to achieve their objectives.*

Unions have supported such legislation as minimum
wages and maximum hours of work, safety regulations,

[1] In a closed shop, only union members are hired; in a union
shop, new workers must join the union; and the check-off means
the employer collects the dues for the union.

and workmen's compensation. Through their political action groups, they tend to support friendly candidates and oppose those they consider to be unfriendly. Their interest in legislation and public policy ranges beyond the trade union field. The major objective of unions is still to get more for their members, but on some issues this can be done only by getting more for others by governmental action. Thus unions have generally supported social welfare programs of local, state, national, and even international magnitude. However, union members do not present a solid political front. On such issues as tariff reduction or the role of government in labor affairs, union workers have a variety of political views and, like any other group in the economy, their voting decisions reflect a number of considerations.

Today, the typical collective bargaining contract covers two major types of issues: those that pertain to the worker, and those that pertain to the union. The contract sets forth the wage rates to be paid, the hours to be worked in a normal work week, payment for overtime work, vacation rights, and various other conditions of employment. These provisions cover the issues that first led workers to join unions.

The contract also includes provisions affecting the survival of the union. The union has objectives of its own in addition to those affecting the welfare of its members. It seeks to protect its status as the bargaining agent, to maintain its membership and financial solvency. The union leader may recognize that in the long run these provisions are as important as those governing conditions of employment.

Frequently, conditions of employment—wages, hours, and so on—are not the key issues in a dispute. If the strength of the union is at stake, the so-called group objectives of the workers may take precedence over their immediate economic objectives. Thus the union should be viewed not only as an economic group but also as a social and political institution that holds the loyalty of its members. In the eyes of many workers, the union gives the laborer a chance to "speak up"; it serves his desire for self-respect; it promises security and protection from some of the economic and social forces of the modern world; and it gives him the feeling of belonging to a group—a basic desire of all of us. For these reasons, it is generally irrelevant arithmetic to calculate the length of time it will take a worker to make up the income lost as a result of a strike.

To achieve their goals by direct action or at the bargaining table, unions have developed many tactical approaches. Some unions have imposed restrictions on the number of apprentices entering a trade or used high union dues or opposition to immigration in order to limit the number of available workers. These measures (found mainly in craft unions) are based on awareness of the union of the principle of supply and demand. Some other aims and practices of unions are:

To achieve uniformity in wage rates—the slogan is "equal pay for equal work"—some unions have used an agreement with one employer as the basis of negotiation with another (pattern bargaining). Such bargaining is not only less complicated, but it eliminates competition among employers at the expense of workers.

To organize nonunion workers, they have employed full-time organizers and launched extensive organizational drives.

To maintain the interest and support of their members, they have established newspapers and published educational material.

To simplify the collection of dues, some unions have negotiated the check-off, whereby dues are deducted from the worker's pay and turned over directly to the union.

To maintain membership, some have sought "union shop" or "closed shop" contracts, seniority rules, and other rules governing the discharge or demotion of their members.

The strongest and costliest weapon of a union is the strike. When collective bargaining fails and the existing agreement has expired, the union may attempt to halt production by withholding the supply of labor. In general, it does so because it expects that the loss of income and markets will prove more costly to the employer than the loss of wages will be to the worker. The employer, on the other hand, may attempt to stay in operation with a skeleton work-force or nonunion labor. Any strike thus raises two major questions: (1) whether the union can effectively withhold the supply of labor and (2) whether the workers or the owners can best stand the losses if a work stoppage occurs. A strike can be made effective or "broken" on the first issue; on the second issue, it may evolve into a contest of endurance.

Because the strike causes economic loss, it is frequently criticized. But the right to strike is firmly established in public policy and law. It is a legitimate and necessary part of a free economic system. It represents the final test of bargaining power between the union and management. Indeed, it is often the threat of a strike that forces the opposing sides to reach a meeting of minds at the bargaining table. No other alternative short of government regulation of industrial relations appears available.

To offset the efforts of the employer to "break" the strike, a union may take additional steps to make the strike effective. For example, it may resort to *picketing*, stationing workers at the entrances to the plant with placards charging the employer with unfair practices. On occasion, the entire union membership has barricaded the plant to prevent workers or customers from entering. Another supporting weapon has been the *boycott*. Unions have discouraged their members and the public from buying the products of the firm engaged in the dispute. An extension of this device is the outlawed *secondary boycott*, which is the refusal of union members of one firm to work on materials purchased from a firm that has a dispute with a union. These are actions that help make the strike effective; they are actions to prevent the employer from conducting "business as usual."

WHAT HAVE THE UNIONS ACHIEVED FOR WORKERS?

Organized workers look primarily to their unions to obtain higher wages, better working conditions, and protection from the power of management. In the long run, the stability and further growth of union membership is likely to depend on how well the unions can fulfill these expectations. Therefore, let us examine two questions in more detail: Do unions raise wages? Do they protect the workers from the possible abuse of power by management?

On the face of things, it seems a foolish question to ask whether unions increase wages. Daily newspaper reports of wage increases negotiated by unions suggest that the answer is obvious. But is it? We know that wages tend to be higher in unionized industries—but they were generally higher in these industries before the unions came into being. Recent studies show that union wages tended to increase slightly faster than nonunion wages after the Second World War—but some of the largest increases occurred in some of the low-wage, nonunion occupations (domestic workers, for instance). But, actually, comparisons between union and nonunion wage rates are not too helpful; the existence of unions has influenced *all* wages. For example, in some of the nonunion industries, employers have granted wage increases to prevent unionization of their firms, and some nonunion firms have been forced to increase their wages in order to keep their employees from taking more attractive union jobs elsewhere.

Union workers and employers will seldom question the view that unions increase wages. However, some observers argue that wages are necessarily determined by the supply of and demand for labor; that regardless of union pressure, wages rise and fall as the national income and employment rise and fall. Thus they argue that the wage increases of the postwar years merely reflect the fact that the demand for labor was high. Others argue that wages would not have risen as sharply if unions had not maintained pressure on employers. Unions, they say, shorten the lag between the time the employer is willing to pay more and the time the market makes him pay more. But there is general agreement about the fact that some union workers have from time to time been able to gain relative to other wage earners.

As the compensation of all employees comprises roughly two thirds of the national income, it follows that the general level of "real" wages and salaries (the goods and services the income will buy) cannot advance for long without increased productivity. Wages can, for a time, grow at the expense of profits or other shares, but in the long run the rate of increased productivity sets a ceiling on the increase of real wages.

This truism has been translated into a statement of public policy by the President's Council of Economic Advisers. In 1962, the Council introduced wage-price guideposts to provide standards for noninflationary wage and price behavior. The general guide for wages was that the rate of increases in each industry, including fringe benefits, should be equal to the rate of productivity increases for the economy. The need for specific modifications was recognized; for example, more rapid rates of increase would be justified in low wage industries or in industries that needed to attract additional labor. Opinions differ on the role of the guideposts, but for the period 1962–66 the pattern of wage and price changes did approximate the Council's description.

In the long run, competition for labor might cause real wages to keep pace with rising productivity, but there is no assurance that it will. Certainly, the bulk of organized workers are not likely to resign themselves either to the benevolent dispositions of their employers or the gradual workings of a free, nonunion labor market. The role of unions then is to maintain pressure on employers to keep wages rising. From industry to industry and from plant to plant, differences in productivity and the relative economic strength of labor and management will yield wage differences. But the over-all effect of the unions will be to strengthen the long-run tendency for wages to rise with productivity.

Wages alone do not tell the full story of employee compensation because "fringe benefits" have accounted for an increasing share of the wage bill in recent years. These supplements to regular wages are now an important part of the payroll of American business. Indeed, they have become so large that the term "fringe benefits" is hardly appropriate. These benefits include pay for time not worked (such as vacation pay, sick leave, and voting time), monetary awards and prizes, bonuses, profit-sharing plans, educational subsidies, pensions, payments for death, hospitalization, medical, and surgical insurance, and special services such as credit union facilities and employee discounts.

Some of these wage supplements have resulted from legislation (old-age and survivors' insurance, unemployment insurance, and workmen's compensation), and some from the greater concern of management with employee morale. There is little doubt, however, that the growth and prevalence of these supplements largely reflects union bargaining power. Much of the growth in wage supplements took place during the wage stabilization programs of the Second World War and the Korean conflict. When unions were unable to obtain increases in wage rates, they sought instead to obtain non-wage payments. By 1960 negotiated health and insurance plans covered 14.5 million workers and pension plans 11 million (or 80 per cent and 60 per cent, respectively, of all workers covered by union contracts.)

In recent years, unions have also shown a growing interest in a more stable income and protection against the impact of technological change. For example, demands for a "guaranteed annual wage" in recent years have led to the introduction of supplementary unemployment benefits in labor contracts. These SUB plans generally provide for employer contributions to a trust fund that makes weekly cash payments to employees who are out of work and eligible for state unemployment compensation.

To workers, one of the most significant contributions of unions has been the improvement of working rules, protection from employer dictation, and an increase in security. Some observers contend that the orderly and judicial procedure for settling grievances is the most important union contribution to the welfare of the workers and to industrial relations in general. The grievance procedure is the machinery for handling the disputes and complaints that arise out of the interpretation and enforcement of union contracts. Collective bargaining contracts usually provide for procedures whereby individuals—representing the company or the union—can appeal for redress. Procedures provide that the worker and his shop representative can appeal to foremen and then to successive levels of authority up to representatives of top management and the national union. Finally, there is wide acceptance of the right of either side to appeal to an umpire or arbitrator whose decision may be accepted as final and binding on both parties.

For the individual worker, the singular importance of the grievance procedure negotiated by his union is that it assures him full and just consideration of his complaints. Most companies, too, have been equally interested in perfecting workable grievance procedures, as they help to maintain employee morale, eliminate many causes of industrial unrest, and avert work stoppages resulting from unsolved issues. Seniority rules may provide additional protection to the workers by assuring a measure of job security and a chance for promotion. These rules play much the same role as civil service regulations and tenure for teachers. They serve the desire of the workers for security.

But not all unions are equally concerned with the welfare of the workers. Like any group they may occasionally fall under the domination of unscrupulous leaders. Fortunately, however, most American labor unions have responsible leadership. The AFL-CIO has taken strong measures in recent years to deal with crooked union leaders and has expelled several unions from membership in the national organization. The racketeers in unions may get some of the headlines, but they represent only a minority of unions.

HOW DO UNIONS AFFECT MANAGEMENT?

To the employer, the growth of unionism has often resulted in some loss of managerial control. He has lost the power to set wages unilaterally, subject only to the factors of supply and demand of the market place; his power to promote or fire workers has been limited; his power to discipline employees has been curbed. Moreover, he has frequently been forced to fall in line with the wage pattern set by a dominant firm in the industry. He has been persuaded to change his organizational structure to include a division or department of industrial relations, and at times to accept the decisions of outside arbitrators regarding working conditions in his plant.

Observing the spread of collective bargaining contracts into areas that once appeared to be the sole prerogatives of management, we may ask: How far can labor be allowed to assert its voice in the formulation of policies that were once the exclusive concern of management? At what point will the ability of management to manage be dangerously hampered?

There are few laws or accepted rules limiting the range of collective bargaining. Therefore, these questions are not readily answered. It is not easy to determine the point at which union demands for self-determination seriously obstruct the operations of management. Fifty years ago, the attempts of unions to bargain over wages were opposed as an invasion of the rights of management. Today, bargaining over wages has become established, while union bargaining on the rate and timing of production is generally being resisted.

For the most part, unions have sought a role in deciding affairs they believed affected the welfare of their members. Over the years, they have expanded their notion of what affects the welfare of their members. Consequently, the scope of collective bargaining has increased. It seems likely that unions will continue to press for a greater voice in affairs that affect their members. However, there is little evidence that they desire real joint management-labor direction of enterprise. Generally, American union leaders feel that they can better serve the workers by bargaining with management than by assuming the managerial role.

Although labor usually appears to be the aggressor, it is not always. During a period of rising income and employment, demands for wage increases and other benefits tend to be initiated by the union. If the economy is prosperous, unions have a better chance for success in their bargaining. However, in a period of declining income, many of the pressures generated at the bargaining table will arise from management. When incomes and sales are falling, employers may seek to reduce expenses by cutting wages and other labor costs. A sustained period of such negotiations initiated by management would make management appear, in the eyes of labor, as the party that is "encroaching" on the other.

The failure of firms has occasionally been blamed on unions. From time to time, firms have announced that they were going out of business because "unreasonable demands" by labor had made operations unprofitable. It has seldom been clear, however, whether the union demands were *the* cause, or the final straw, or merely an alibi. There is no doubt that a strong union has the power to impose demands that would make profitable operations impossible. On occasion, especially when the union has greatly miscalculated the ability of management to meet higher labor costs, unions have probably caused significant business losses. But when the union is merely trying to raise wages to a level being paid by competing firms, the failure of a firm may not be attributed to abuse of union power. When wages are the same in competitive firms, business failure is generally a result of the inability of management to meet business competition.

On the positive side, management has often found the union a helpful ally. The union may provide management with useful information about the status of employee morale. Co-operation in the grievance procedure can prevent minor complaints from growing into major issues. Some unions maintain expert staffs that seek ways to improve production. It is not unusual to find labor and management combining to lobby for the passage or defeat of legislation that affects the interests of their industry.

In some instances, unions have accepted lower wages in an attempt to keep some firms in operation. For example, some New England textile workers accepted wage cuts in order to prevent manufacturers from closing down their plants in New England and moving to the South. At the same time, unions have attempted to raise wages in the South. Generally, unions attempt to maintain the same scale throughout a given industry—preventing one firm from gaining an advantage over another in wage rates.

It is not possible to catalogue all the ways in which unions affect management. The rapid growth of the field of "industrial relations" reflects the importance of their influence. Even firms that are not unionized are affected by the existence of unions. They usually have to meet the prevailing wages and conditions of employment established by bargaining elsewhere, and some firms modify their employment practices in an effort to keep employees out of the unions. The labor union, like the corporation, has become an institution affecting the operation of most American businesses, and it is the task of each firm to deal with this institution in a way that will best serve the objectives of the firm.

THE IMPACT OF UNIONISM
ON THE ECONOMY

The union may affect the productivity of the economy, its prices and employment, the distribution of its national income, and its industrial peace. With union influence becoming more and more a part of our national economic life, there is no doubt that the public interest is increasingly concerned with the day-to-day operations of labor unions, with the conduct of their collective bargaining negotiations, and with the provisions of their collective bargaining contracts.

Some unions use practices that clearly reduce labor productivity. Union controls over hirings, layoffs, and promotion by seniority may have an indirect adverse effect on productive efficiency. More direct limitations on productivity come from union make-work or "feather bedding" rules. Restrictions on the amount of bricks a bricklayer can put in place per day, extra stand-by musicians for radio stations, extra workers on railroads, and restraints on the operations of out-of-town truckers are familiar illustrations of such union practices. On occasion, union opposition to technological advances has retarded the expansion of labor productivity. Unions support these restrictions on the ground that they are necessary for the health, safety, or security of their members. Whether we always agree with this reasoning, we must recognize that these practices tend to curtail production.

Union restraints on productivity, however, are not universal. Some of them are a heritage of the early struggle for recognition. Some result from a fear that new jobs may be hard to find. As the conditions that lead to restraints are more pressing in some industries than they are in others, union policies toward them differ from industry to industry. However, most union leaders recognize that economic growth requires technological change and increased productivity. As one labor leader expressed it, "Nothing could

98

be more wicked or foolish [than to restrict replacement of men by machines]. You can't stop technological progress and it would be silly to try it if you could." The major concern of most unions is to see that the adjustment to new technology is made without serious harm to the welfare of the workers.

Union wage policy—the pressure for more labor income —is often a stimulant to economic growth. It induces management to find new and better ways of reducing costs. In other words, by seeking greater income, unions actively stimulate management to accelerate technological advancement. Mechanization of the coal mines and dieselization of the railroads, for example, are generally considered to be partially the result of union pressure for higher wages. Similarly, unionization of the clothing workers eliminated the "sweatshop" and forced employers to adopt more productive means of operation. Demands made by unions for shorter hours, sanitary and safety standards, and other better working conditions have likewise at times contributed to increased productivity and larger total output. But not all economists accept this "shock" theory of increasing productivity. Some believe that strong unions can force employers to share the gains of new technology with workers; if they do, they argue, it will reduce the incentive for innovation.

The impact of union policies on prices and employment is difficult to assess. If unions succeed through collective bargaining in raising wages only by the amount of increased productivity, the effect on prices or employment will tend to be slight, although, as shown later, there may be an effect on the distribution of income. If, however, the increased wages (the cost of labor) are not matched by increased productivity, the effects on prices and employment may be far-reaching. Confronted by higher labor costs, management must either absorb them, pass them on through price increases to consumers, or cut costs elsewhere.

If the wage increase occurs in an industry where the

product involved has a highly elastic demand, that is, where a price increase would deter a large number of buyers, the firm will generally have to absorb the increase. A firm with profits large enough can do this, and the effect will be a shift in the distribution of income. However, if the profits of a firm are small, a wage increase may have to be passed on. One of the debates between labor and management since the Second World War has dealt with this point—whether wage increases can be absorbed or have to be passed on. The arguments over "the ability to pay" have never been resolved, largely because people, even those on the same side, can not agree on what is a "necessary" profit or how much of the additional cost can be passed on.

When the cost of wage increases is passed on to consumers, the output of the firm may be affected. Except where the demand for the product is inelastic—that is, where sales do not appreciably change when the price changes—price increases by an individual producer will tend to reduce his sales; consumers will tend to reduce their purchases and spend their money for other items. A decline in sales will lead to a decline in production; a decline in production will result in the layoff of some workers. These workers may be absorbed by the firms whose output has expanded. But if the demand for labor in other firms does not increase, the workers will remain jobless. As the saying goes, they will have been "priced out of the market."

But a firm's output and employment do not always change when wages change. Reductions in profit margins, in other production costs, or increased productivity of workers may offset the rise in the wage bill. Declining production and employment may also be averted if the wage increase becomes widespread—that is, if a wage increase in a pace-setting industry is followed by wage increases in other industries. The cost of these increases may be passed along to consumers, leading to a general rise in prices that leaves the firm's relative position unaffected. Indeed, higher wages may help sustain the higher prices;

if this income effect is sufficiently widespread, total demand and total output may remain unchanged.

When labor is fully employed, widespread wage increases that outstrip the growth in labor productivity will tend to feed inflation. Monetary gains will be illusory to the degree that they are offset by rises in the price level. For example, after the Second World War successive "rounds" of wage increases did not lead to unemployment, but rather contributed to an increase in incomes and prices. Each union generally felt that it had to get more to "catch up." When it did "catch up" under a new contract, other unions had to do the same.

Because it is hard to forecast the effects of wage increases, it is understandable that union leaders give relatively little attention to the effect of a wage demand on employment. A wage increase occurs in the present, and the price and employment effects generally occur in the uncertain future.

Unions have encouraged "the downward rigidity and the upward flexibility" of wages and prices. When national income is falling, wage and price cuts are less likely to occur in organized industries. The union may foresee future difficulties in restoring a wage cut, but it is less able to foresee how much a wage cut may help or harm employment. Thus it will generally resist wage cuts—even in the face of a general decline in economic activity. The fact that workers can fall back on unemployment compensation encourages unions to allow the pressure of a recession (lower national income) to fall on employment rather than lower wages. In the industrial sphere, this behavior reinforces the tendency of firms to hold their prices relatively stable and adjust to the recession by curtailing production and employment.

Unions maintain upward pressure on wages to increase the share of their members in the growth of the national product. Theoretically, labor can share in the increased output of our economy without getting increased wages. For instance, if our economy becomes more productive, that is, if more goods and services are produced per worker, the prices of goods and services may fall. If prices are lower, workers will obtain more with the same money income. In other words, workers with stable wages will share the gains of greater productivity if the economy is so competitive that producers must reduce prices in order to sell their larger output.

Broadly speaking, however, unions are not likely to rely on this process; first, because they doubt whether lower prices would result; second, because even if they believe that price cuts will increase the real value of money wages, each union wants to improve the incomes of its own workers a little bit more; third, because a union leader who tried to sell his members on the prospects of future price cuts in the things they buy, instead of higher wages, would soon be out of a job.

Work stoppages are another way in which unions affect our economy. Work stoppages usually result from a breakdown of collective bargaining. Therefore as both unions and management are involved in the bargaining, we can seldom say a stoppage has been "caused by the union" or "caused by management." Actually, most work stoppages result from miscalculations in the collective bargaining process. There are exceptions, however; for instance, the "wildcat strike" (workers defy their leaders and bypass collective bargaining in order to stop work over some grievance), the "racketeering strike" (a few unions have been controlled by racketeers who use the strike for extortion), or "union busting" (employers refuse to bargain in the hope that a prolonged strike will break the power of the union). The work stoppages that result from these conditions occur because collective bargaining is not used in good faith.

But most collective bargaining sessions are concluded without a strike. Estimates of the United States Bureau of Labor Statistics show that even during the great "strike year," 1946, over 1,000 new labor contracts were peacefully settled each week and strikes resulted in a loss of only about 1.4 per cent of total man-days worked. In 1947, about 100,000 labor contracts were negotiated, 24 out of 25 of them peacefully. Between 1955 and 1965, the average loss of time from strikes was less than ¼ of 1 per cent of the total man-days worked. The number of work stoppages has not declined, but fewer workers have been involved and most strikes are settled promptly (in 1965 three out of five lasted two weeks or less).

A major contribution to industrial peace in the postwar period has been the trend toward agreements lasting two years or more. The one-year contract once typical of collective bargaining had become the exception to the rule by the early 1960's. These long-term contracts frequently provided for automatic wage adjustments during the life of the contract geared to changes in productivity or the price level, or both.

There is no doubt that the economy has come a long way from the time when the desire to "bust the union" was a part of the every-day creed of business, and union leaders claimed that the businessman was a "soulless exploiter of human suffering." Today, the old phrases are sometimes brought out again in the heat of battle, but they generally do not have the ring of an earlier period.

This brings us to the question of government policy toward public emergency strikes. We shall use this question to illustrate again the steps in economic analysis.

The Problems and Issues

An important task of public policy toward labor has been to help establish an environment in which labor and management will reach a bargain that will be mutually advantageous and fair to the public. The legal framework that has developed encourages the formation of unions and the use of collective bargaining by labor and management. The Wagner Act, for example, established the basic "rules of the game" by saying that employers must allow workers to organize into unions, must not make attempts to break the power of the union, and must bargain with the union in good faith (that is, must honestly attempt to reach a settlement). The law said, in effect, that labor unions are legitimate economic bargaining units that must be treated by the same rules that apply to any bargaining unit in a competitive economy, and efforts to destroy them are illegal.

The Taft-Hartley Act and the Landrum-Griffin Act placed restraints on the powers of the unions—saying, in effect, that they, too, must abide by certain rules. They must reflect the actual desires of their workers, they must not impose certain restraints on the ability of workers to obtain employment, they cannot employ certain "unfair labor practices," and they must disclose certain information about the officers and the finances of the union. Also, strikes in vital industries were made subject to certain controls.

As we noted earlier, one of the weapons in industrial conflicts is the strike. Most of the time it is not needed, but occasionally it is used. When a strike occurs in a major industry, the whole economy feels some of the effects. When most of the coal industry is shut down, or the railroads or airlines are tied up, or milk deliveries are halted, the impact on the public is great.

Occasionally, a strike means that the public may be deprived of goods and services that, even if not essential for health and safety, are important to comfort. In addition, employees are deprived of employment and income, and this loss may depress business activity in the affected area. The consequences of a strike may also spill over into other industries: a strike in the steel industry, for example, can cause loss of work in the automobile industry. Under many conditions, therefore, a strike is a public calamity rather than a purely private contest over wages, hours, or working conditions.

Public pressure for settlement of industrial disputes always exists. Generally, the public is less interested in the terms of settlement than in the settlement itself. Both labor and management recognize this. They recognize that there are three parties to the dispute, not two, and that the third party—the public—grants labor and management the right to pursue free collective bargaining in the expectation that both sides will actively seek agreement.

In general, the public is willing to bear some occasional inconvenience in order to allow labor and management to settle their differences by negotiation, but there are limits to public forbearance. The public has generally indicated that it will not tolerate a shutdown of vital services like electricity or a sustained breakdown in the delivery of vital goods like steel or milk. In such emergencies, the public has shown many times that it will not allow the government to stand idly by while labor and management engage in a test of strength.

When public health or safety is endangered or when an important part of the production of the nation will be halted by a strike, some action must therefore be taken. The major issue then is to determine what steps may be taken. The principal questions to be answered are: What will different measures do to our system of collective bargaining? How effective will different measures be in ending the work stoppage? What measures will be most fair to all parties?

Objectives

The basic objectives of the public when a strike has curtailed the flow of indispensable goods or services is to restore the flow of production. At the same time, the public also has the goal of preserving our pattern of free collective bargaining. Consequently, an emergency strike forces the public into a choice in which it tends either: (1) to preserve and assist free labor-management relations—thus risking the loss of vital goods and services; or (2) to maintain the flow of vital goods and services with governmental order—thus sidestepping the bargaining process.

The requirements for a solution to the problem might be that neither labor nor management will receive any special advantage, that the government will not continue to intervene indefinitely, that any government action will not hinder a private agreement, or that force will or will not be used. Here again, there may be conflicts; conflicts that will have to be settled in order to reach a decision.

Alternatives and Consequences

First, the importance of preserving free and voluntary solutions of industrial conflicts suggests the use of *mediation and fact-finding*. Mediation in a labor dispute is the intervention of a third party—usually appointed by the government. The go-between may enter the dispute at the request of either side or when the government offers mediation in the public interest. The mediator uses his skill to find a compromise solution, but he is not empowered to compel either party to accept the compromise. He tries to keep tempers down so that both sides can continue to work toward a solution. In general, he uses his understanding of the issues, the individuals, and the bargaining process to bring the parties together so the deadlock can be broken.

Fact-finding involves the appointment of an impartial board to investigate and report on the facts of the dispute. Fact-finding boards at times recommend solutions, although they do not have the power to enforce them. The purpose of these fact-finding reports is to clarify the issues and to help build up public opinion that will put pressure on the parties to accept a solution.

Both methods have been used to deal with emergency strikes, and sometimes they have been useful in expediting a solution. They have the advantage of preserving the freedom of union-management relations. But they do not meet the other requirements of a policy to deal with the public emergency strike. They do not guarantee the continued flow of indispensable goods and services. If they fail to bring about a solution, the public may demand more drastic action.

Second, to compel the performance of indispensable services or the production and delivery of essential goods, *compulsory arbitration* is sometimes proposed. Several states have passed laws calling for compulsory arbitration of disputes involving public utilities. These laws generally provide for the appointment of an impartial board that investigates the dispute and decides on a settlement that the state can enforce. However, in some states where these laws have been tested in the courts, compulsory arbitration has been held unconstitutional when it affects interstate commerce.

Generally, proposals for compulsory arbitration have not had wide support. One reason is the feeling that it would concentrate too much power in the hands of a few people, and, as it is a government program, these people may be involved in politics. A more basic objection is the view that if labor and management can get along well enough to make the system work, they probably do not need it. In brief, this approach has received little use and little support in this country.

Third, the *injunction* is a court order that prohibits both employers and employees from shutting down operations. It usually requires operations to continue under existing conditions. The Taft-Hartley Act, for example, empowers the federal government to obtain an eighty-day injunction against a work stoppage in an essential industry. This injunction is intended to provide a "cooling-off" period during which labor and management will have additional time to resolve their disputes. In practice, however, the injunction has not always proved to be effective, because the union is free to strike when the injunction expires. The injunction may merely change the deadline for a strike. Another criticism of the injunction is that it works to the benefit of the party resisting change. Typically, this has been the employer, but in a period of declining business activity, it could act to the disadvantage of an employer who seeks a reduction in pay or an increase in hours worked. An injunction of indefinite length obviously would be grossly unfair in a society in which economic conditions change as they do in the United States.

Fourth, by *seizing* a strikebound firm, the government can safeguard the flow of production. When the government seizes a plant, it continues operations either under existing conditions (with a deduction of a percentage of net income as compensation for its services), or under temporary new wage scales established by a special board. The advocates of seizure as a weapon of last resort point out that it averts public hardship, while leaving to the union and the company the task of arriving at a final settlement by the bargaining process. When agreement is reached, the firm is returned to the management of the company.

However, the terms of seizure do not make agreement equally urgent to both parties. If the seizure provides for maintaining the status quo, it is open to the same objections that are raised against the injunction: it works to the benefit of the party resisting change; this party has little incentive to push for a solution that would involve important concessions. If the terms of seizure allow for changes in wage rates and working conditions, the party that benefits has no incentive to seek a permanent solution. Moreover, a change in the working conditions may have the effect of compulsory arbitration; that is, the new terms would represent the minimum acceptable to the favored party. In this instance, the claim that seizure preserves the free bargaining process would be illusory.

In public policy toward emergency strikes, the government must consider not only the alternatives available but also the way in which they are used. If the government lets the parties to the dispute know which weapon it will use to compel fulfillment of the demands of the public, it will tend to weaken the chances for settlement. For example, if the employer feels assured that the government will resort to an injunction that will favor him, he will have less incentive to bargain in good faith. The same is true in the case of the union. If it is assured that the weapon of compulsion will work in its favor, it will have less incentive to bargain in good faith.

Choice of Alternatives

The threat of governmental action stresses an important aspect of collective bargaining—that it is a contest in which economic strength, the persuasive abilities of the parties, the ability to bluff, the backing of workers or other employers, and many other economic and noneconomic factors all play a part. To resolve such a contest, both parties must strongly desire a settlement. The function of public policy is to increase the desirability to both parties for settlement and thereby to reduce the probability of a strike.

The *threat* of an arsenal of government weapons can help the situation, but it cannot provide a complete solution. In some cases, each disputing party may foresee, correctly or incorrectly, governmental intervention as an aid to its position. Each party may feel it is futile even to consider such an uncertainty as governmental control, or may not strongly care whether there is a strike or not. Eventually, therefore, such stoppages may have to be settled by the only alternative—compulsion.

Each of us must decide for himself whether compulsion is or is not necessary. If compulsion is deemed necessary, which of the alternative forms of compulsion best meets our needs? Also, what about the specific conditions to be imposed? Shall the existing wage level continue while the government has control? How can we bring equal pressure on unions and management to settle their differences? Our ultimate decision on such questions will be based on our objectives and our understanding of the consequences of different courses of action.

This chapter has stressed the following basic ideas:

1. Labor unions are one of the most important groups in this country; they play an established role in our economic system. Like many other economic groups, their primary objective is to enhance the welfare of their members. However, they are not motivated solely by economic

considerations; they have their own internal political objectives, and they have social objectives. Occasionally, these other goals actually conflict with their economic interests.

2. One of the most important achievements of unions is the maintenance of pressure on employers for wage increases and other economic benefits. Unions have also provided the individual worker with a greater degree of control over his working conditions. Many decisions formerly made exclusively by management are now influenced by unions. The economy has thus shifted from an arrangement in which management provided most of the directive influence over economic activity to an arrangement in which both management and labor direct economic affairs.

3. Wages, employment, and prices are affected by collective bargaining. However, wage increases gained by collective bargaining may or may not be inflationary—they may contribute to price increases or they may contribute to falling prices. Similarly, wage increases may result in an expansion of employment or unemployment. Their effects at any given time will depend on a number of other factors: how much employment already exists, how much output per worker has changed, whether consumers are willing to pay higher prices for a given amount of a product, and so forth. In order to evaluate the economic effects of the demands of the union for wage increases or the demands of management for wage cuts, it is necessary to understand many relevant circumstances.

4. As work stoppages halt production, they can be considered an economic loss. However, this loss may be measured against the gains that result from free collective bargaining. Broadly speaking, the American people have decided that the gains outweigh the losses. However, there are occasions when the effects of a work stoppage extend far beyond the immediate area of union-management conflict, and the cost exceeds the gains. These cases raise some of the most difficult issues of public policy toward labor.

Suggested Reading

Paul A. Samuelson, *Economics: An Introductory Analysis*, Chap. 7, pp. 123–38, Chap. 29, pp. 542–69. George L. Bach, *Economics: An Introduction to Analysis and Policy*, Chaps. 31–32, pp. 491–527. These selections explore the practices and goals of labor unions and some of the economic consequences of union policies. (In a few sections the discussion may be somewhat advanced for those who have not read earlier chapters in the books). See also "The Impact of Unions on the Level of Wages," by Clark Kerr; "Minimum-wage Rates," by Milton Friedman; "Labor Unions Are Worth the Price," by Max Ways; "Can Union Power Be Curbed?" by Edward H. Chamberlin in *Readings in Economics* (Samuelson et al., ed.), pp. 248–73.

Chapter 5

DEBTS AND MONEY

The preceding chapters have described some characteristics of our "mixed economy." They have indicated the way the market regulates production and distributes economic rewards. They showed the roles that competition, governmental controls and regulations, labor unions, and a variety of other influences play in economic life. Now we turn to a new topic—the role of money and debt in our economy.

American economic growth has been accompanied by an increase in public and private debt. By the end of 1965, the debts of consumers, business firms, state, local, and national governments, and the private financial institutions of this country were an estimated $2150 billion. They had increased six-fold in twenty-five years, and they were still rising. By 1970, these debts will probably exceed $2.6 trillion.

As the chart on page 114 shows, financial institutions—banks, insurance companies, and other financial organizations—have the largest debts, and governments and businesses owe considerably more debts than they hold. As a debt is merely the promise of a person, group, or institution to pay another at some future date, the graph also shows the obvious fact that for every borrower there is a lender. For the whole economy, the volume of debt is equal to the volume of credit.

Surprisingly enough, this total volume of debt has been built up faster during prosperity than during recessions.

As individuals, we might expect to go into debt in bad times and to pay off in good times. But actually this offhand, common-sense expectation does not hold for the economy. Total debt (public and private) has tended to grow as gross national product has grown.

TOTAL DEBT 1965ᵃ

WHO OWES IT?

CONSUMERS $340 billion

TOTAL $2150 billion

CONSUMERS $780 billion

WHO HOLDS IT?

BUSINESSES $570 billion

GOVERNMENTS $370 billion

FINANCIAL INSTITUTIONS $870 billion

BUSINESSES $310 billion

GOVERNMENTS $115 billion

FINANCIAL INSTITUTIONS $945 billion

ᵃ These figures are estimates based in part on flow of funds data in the *Federal Reserve Bulletin* (May 1966) and "Net Public and Private Debt," *Economic Report of the President, 1966*, p. 272. All figures are rounded to the nearest $5 billion. Nonprofit associations and trust funds are included in the group labeled "consumers."

Basically, the growth of income and the growth of debt go together, because the amount that many people want to spend is influenced by their incomes. Businessmen, for example, are optimistic about the future when their income is growing; thus, they are more willing to borrow during prosperity. At the same time, many people tend to save more as their incomes increase. As their incomes rise, their spending rises, but not as rapidly; hence, their savings also rise. The growth of debt is the way that the deficits of one group and the surpluses of another are brought together. As these surpluses and deficits tend to grow with income, the growth of income contributes to the growth of debt.

One of the most important things to learn about our economic system is that it requires the use of debts. The objective of public policy is not to eliminate debt, but to manage it so as to maintain the flow of income and production. We shall see later what specific functions debts play for various groups, but let us list here the major functions they play for the economy as a whole.

Debt enables us to adjust the timing of our spending. By freeing us from the day-to-day restraint imposed by our income, debt enables us to meet emergencies and to enjoy consumption, build factories, or make major governmental outlays when we most want them and then pay for them out of future income.

Debt enables us to build new productive equipment. Savers are not necessarily directly interested in creating capital (building factories, tools, or other productive equipment), hence debts bridge the gap between them and the people who create capital. Moreover, debts enable a large number of persons to pool their savings to buy equipment that would be too expensive to be financed by a few. It also helps existing enterprises over temporary periods of inadequate income. In each of these respects, debt facilitates economic growth.

Debt provides us with our money supply. Not only our currency but our main medium of exchange, commercial bank deposits, is a form of debt. In the specialized industrial economy based on exchange, this money provides a convenient and readily acceptable means of payment.

We can see how these functions are performed by looking at the debts of the four major groups—consumers, business, governments, and financial institutions. Of course, each of these groups contains some borrowers and some lenders, and each does some borrowing from the other groups. Each borrows for different reasons, and when it borrows, it has different effects on the economy.

THE ROLE OF CONSUMER DEBT

The opportunity to "buy now and pay later" has radically changed the living conditions of American consumers. Without the use of credit, the consumer might have to put off buying a house, a car, or a kitchen range until he had saved enough money for the purchase. With credit, he enjoys the use of the house, car, or range while paying for it.

Debt, in short, enables the consumer to enjoy a richer way of life. Is he "living beyond his income"? For the most part, he is not. If a man has an income of $5,000 per year, he obviously cannot buy an $18,000 house with that year's income. But over a twenty-year period his income will total $100,000—quite enough to permit an $18,000 purchase—and a twenty-year mortgage recognizes this fact. A consumer may appear to live beyond his income because he goes into debt for a major purpose, but he generally does not live beyond his present-plus-future income; only those who consume their inherited wealth and those who die in debt, live beyond their income over the long run.

Some people argue that if individuals would save as much before they buy as they do after they go into debt, they could still have what they want—without paying interest. But it is not quite that simple.

In the first place, unless people can borrow, frequently they will have to wait before they can buy. Debt enables them to buy more nearly at the time they choose. In addition, many people apparently will not or cannot save except under the pressure of an overhanging debt. If they could not borrow to buy a car, they might never have a car at all, for they might never put aside enough money beforehand to buy it.

Debt is especially useful for the purchase of houses. The people who most want housing are young couples with growing families. Most of them have not saved enough money to buy outright the kind of house they need. By the time they could save enough, they would no longer want big houses: their children would have grown up, married, and moved away, and would probably be buying homes of their own—on credit. So they go into debt. Consumer credit enables families to grow up in bigger and better homes by permitting the bit-by-bit purchases of houses.

Despite their borrowing, consumers on the average spend less than their total income. Although they owed

TOTAL DEBT 1965

WHO OWES IT?				WHO HOLDS IT?
CONSUMERS $ 340 billion	TOTAL $ 2150 billion	CONSUMERS $ 780 billion		
BUSINESSES $ 570 billion				
GOVERNMENTS $ 370 billion		BUSINESSES $ 310 billion		
FINANCIAL INSTITUTIONS $ 870 billion			GOVERNMENTS $ 115 billion	FINANCIAL INSTITUTIONS $ 945 billion

$340 billion in 1965[1], they held debt or claims on others amounting to $780 billion. They are, as the chart above shows, a group with surplus income—although some of the group borrows, as a whole, the group has tended to spend less than its income. Consumers hold some of the debts of other consumers. They hold a large part of the business debt and a large part of the debt of the federal government. They also hold a large share of the insurance policies and bank deposits, which are the debts of financial institutions. In other words, consumers as a group have transferred (loaned) their surplus to the other groups.

THE ROLE OF BUSINESS DEBT

Unlike consumers, business owes more debt than it holds. As the chart on page 119 shows, in 1965 business owed $570 billion, mainly to individuals (consumers) and financial institutions.[2] It held only $310 billion of the debts of others, and some of that includes the debts of individual businesses. These figures do not mean, however, that business is "insolvent." Each business has other assets, such as plants, machines, and its position as a going concern, which generally more than offset its debts.

Business debts are commonly considered the most desirable debts in the American economy. Most of us understand and approve debts to increase the production and distribution of goods; for example, when a department store borrows a hundred thousand dollars to finance the purchase of new stocks of merchandise or when a steel company sells $10 million in bonds in order to modernize its blast furnaces.

[1] This was about $220 billion in housing mortgages, $85 billion for purchase of durables, personal loans, charge accounts, etc., and $35 billion for so-called "financial loans" from banks and insurance companies.

[2] About $285 billion in mortgages, bonds, and other long-term debts and about $285 billion in short-term notes, tax accruals, and bank loans. As defined here business includes corporate, noncorporate, and farm enterprises.

TOTAL DEBT 1965

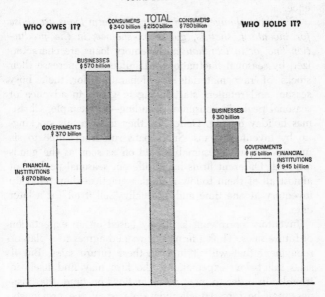

WHO OWES IT?

CONSUMERS $340 billion

TOTAL $2150 billion

CONSUMERS $780 billion

WHO HOLDS IT?

BUSINESSES $570 billion

GOVERNMENTS $370 billion

BUSINESSES $310 billion

GOVERNMENTS $115 billion

FINANCIAL INSTITUTIONS $945 billion

FINANCIAL INSTITUTIONS $870 billion

Businessmen, however, do not go into debt merely for the sake of increasing production. They have another, more basic motivation. They want to make profits. Whether a loan is for a steel plant or a dance studio, the ultimate test will be whether it can make an adequate return. That is the test that will be posed by both borrower and lender.

Business borrows for two broad purposes: to maintain day-to-day operations and to finance major capital improvements. Day-to-day borrowing is necessary because workers must be paid promptly, materials have to be purchased, inventories have to be held for certain periods, and slow-paying customers must be financed—in short, a steady stream of bills must be paid when due. Few businesses can schedule their operations so that incoming revenue can always be counted on to meet the demands for outgoing cash. Therefore, most enterprises find it necessary to borrow additional funds to make up the difference.

The most changeable of these short-term loans are those for inventory, that is, goods on shelves, in the production line, or in warehouses. Inventory loans are characterized by seasonal fluctuations. Manufacturers increase their stocks of raw materials in preparation for their busy season, and retailers start laying in goods in advance of seasonal peaks in consumer spending—for example, Christmas holiday buying. Generally, they finance this stocking-up by inventory loans. Such loans run from three to six months and are presumably paid off as soon as the goods are sold. Different firms have different seasonal peaks, but almost all of them follow a similar practice—they build up inventory at one time and gradually "sell it off" at a later date.

Inventory borrowing is clearly based on an expectation of future sales. Thus a firm borrows and agrees to a plan of repayment that will fit in with these future sales. But if sales fall below expectations, the firm may find itself in trouble. In order to meet its obligations on time, the business may be forced to liquidate a part of the previously acquired inventory at reduced prices. Unfortunately for economic stability, the businessman tends to follow this erratic pattern because he must (1) anticipate his sales on the basis of forecasts and (2) meet his fixed credit obligations. Of course, without inventory debts, the occasional pressure to get rid of inventory would be milder, but apparently we prefer to pay the price of this instability for the convenience of having our businesses well-stocked.

The economic decline that occurred in late 1957 and early 1958 was due partly to a cutback in business buying for inventory. Before the decline began, business was adding to its inventories at a rate of about $2 billion a year. During the worst of the recession, however, business not only stopped buying the $2 billion in new inventory but also began selling off the stocks it already had on hand—at the rate of over $8 billion a year. In other words, business not only stopped buying goods to add to stocks in its warehouses, it didn't buy even enough to keep the stocks at the old level.

Business debt incurred for the purchase of plant and equipment also changes from time to time. It tends to increase more rapidly during prosperity than during periods of declining income. Businessmen wax optimistic and pessimistic like the rest of us, so they tend to expand their equipment when sales are growing and to put off new capital purchases when they are having trouble disposing of all the goods produced with equipment on hand. Their rate of borrowing and spending is therefore highly dependent on their expectations of changes in the level of our national income and employment.

But this is a circular process. Business spending is also an important part of our total spending. Thus a change in the level of investment spending can lead to a change in the level of income and employment. This circular process is discussed in Chapters 6 and 7.

Some of our most prosperous businesses have always been "in debt." They can remain "in debt" because their earning power continues, and people are willing to lend them their money. A business corporation does not have to plan on getting "paid up" when it becomes old. Because it does not have to die, it can remain in debt indefinitely. A person, of course, must redeem his debts during his lifetime or leave an estate to pay them. He may borrow during his lifetime, and he may even "refund" his debts (borrow to pay debts that are coming due) for a while, but a corporation can continue to grow and accumulate new equipment and new debts indefinitely—as long as the way it uses the funds is economically useful.

THE ROLE OF GOVERNMENT DEBT

Most of the outstanding government debt is owed by the federal government. About one sixth of the total government debt is owed by state and local governments. The

121

federal debt—swollen by the cost of fighting wars and meeting various emergencies—accounts for the rest. But this has not always been the case. Throughout most of our history, state and local government debt tended to exceed the federal debt. Since the First World War, however, the federal debt has generally been larger and more important to our economy.

Like business, government borrows more than it lends. In other words, over the years, it has spent more than its income. As the chart on page 123 shows, in 1965, governments owed $370 billion and held only $115 billion of outstanding claims against consumers, businesses, and financial institutions. But also like business, it cannot be said that government is insolvent. Government has vast investments in roads, land, military equipment, schools, and many other tangible and intangible assets, including the power to tax.

The $370 billion is actually the "net debt" of governments. The total amount of outstanding government debt in 1965 was really about $475 billion. Of this, $105 billion was held by agencies and trust funds of the governments, and thus is subtracted from the total.[3] The federal government, for instance, owed $321 billion in 1965 but $61 billion was held by its own trust funds; therefore its obligations *to others* actually amounted to only $260 billion.

State and local government debts arise for the most part, from spending for tangible things: schools, fire houses, parks, playgrounds, and streets. Most state and local governments cannot pile up large funds out of tax revenues with the idea of spending the funds later in a lump sum for some major project. If they do accumulate funds, pressure for tax reduction tends to curtail their savings. So they pay for such projects by issuing bonds and then pay off a certain amount of the bonds year by year.

Unfortunately, state and local governments generally

---

[3] This same calculation was made in adding up the debt of corporations that owe money to their subsidiaries.

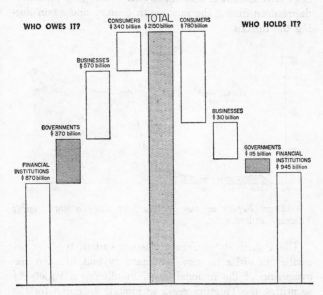

tend to borrow and spend when most of the rest of the economy is doing the same thing. When incomes are high and people have jobs, tax receipts are high, and cities and states have more income available for servicing bonds. Therefore, they borrow during periods of prosperity and cease borrowing in periods of depression when tax receipts fall off. In following this pattern, they tend to aggravate our cycles of prosperity and depression. In addition, this pattern is uneconomical. A local government unit often ends up buying some of its projects when they cost the most—and paying for them when incomes are lower.

As shown by the accompanying chart, most of our present federal debt arose during the Second World War. The pattern of sharp increases brought by the two world wars holds for similar times of crisis, including the Revolutionary War, the War of 1812, and the Civil War. The debt also increased occasionally as a result of panics or depressions during the nineteenth century and again during the thirties.

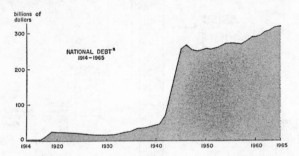

a *Annual Report of the Secretary of the Treasury, 1965;* Treasury Bulletins.

The United States Treasury issues various types of securities in order to vary the maturity and broaden the ownership of the national debt. In offering a variety of securities, the Treasury seeks to provide an outlet for the surplus cash of many different types of investors.

The direct owners are individuals or institutions who have transferred a part of their spending power to the federal government. When we as consumers decide to put some of our funds into government securities, we are, in effect, saying to the government: "Although we have enough money to buy some of the things available in the market place, we don't want to spend it, so you take the money and buy some of the goods you need. Later, you can return the money to us—with interest." The effect of such a transaction is to switch the pattern of spending from the consumer goods we would have purchased to government goods. From washing machines, perhaps, to spacecraft. The same type of transfer takes place when corporations or other investors buy government securities.

OWNERSHIP OF THE FEDERAL DEBT, MARCH 1966[a]

Owner	Amount (In Billions)
Direct Owners	$177
Individuals	$74
Corporations	17
State and Local Governments	24
U. S. Treasury Trust Funds	62
Financial Institutions	145
Commercial banks	$57
Federal Reserve Banks	41
Savings Banks	6
Insurance Companies	10
Other	31
Total Federal Debt	$322

[a] Board of Governors of the Federal Reserve System, *Federal Reserve Bulletin* (May 1966). Figures rounded.

They decide to hold government securities rather than the other things they might have purchased.

The federal government therefore can borrow from the public when it wants to control private spending. In wartime, for example, the government wants to divert much of the resources of the nation from production of consumer goods to war goods. So it asks the public to buy bonds "to help in the war effort." The request is not made because the government cannot get along without our money. It is made so that the public will stop trying to buy consumer goods—stop trying to bid materials away from the government. In wartime, the government will get the things it wants anyway, but it prefers to get them at stable prices in order to avert a general inflation.

Superficially, it might seem that all that should be necessary in such circumstances would be to tax the spending power away from people. But the problem is not that easy to solve. One of the ways war industries persuaded people to move from garages in Iowa to airplane plants in Los

Angeles and induced housewives to become welders, was to offer them more money. If the government had then turned around and taxed all of the extra money (it did tax some of it), people would have had little reason for making the changes. Therefore, the government did the next best thing—it tried to persuade people to save their new earnings until after the emergency was over. It asked them to buy government securities.

The key to public debt policy is to borrow from the right people at the right time. In depression, the government should attempt to borrow from people who are not planning to spend much of their income. Actually, as we shall see later, it should try to borrow from banks. It would do the economy little good, and might even do harm, to borrow from people who planned to spend their money anyhow.

During a war or inflation, the government should attempt to do the opposite; it should try to borrow funds that otherwise would have been spent. Of course, if people are already saving and holding their cash idle, the government would not need to borrow to put a damper on consumer spending, but if people tend to spend their incomes as fast as they earn them, the Treasury could help prevent price inflation by getting them to buy bonds instead.

The other group of government debt holders—financial institutions—permit the "indirect purchase" of government securities by providing the public with their own debts. The government regularly invites commercial banks, insurance companies, savings banks, and savings and loan associations to take some of its securities. These institutions are able to buy them because the public buys life insurance policies and holds accounts at savings institutions and commercial banks.

The public, which may not want to purchase any more government securities, purchases them indirectly. The financial institutions create liquid assets for the public as a substitute for the government securities that the financial institutions hold. This is possible because the public prefers to hold these bank deposits, life insurance policies, and other liquid assets that can be converted to cash quickly and without any loss in value.

A portion of the government debt, called "Treasury Currency," plays a special role in the economy. This is the coin and currency issued by the Treasury, which says, in effect, "the United States Government will pay the bearer on demand so and so many dollars." Because we use these "securities" as money, very few people regard them as a part of the government debt. Nevertheless, they are in fact a very special kind of government debt. By custom and by law, we have decided to use them as money—as our medium of exchange and our unit of value—and close to $5 billion of coins and currency of this type were being used this way in early 1966.

We use different things as money. At one time, we used only gold and silver coins, and now we use Treasury coins and currency and several other kinds of paper money. Actually, money can be almost anything—as long as most people will accept it and agree to use it in setting the prices of what they buy and sell. Wampum, furs, stones, and metal have all been used as money at one time or another—and this frequently had very little to do with their usefulness to people.

Money is not mysterious (as some people claim) unless we persist in assuming that there is something tangible and physical "to back it up." In fact, it only requires a sort of social acceptance. In our economy, and most other modern societies, we have decided to use *debts* for our money—not all debts, but only certain types. Treasury currency is one type, but as we shall see later, there are several others.

The federal government's debt—the national debt— often worries people. Too often, however, they worry about the wrong thing. The size of the debt is sometimes said to be a threat to our national solvency. But the fact is that we do not know how large the national debt can become before we might run into trouble. We do know, however, that it can be much higher than today—even though we do not know the precise amount.

We should remember that one hundred years ago or even twenty-five years ago, most Americans would have said (and many economists would have agreed with them) that a debt of $320 billion would pose insuperable problems for the American economy. Yet the problems were dealt with, and the nation is prospering as never before in our history.

The national debt *is* large but it must be viewed in the perspective of a growing economy in which the use of credit is an important element. In the twenty years since the end of the Second World War, the net federal debt increased by $18 billion, but in the same period state and local government debt increased by $79 billion, consumer debt by $80 billion, private mortgage debt by $255 billion—and corporate debt increased $350 billion! Compared with other borrowers the federal government has used its credit sparingly in recent years.

Our capacity to bear a national debt is influenced by a number of conditions: how the debt is distributed, how we use the financial institutions, how fast we allow the debt to grow, what happens to private debt, and the rate of growth of the economy itself. This much is certain: the ratio of the public debt to the growing national income can at least remain about the same as it is today; if required by future events, the debt can expand along with the rest of the economy.

But what if future events require a dramatic increase in the national debt? Would this jeopardize our national solvency? To explore this issue, we must first clear away some verbal underbrush. Insolvency means that a debtor does not currently have the ability to pay his debts. Bankruptcy is the legal condition that may result from insolvency; it is the device society uses to decide how much an insolvent borrower can pay to each of his creditors. In the legal sense, these terms cannot be applied to the debts of the federal government to the public. The capacity of the federal government to pay its debts is virtually limitless—it can use taxes or it can create the funds necessary to pay whatever it owes to its citizens. For these and a host of other reasons the state of bankruptcy is not applicable to a national government.

THE ROLE OF THE DEBT OF FINANCIAL INSTITUTIONS

Financial institutions channel funds from savers to borrowers. As intermediaries in the flow of savings, their role is vital to the steady growth of national income. They also provide the economy with most of its money supply as well as other liquid assets. Savings and loan associations, savings banks, insurance companies, and commercial banks owe a variety of debts to the people who have funds deposited with them. These debts occur in many forms.

Savings accounts, sometimes called time deposits, are claims against a savings bank. They do not have to be paid by the savings bank at once. The savings bank may require several months notice. For this privilege, the savings bank generally pays *interest* to the owner of the account. Savings and loan shares work the same way, but the time before the savings and loan association makes payment may be longer. Most life insurance policies grow in value as premiums are paid, and on very short notice, the owner can obtain the accumulated value by surrendering his policy.

Checking accounts (sometimes called demand deposits) are claims against a commercial bank. They must be paid immediately on the request of the owner. A check is an order from the owner of a deposit to the bank; it orders the bank to pay so and so much to the holder of the check. Some commercial banks also owe savings accounts, but a savings bank cannot owe a demand deposit. If a bank has demand deposits, it is a commercial bank.

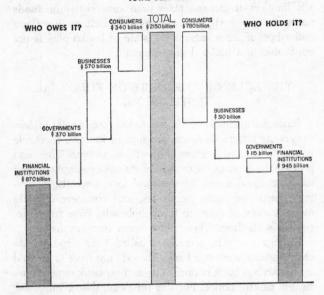

TOTAL DEBT 1965

WHO OWES IT?

CONSUMERS $340 billion

TOTAL $2150 billion

BUSINESSES $570 billion

GOVERNMENTS $370 billion

FINANCIAL INSTITUTIONS $870 billion

CONSUMERS $780 billion

WHO HOLDS IT?

BUSINESSES $310 billion

GOVERNMENTS $115 billion

FINANCIAL INSTITUTIONS $945 billion

As the above chart suggests, financial institutions perform an intermediary function; they create one form of debt in exchange for another. They exchange their debts for those of others. If the people of a community want to save $100,000 and put it in a savings bank, they will receive $100,000 credit in their pass books. The savings bank can then loan the $100,000 to borrowers who will spend it. So the savings bank gives two things to the public—a pass book credit and $100,000. It has also received two things from the public—an IOU from the borrowers and $100,000. The whole transaction has transferred spending power from the depositors (those with a surplus of funds) to the borrowers (those with a deficit of funds).

Financial institutions are necessary because people do not want to invest all of their savings themselves or to lend

their funds directly to the people who want to borrow.
Some people do not like to hold the IOU's of other people
or the bonds and notes of business or government. They
prefer to hold their savings in bank deposits or insurance
policies—they prefer the IOU's of financial institutions. The
main function of financial institutions is to supply these
savers with the kinds of assets they want to own and at
the same time to provide funds for the people who want
to borrow. Thus when people hold more bank deposits, this
indicates that banks have done more lending. If people
hold something else, some other institution has done more
lending.

But are the financial institutions purely passive in these
transactions? Not at all! A commercial bank, for instance,
can go out and find customers to whom it can lend money
and so can the savings institutions. The commercial bank
can offer to take the customer's IOU, and, in return, give
him a checking account (a debt of the bank). The other
financial institutions also make loans, but not quite in the
same way. Savings banks and insurance companies must
first find someone who will deposit money and hold a
savings account or an insurance policy.

This tells us that there is something special about the
commercial bank. A borrower will accept a checking account from a commercial bank, but he will *not* accept a
savings account if he borrows from a savings bank. Why?
Because a borrower wants money that he can spend.

Let us look into this idea of money. As stated earlier,
money can be anything that is generally acceptable as a
medium of exchange. It eliminates barter; it permits each
of us to exchange our specialized output for a wide variety
of other things. The Treasury currency described earlier
and the checks that people write on their bank accounts
perform this function. (The fact that some people will not
accept checks for payments does not alter the fact that
they are *generally* acceptable. In earlier times, some people would not accept gold coins unless they could weigh
them on the spot, yet coins were still considered money.)

But money is more than a medium of exchange; it is also an abstract unit of measure. As an inch is a measure of length, and a pound is a unit of weight, the dollar is the unit we use to measure value. And the money we handle is merely the thing that shows we have a claim for so and so many dollars' worth of goods and services. The fact that money is a generally acceptable *claim* also means that it is a "store of value." Instead of collecting a lot of goods and services for the future, we can hold money with the expectation that we can buy the needed goods and services when we want them.

Certainly, the balance we hold in a checking account at the commercial bank performs the functions of money. But what about the balance we hold in a savings account or in an insurance policy? Is this also money? Almost, but not quite. It is a "store of value"—a claim for a certain amount of dollars—but it cannot be used for the purchase of goods and services without some intermediate steps. We cannot exchange our savings book for groceries, nor can we use our insurance policy to buy a car—but we can convert them to the cash needed for such purchases. For this reason, these other debts of financial institutions are sometimes called *near-money*. They are similar to currency and demand deposits in some ways, but they are not a means of payment.

To summarize, a commercial bank creates new money because it gives its customers checking accounts. As a checking account is money—it can be spent—a depositor has not given up his money when he deposits cash in a commercial bank. He has only changed its form. But when a depositor puts his cash in a savings bank, he gives up cash for a savings account—which cannot be spent. He has exchanged his money for near-money. Thus most financial institutions must issue more near-money in order to obtain the funds with which to make loans, but commercial banks may issue more money at the same time as they increase their loans.

132

There are two principal ways in which commercial banks may increase the money supply outstanding. The first is to lend more to borrowers; the second is to buy more of the existing debt already held by the public. But, at a given time, there are limits on their ability to create money.

The rate at which commercial banks can create money is limited partly by the willingness of the public to borrow. At any time the number of people who are willing to borrow is limited. Borrowing costs something—interest—and some people are not willing to pay this cost. Also, some people are too uncertain about the future to know whether they will be able to repay the loan on schedule—and some people do not even bother to ask for loans because they know the banker would not regard them as sound risks. Whatever the reason, when the public becomes less willing to borrow, it will put a damper on the creation of money.

Banks can, of course, attempt to influence the attitude of the public toward borrowing. They can raise or lower the interest rates they charge, or they can ease or tighten their standards for acceptable loans. But the response to these changes is not always prompt or substantial.

If banks cannot increase the demand for loans, they can still create deposits by buying outstanding debts. When banks buy government securities or other debts that are held by the public, they pay for them with increased bank deposits.

The ability to expand total deposits this way depends upon the attitudes of the public and the banks toward holding deposits and other debts. Bankers may be unwilling to buy securities, as they were in the 1930's, because their yields are too low to offer a satisfactory return. And there are times when the public prefers to hold other debts instead of bank deposits. When a person sends a check to be deposited in a savings and loan association he is saying, in effect, "I prefer to hold savings and loan shares instead of a checking account"; when he buys a government bond he is saying he prefers a bond to a demand deposit; when he draws a check on his account to pay off his note at the bank, he is saying that he prefers less debt rather than more deposits.

Let us use an illustration to show why, if demand deposits are to grow, the public must be willing to hold them. Suppose Mr. A decides to pay off a $1,000 loan he owes the bank; he will write a $1,000 check, payable to the bank, and get back his IOU—the bank will cancel the $1,000 deposit and the $1,000 debt.

Because Mr. A wanted to cancel his IOU rather than hold a bank deposit, he made total deposits fall. And the bank, in order to restore its deposits to their former level, must now try to obtain another security to take the place of the one retired by Mr. A. But this may not be easy. If many people act like Mr. A, the supply of debts will become more scarce, their prices will rise, and the banks may decide that their yield is not worth the price. Thus when the public becomes less willing to hold deposits the willingness of banks to buy securities and create deposits may also be restrained.

The impact on the banks will be similar if Mr. A wants to buy government bonds, savings and loan shares, or any other type of IOU. His funds may compete, directly or indirectly, for the same things that the bank needs to create deposits. Banks can, of course, attempt to persuade depositors to keep their funds in the bank. They may advertise and offer their customers a variety of services to induce them to hold bank deposits. But there are limits to the amount of competition banks can afford and still make a profit. Therefore, if their customers do not readily respond to these efforts, the growth of bank deposits will tend to be retarded.

Legal controls impose an important limit on the ability of the banks to create deposits. For most banks, this limitation is imposed by the Federal Reserve System.[4] The

---

[4] About 85 per cent of our commercial bank deposits are owed by members of the Federal Reserve System—the rest are under state regulation.

banks that are members of the Federal Reserve System can only create deposits if they own some of the debts of the Federal Reserve Banks. Generally speaking, the more debts of the Federal Reserve Banks the commercial banks own, the more deposits they can create.

What is the Federal Reserve System? It is a group of twelve banks (Federal Reserve Banks) located in different sections of the country and operated under the central direction of the Board of Governors of the Federal Reserve System in Washington, D.C. The Federal Reserve System is not a part of the Treasury or any other agency of the federal government; it is a separate agency the primary purpose of which is to supervise the activities of commercial banks. The Board of Governors consists of seven men, appointed for fourteen-year terms by the President with the consent of the United States Senate. These terms are staggered so the Board will be relatively free from control by any single presidential administration.

Each of the twelve Federal Reserve Banks is actually "a banker's bank." Commercial banks use a Federal Reserve Bank in much the same way that we use a commercial bank. The commercial banks own deposits—debts of the Federal Reserve Bank—and they can obtain currency by writing checks on their deposits. They can also write checks to pay what they owe to other banks. They can also borrow from the Federal Reserve Bank in order to build up their deposits.

The important control exercised by the Federal Reserve System is its requirement that each of its member banks must have a deposit of a certain size in a Federal Reserve Bank. This deposit is called its *legal reserve*. The amount of reserves that a bank must own is a prescribed percentage of its deposits. In other words, if a bank has $1 million of demand deposits and a 20 per cent reserve requirement, it will need a $200,000 deposit at the Federal Reserve Bank. If the bank wants to increase its customers' deposits, by receiving cash from the public or by accepting the IOU of a borrower, it will have to increase its reserve account at the Federal Reserve Bank. If it cannot do this, it cannot increase its deposits—that is the law.

By controlling the amount of reserves, the Federal Reserve authorities can impose a limit on the amount of deposits commercial banks can create. We shall not stop here to go into the various ways that the authorities can change the amount of reserves—this is discussed in Chapter 7—but we should note that the control over these reserves is one of our principal means for influencing the level of national income and employment.

In summary, there are certain requirements for issuing the debts (money or near-money) that financial institutions can create. They can create them only if: (1) they are willing and able to lend to consumers, business, and government, (2) the public wants to hold the money or near-money, and (3) the regulating authorities will permit the institutions to create them.

There is one more financial debt that should be mentioned—Federal Reserve Notes. These are another part of our money supply—currency issued by the Federal Reserve Banks. Our total supply of coins and currency was about $41 billion in 1966 and, as we mentioned earlier, about $5 billion of this is a debt of the United States Treasury. All the rest is a debt of the Federal Reserve Banks. The Federal Reserve Banks create these notes when the banks ask for them. All the banker has to do is to write a check on his deposit at the Federal Reserve Bank and he can get the cash.[5] The note is merely a paper evidence of the IOU of the Federal Reserve—another debt that we use as money.

We can now see that our money today is a mixture of debts of banks (deposits), debts of the Federal Reserve System (currency), and debts of the government (cur-

---

[5] There are also reserve requirements for the Federal Reserve Banks in issuing its notes and deposits. However, these requirements are not discussed in this volume but can be found in most standard textbooks on money and banking.

rency). Most of our currency comes from the Federal Reserve System. Some of it comes from the Treasury. However, deposits on which the public can write checks are the most important form of money in the United States.

As shown in the accompanying tabulation for March 1966,[6] deposits of commercial banks account for over three quarters of our money supply. All of this money is a form of debt obligation—but by law and by custom these debts are accepted as our medium of exchange.

Currency and Coin		
Treasury		$ 5
Coins	$3.5	
Notes	1.5	
Federal Reserve Notes	36	
Total Currency and Coins in Circulation		$ 41
Demand Deposits at Commercial Banks		130
Total Money Supply		$171 billion

We turn now to examine briefly a problem dealing with money and debt: What shall we do about the size of the debt of the United States Government? As in the earlier chapters, we shall explore this problem by following the outline used in Chapter 1.

The Problem and Issues

After each major war, the federal debt has been reduced somewhat, and on one occasion (1836) it was completely paid off. However, after the Second World War, the debt was reduced only slightly and later, increased. As a result, twenty-one years after the war the federal debt amounts to about $320 billion.

The annual interest cost of this debt is around $11 billion—a sizable item in the federal budget. Many people consider this a "dead-weight" burden that should be reduced. They say that the debt may have been necessary during the war, but there is no sense in paying for it so

[6] *Federal Reserve Bulletin.*

long after the war. We should, they argue, pay off the debt. Others claim that the debt is still providing us with many useful services and that it would be poor policy to pay it off.

The primary issues we might explore then are as follows: What are the possible effects of a substantial reduction in the federal debt? What are the possible consequences of permitting the national debt to remain at its present level? For the present, we shall assume that the question of increasing the debt further is *not* one of the issues, although it may be explored as a separate problem.

The Objectives

Our broad objective is to maintain an expanding economy in which production and employment will gradually grow from year to year. As an additional requirement, we may also want gradually declining prices for the things we buy—or we might prefer the price level to remain stable or to rise very slowly. One requirement is certain: we should not want our economic growth to be accompanied by wide fluctuations in prices.

Alternatives and Consequences

One of the benefits of our outstanding debt is that it is now built into our financial structure. Obligations of the federal government are virtually riskless—we know the government will pay them off when they come due—hence they are a fairly reliable asset for investors. In other words, because there are over $320 billion in IOU's that are guaranteed by the federal government, the American people can feel stronger financially than they would without this volume of riskless securities. Moreover, this financial strength extends beyond the direct owners of the debt. The banks, for instance, have cash and government securities equal to about a third of their deposits; as a result, our banks today are stronger than they were thirty years ago when less than a fifth of the assets of commercial banks were as safe as government securities.

Those in favor of keeping the debt large point out that we do not know whether the interest payments are good or bad for the economy. They argue that even though taxes must be $11 billion higher because of the debt, some people are also receiving this $11 billion as income. They recognize that the tax effect and the income effect are probably not perfect offsets to one another, but they note that we do not know for certain whether the net effect is an aid or a hindrance to our economy. In any event, they claim that if we raise taxes to pay off the debt, we shall be making the same kind of transfer—for $320 billion instead of $11 billion per year.

They also argue that if, as a result of the reduction in the federal debt, total debt, public and private, should not keep pace with the growth of production, the price level will tend to fall. Eventually, this may cause our rate of growth to slow down. In other words, as a contraction in debts may lead to a contraction in spending, it may also bring about a contraction in production and employment.

Some of the people who argue for reduction of the debt state that if we reduce the debt, we shall help wipe out some of the inflation caused earlier by the growth of the debt. They say that if the government collects more in taxes than it spends, it can use the balance to reduce the debt held by the banks—and this in turn will wipe out some of the "excess money supply." The process would be as follows: the taxpayer sends a check to the government, the government deposits the check in a bank, then the government says to the bank "cancel out the deposit you owe the government and return the government bond to the Treasury." The taxpayer's deposit has disappeared and so has the bond.

Other proponents of debt reduction say that reducing the federal debt will release more credit facilities for private borrowers, putting more emphasis on private economic activity and less on the government. On the face of things, it might appear that if the government pays off some of its debt, lenders will be more able to lend to private borrowers. However, we cannot be certain they will be as willing to make private loans, when they no longer have safe government securities to go with their private securities. Moreover, if private loans do not fill the gap, the government may have to spend more money to keep national income from falling.

Those who argue for reducing the public debt also note that the debt can provide a new wave of inflation at any time. If the Federal Reserve Banks, which have the power to buy government securities, purchase a government bond from, say, a commercial bank, they give the commercial bank more reserves. More reserves mean the commercial bank can make more loans and create more deposits. When banks create deposits faster than the growth of income and production, the price level tends to rise.[7] The opponents of debt reduction agree that this *can* happen. But they point out that the Federal Reserve Banks can also increase bank reserves in other ways—thus the place to watch is the Federal Reserve System, not the national debt.

Appraise the Alternatives

Actually, it would not be possible to determine our public debt policy on the basis of these issues alone. Nevertheless, they illustrate some of the reasoning we must do. We have concentrated here on some of the financial effects in order to throw additional light on our debt structure. The national debt, we have seen, must be viewed along with all of our other debts; and, like all debts, it has an impact that may extend far beyond the borrower and lender. In deciding what should be done with it, we must have some understanding of these effects.

[7] When we have extra deposits what do we do? We spend them ourselves, or we lend them to others who want to spend them. And the more we have, the more eager we are to spend or lend.

This chapter has stressed these basic ideas:

1. Debts are a necessary part of our economic system. They represent an economic relationship between those who wish to spend more than their income and those who wish to spend less than their income. Our arrangements for borrowing and lending contribute to the growth of our income and production. The fact that some people abuse this arrangement by incurring debts that they are unable to meet causes some individual problems, but it does not indicate that the over-all arrangement is economically unsound.

2. There are different types of debts for different borrowers. They perform different functions, and they have different effects. Consumers buy automobiles, businesses buy raw materials, governments buy roads, and financial institutions buy the debts of everyone else. They all foster the growth of spending, the growth of markets, production, and employment.

3. When financial institutions buy the debts of consumers, business, and government, they contribute to the growth of liquid assets. Some of these liquid assets are called *money*. For this reason, the role of the financial institutions is particularly important. They do more than merely transfer funds from one person to another—they create a particular type of debt that has special effects of its own. The growth of the money supply influences our spending and, in turn, the level of production for the entire economy.

Suggested Reading

Paul A. Samuelson, *Economics: An Introductory Analysis*, Chaps. 16 and 17, pp. 275–315. George L. Bach, *Economics: An Introduction to Analysis and Policy*, Chaps. 7 and 8, pp. 95–123. These readings cover two broad topics: (1) our monetary system and the way in which commercial banks fit into the system, and (2) the relationship between prices and money. Two publications of the Federal Reserve System are especially informative: *The Fed-*

eral Reserve System . . . Purposes and Functions (Board of Governors of the Federal Reserve System, 1963) and *Money: Master or Servant* (Federal Reserve Bank of New York, 1966). Both of these books are distributed without charge and both provide a clear, non-technical explanation of the role of money and banking in our economy. *Debt: Public and Private* (Chamber of Commerce of the United States, Washington, 1961) gives an objective discussion of the problems and issues of our debt system.

Chapter 6

PROSPERITY AND DEPRESSION

The American economy has been plagued by short-run instability. It has often moved ahead rapidly for a few years only to slip back temporarily before moving on to new peaks of production. Many names are given to these fluctuations in production, prices, and employment: "business cycles," "prosperity and depression," "inflation and deflation," or simply "boom and bust." They all signify disturbances that interrupt the long-run improvement in the level of living.

The preceding chapter gave us some indication of how money and debt can contribute to these disturbances. One of the purposes of this chapter is to identify some of the other causes of changes in the level of business activity. To do so, it will be necessary to explore more fully the nature of business cycles—to look inside them and see how they come about.

WHAT ARE ECONOMIC FLUCTUATIONS?

All of us know something about economic instability from our own experiences. Older people remember the inflation that followed World War I. In 1919, the cost of living almost doubled, and the average citizen had to try to make ends meet on an income that failed to keep pace with prices. Then, in the middle of 1920, farm prices fell precipitously, and many businesses failed. During 1921, unemployment averaged 10 per cent of the labor force.

Gradually, the nation recovered, and the late twenties saw most people, but not most farmers, enjoying higher levels of living than before. This upswing reached a peak in the hectic get-rich atmosphere of the stock market boom of 1928 and 1929 when many people thought America had at last attained permanent prosperity.

The 1929 crash and the great depression of the 1930's are still vivid memories to many adults. The bank failures, the bread lines, the farm surpluses, the vast army of unemployed made many people think our economic system had disintegrated, that capitalism was through. By 1940, however, the United States was rearming. War entirely changed the economic picture. Ten years after the unemployment crisis of 1933, the United States found itself trying to hold down prices, rationing food and gasoline, and recruiting housewives and others to meet a labor shortage.

The fear of depression was well entrenched, however. Long before V-E or V-J day, there were many predictions of a postwar collapse that would throw millions out of work. But it didn't occur. After the Second World War, employment remained high, shortages continued, and prices soared. In the summer of 1948, Congress was called into special session to deal with price inflation. But a year later we were in a "recession" and unemployment rose above the 4 million mark (over 6.5 per cent of the civilian labor force).

During the 20-year period following the Second World War the economy escaped a major depression but it suffered four recessions—the recessions of 1948–49, 1953–54, 1957–58, and 1960–61. In 1949 the rate of industrial production fell to a level 10 per cent below the previous year. Business improved again in early 1950, and then came the Korean War and a new surge of price inflation as well as new records in employment and production. By the fall of 1953, however, the nation began to curtail defense spending, and business activity began to decline. By March 1954, unemployment had risen to 3.7 millions (5.8 per cent of the labor force), and industrial production had declined about 10 per cent. In 1955, however, production and employment once again broke all records. Between September 1957 and April 1958, industrial production fell by 12.5 per cent and unemployment more than doubled, reaching 7.5 per cent of the labor force. By March 1959, however, industrial output was exceeding the pre-recession level and GNP was at an all-time high. In the presidential election campaign of 1960 a new slowdown in economic activity became a major issue, but, by July of 1961, industrial production had regained its previous peak, and it continued to expand for the following five years.

The business cycle is a highly complex process, and no two cycles are alike. The great "peaks" of prosperity such as 1929, the inflationary crises such as 1920, 1948, and 1951, and the deep "valleys" of depression such as 1933 are spectacular events that nearly everyone remembers. It is more important, however, to understand the continuous and varied nature of the business cycle and to recognize that the term "business cycle" is not a description of evenly spaced changes in business activity. Business activity does not fluctuate rhythmically between the extremes of price inflation and depression, nor does it fluctuate around a norm of full employment. In order to understand what does happen, let us now distinguish the phases of the business cycle as follows:

> The Upswing (prosperity phase, expansion)
> The Upper Turning Point (downturn, crisis)
> The Downswing (depression phase, contraction)
> The Lower Turning Point (upturn, revival)

Keeping this division in mind, we should note that the upswing does not *necessarily* culminate in inflation. It did in 1920 and in 1948, but it did not in 1926 and 1937. In 1937, for example, an upswing terminated, and a downswing began when unemployment was still over 7 millions. Nor does the downswing *necessarily* culminate in deep depression. It did in 1921 and in 1933, but it did not in 1949, 1954, 1958, and 1961.

On the basis of historical knowledge, we can say that economic fluctuations vary in length, amplitude, and scope. Some downswings and upswings, like the cycle from 1929 to 1937, can be measured in years. Others, like the "recessions" of 1949 and 1961, can be measured in months. Some cycles have reached extremes such as the crisis of 1933 and the postwar inflation of 1946–48; others such as the recession of 1954 have been mild and have even gone unnoticed by large sections of the population. Finally, some recessions have involved all kinds of economic activity—manufacturing, construction, agriculture, and so on—as in 1933, while others have touched only particular areas, such as the so-called "inventory recession" of 1949.

Sections of the economy are affected in different ways by these fluctuations. For example, agricultural production and employment do not change rapidly, but the prices of farm products tend to fluctuate widely. On the other hand, in the steel and automobile industries prices do not go up and down as much, but production and employment fluctuate widely. In fact, in recent years there has been an increasing tendency for all prices to become "sticky"—to resist downward adjustment. Many farm prices are supported by the government; minimum wage laws and long-term union contracts put something of a floor under wages; many prices, including utility and transportation rates, are regulated by governmental agencies. Thus one big difference between recent business recessions and those of thirty or more years ago is that the price level seems to go down much less than formerly; a recession is now likely to affect industrial output and employment more than the price level.

Why worry about these short-term fluctuations if in the long run each generation is better off than its predecessor? The answer, of course, is that depression means idle production facilities, men and women out of work, businesses failing, and farmers unable to get satisfactory prices for their crops. Inflation means housewives are unable to stretch their dollars far enough at the grocery store. It means that retired people and others who receive fixed incomes suffer a decline in real purchasing power.

In addition, the effects of these ups and downs in employment and income in the United States are often felt well beyond our borders. As a result they may have a significant impact on our relations with the rest of the world. The world is now witnessing a struggle between the rival economic, political, and social systems of the Soviet Union and the United States. Few events could do more to undermine our leadership in the free world than a serious American depression. To many in the rest of the world, our attempt to operate a free society would seem a failure, and Soviet communism could win an important victory in the cold war.

EXPLAINING ECONOMIC FLUCTUATIONS

Unfortunately, a simple statement of the cause of business fluctuations is not possible. In the first place, there seems to be no single "cause." The American economy is extremely complex, and a variety of factors influence its operation. Many theories "explaining" business cycles have been put forward over the years, but not one of them is accepted alone as an adequate answer. For example, some economists have viewed the banking system as a major source of instability. Others have attributed economic fluctuations to under-consumption—the inability of consumers to buy continually all the goods produced; to psychology—alternating "waves" of optimism and pessimism; to distortions in "the structure of production"—changes in the balanced relationship between capital goods and consumer goods industries; to the irregular rate of industrial innovations, and even to cycles of sun spots!

Economists are generally agreed that no single one of these theories provides *the* explanation; they agree that there is an element of truth in most of the theories. And, as a result of the research that has been done, there is a better appreciation today than ever before of the key elements and relationships involved in economic fluctuations.

The concept of the gross national product can help us explain economic fluctuations. As described in Chapter 2, the figures for gross national product show us that there are three major groups who buy the things our economy produces for the market—consumers, producers, and government.[1] We refer to the total demand of these buyers as "aggregate demand." The following figures for 1965 illustrate this:

	Billions of dollars
Gross national product	681
Consumers (personal consumption expenditures)	431
Producers (gross private domestic investment and net foreign investment)	114
Government, federal, state, and local (government purchases of goods and services)	136

If aggregate demand is rising—if the three buyers are trying to buy more goods and services—total production tends to grow. But if aggregate demand is rising faster than the growth of our supply of goods and services, prices tend to rise, and we have inflation. Inflation, which has been described as "too many dollars chasing too few goods," means that the buyers are spending more than is needed to buy a limited supply of goods and services at prevailing prices. Therefore they bid up the price level. If aggregate demand is falling, if the three buyers are buying less, then prices and production will tend to fall. Declining aggregate demand generally results in falling prices,

[1] In the following discussion producers' purchases and net exports, treated separately in Chapter 2, have been combined for convenience of exposition.

less employment, idle factories, and farm surpluses. Ultimately, it results in depression.

The objective of public policy, then, is to see that aggregate demand is maintained at the right level—not too high, and not too low. The "right level," of course, is not a fixed level. Because our capacity to produce increases about 3.5 per cent a year as a result of growth in the labor force and gains in productivity, the "right level" must gradually increase.

THE SOURCES OF AGGREGATE DEMAND

To the economist "demand" means more than just "want" or "need." It is wanting something and being able to back up that want with purchasing power. During a depression, millions of persons "want" things but are unable to enter the market as buyers because of lack of money. Where then does aggregate demand come from and why does it vary?

The principal source of aggregate demand is current income. As shown in Chapter 2, the production of goods generates income in the form of wages and salaries paid to workers, profits earned by independent businessmen, farmers, and corporations, rent paid to those who permit the use of their property in the productive process, and interest paid to those who lend money. Thus the process of production generates the purchasing power needed to buy the goods and services that are produced.

There is no guarantee, however, that total spending will exactly equal income received. To begin with, a sizable part of income—around one third, in fact—is taken from income earners by the government in the form of *taxes*. Of course, the government usually uses tax revenues to buy goods and services. But its total expenditures will not necessarily equal its total tax collections. It may spend more than it collects, supplementing its tax receipts with borrowed money, or it may spend less. So the government, through budgetary or fiscal policy, can help expand or contract total spending. As we shall see later, fiscal policy is one of the important tools for influencing aggregate demand.

Another part of income is likely to be *saved* rather than spent on consumer goods and services or paid in taxes. Some of these savings may be directly invested by the savers: a consumer may use his savings to buy a house, or a business may use its savings to buy new machinery. As we saw in the preceding chapter, some of these funds also accumulate in the form of bank deposits, savings accounts, insurance reserves, and so on. When the financial institutions lend funds to producers who invest in new capital, these funds are also being spent. They are not being spent by savers themselves; they are being spent by businessmen and are part of gross private domestic investment.

But there is no assurance that at any given income level producers will want to invest the same amount of money that the savers of the community decide to save at that same income level. Producers may want to invest more, or they may want to invest less. The decision to save and the decision to invest are made to a certain extent by different groups and for different reasons. Therefore, it would be a coincidence if the plans of the groups were exactly the same. Producers may want to spend more currently than the public wants to lend; in this case, they may draw on previously accumulated bank balances or on new deposits created by borrowing from the banking system. Or they may want to invest less; in this case, some goods will remain unsold, and the level of income will fall.

In other words, if investors try to spend more than the public currently wants to save, they will tend to increase aggregate demand and thus exert an upward pressure on income, employment, and prices. But if the savers try to save more than the investors want to invest, total spending will tend to decline, and the decline will exert downward pressure on prices, production, employment, and income. What we are saying in both situations, is that upward or downward movements in the national income are likely to result when there are divergences between the plans of investors and savers. It is through these changes in the level of economic activity that savings and investment are made equal.

It should be emphasized that the buyers of the national product can supplement the purchasing power derived from their current incomes by borrowing from financial institutions or by drawing on their own accumulated assets. As we have seen, consumers, businessmen, and the government can and do spend beyond their incomes by borrowing from the banks and other financial institutions. Thus whether aggregate demands go up or down depends in part on government controls over these financial institutions. These controls will be discussed in the next chapter.

WHY DOES AGGREGATE DEMAND FLUCTUATE?

We must now identify the chief influences on spending for investment, consumption, and government services. First, we shall consider changes in the level of investment because these, historically, have been the most dynamic, the most unpredictable, and the most difficult to influence by economic policy.

Investment spending is based largely on the business-man's expectations of profits. Producers invest in the construction of new factories, the purchase of new equipment, and so on, because they believe there will be a demand for the new or better goods and services that will be produced as a result of their investment. Investments, in short, are made because producers expect they will yield a profit. Investment spending, therefore, is affected by technological change—by inventions that improve the output of the firm. It is also affected by the costs and the risks of replacing or expanding plants and equipment. However, experience shows that investments for entering new markets or to use new technology can and will be postponed if expectations of profits are uncertain.

Here we begin to see some reasons for the extreme variability of private investment. For example, it fell from $16.2 billion in 1929 to only $0.9 billion in 1932, and increased from $56.6 billion in 1958 to $69.5 billion in 1961. Investment decisions are made by thousands of producers whose expectations of future profit are affected by many factors. Some of these, such as the evaluation of the international situation or the "friendliness" or "unfriendliness" of an administration in Washington toward business, are quite intangible. That is the reason so much emphasis is often placed on creating a favorable political, social, and economic "climate" to encourage investment. Tax laws designed to encourage the movement of venture capital into industry, harmonious labor-management relations, a rapid population growth, and the development of new industries and products as a result of research are all examples of factors likely to encourage investment. There are also unfavorable factors, which can have the reverse effect. These unfavorable factors were very much in evidence during the 1930's just as the favorable ones have generally been apparent since the Second World War.

The expansion of investment in itself will, of course, generate more purchasing power. The high demand for goods will in turn stimulate more investment. This is the reason that an upturn in one area can lead to a much broader upswing. Isolated cycles in different industries may synchronize into major cycles when each is helped along by the others. A contraction of spending may also lead to a further contraction of spending—especially in spending for capital equipment.

Investment is also influenced by changes in technology. Many economists have pointed out that our economy is extremely dynamic; it is characterized by technological change or "innovation." These innovations take the form of new industries, new products, improved versions of old products, new marketing techniques, and so on. The industrial history of America is full of such stimulating in-novations as automobiles, chemicals, plastics, supermarkets, air-conditioning, frozen foods, motels, automation, and jet aircraft, to mention a few.

These innovations do not occur in a steady stream but come at irregular intervals. When one does come, the eco-nomic chain reaction works something like this: An "in-novator" pioneers with a new product. If it is well received by the public, he reaps his reward in the form of profits. But his success will attract competitors. The upswing or prosperity phase of the cycle of the industry then devel-ops as competing producers vie with one another to bor-row money, hire skilled workers, buy raw materials, build new plants, and develop advertising campaigns. There will be what might be called a "bunching" effect in invest-ment.

Later, however, the market may be temporarily satiated, and increased competition will reduce profit margins. The less efficient producers and the speculators will be squeezed out, the demand for machinery and raw materials will fall, and business activity will decline until some new innova-tion comes along to give fresh impetus to expansion.

In this concept of the business cycle, borrowing also plays an important role. Prosperity—when the imitators are imitating the innovator—will be fed by an expansion of debt if banks and other lenders are able and willing to make loans. If banks have excess reserves and are optimistic about the future of the economy, they can supply new credit at low interest rates and help the expansion of in-come. But when the wave of expansion loses its force, or when the banks run short of reserves, interest rates will tend to rise and new loans will decline in volume. Eventu-ally the business decline may be accompanied by a con-traction in the money supply.

Consumer spending is more stable than investment spending, and it is also much larger. In 1965, when gross private domestic investment was $107 billion, personal con-sumption expenditures were $431 billion, about four times as large as investment expenditures. Personal consumption expenditures tend to remain more stable than investment outlays, but occasionally, under the stress of war or other emergencies, they may also change quickly. It will be useful therefore to look into the factors that influence this largest source of aggregate demand.

Personal consumption expenditures are determined primarily by income, but they are also subject to a variety of influences that are not completely understood. This is particularly true of spending on durable goods like houses, refrigerators, and automobiles. Unlike food and basic services such as gas or electricity, the purchase of these durables can usually be postponed. If millions of persons, for example, decide to make the family car "do" for another year because they expect their income to go down or because they expect automobile prices to go down, their decisions can have a tremendous effect on the business situation. The surveys of consumer spending plans made in recent years by the Board of Governors of the Federal Reserve System and the University of Michigan reveal that we have much to learn about consumer motivations. More than once we have been surprised by unexpected shifts in their behavior.

Sometimes consumers' expectations cause people to act in such a way that what they expected actually does happen. A recent example occurred right after the outbreak of the Korean War in the summer of 1950. With memories of the shortages of the Second World War still vivid, consumers rushed out to buy certain items "before the hoarders got them." This wave of consumer buying created some scarcities that might not have developed during a normal buying period and certainly helped push up the level of consumer prices. Businessmen reacted in the same way and decided to increase their inventories of raw materials, with the result that the prices of these also rose. If consumers expect prices to fall, however, they may hold off their purchases in anticipation of the fall. The consequent decline in demand may then cause the price fall to occur.

Recurring waves of consumer expectations about the future thus can play an important part in economic fluctuations.

Normally, however, consumption expenditures tend to be strongly influenced by the level of disposable personal income. Since the end of the Second World War, yearly consumption expenditures have been between 91 and 97 per cent of disposable income, and from 1951 to 1961, they were between 92 and 94 per cent of disposable income. At times, they have gone as low as 75 per cent and as high as 101 per cent. Consumption declined to 75 per cent during the Second World War, when goods were scarce and the government was discouraging consumer spending. It was over 100 per cent of disposable income in 1932–33, when income and employment were so low that millions of people lived beyond their incomes for several years. However, these extremes occurred in unusual periods—in war and depression. Under more normal conditions, consumption expenditures are more closely related to the flow of income—although the relationship is by no means a fixed percentage.

Levels of government spending change because of changing ideas of what governments should try to do, or because of changing circumstances that force governments to adopt new programs and revise old ones. Spending for roads, schools, old-age compensation, and subsidies to farmers, and a number of "welfare" items, have gradually been introduced into government budgets. The amount spent on them in a given year may vary, yet these programs seem to be a more or less permanent part of government spending. The principal cause of government spending, however, is war, and historically the widest variations in government spending have come with changes from peace to war and vice versa. In recent years, over four fifths of the expenditures in the federal budget have been on items related in one way or another to war—national defense, veterans' expenditures, interest on war debt, and so on. This condition seems likely to continue as long as the "cold war" continues.

Because private spending is changeable, public spending has a special significance: it is the only category of spending that can be directly controlled by the government. It can be deliberately increased or decreased by specific amounts. Thus it may be possible, through changes in the federal budget, to attempt to fashion government spending into a sort of economic "balance wheel." Government spending can be deliberately increased in an effort to boost aggregate demand and deliberately decreased to reduce demand, though it is difficult to alter in the short run.

Summing up, we may say that the motivations underlying private spending are varied and complex. They are not fully understood, and we certainly have not reached the point where we can either accurately predict or precisely control private spending. Nevertheless, a large part of governmental policy today is concerned with efforts to influence private demand or counter-balance its major savings. These governmental programs are the subject of the next chapter.

WHY ARE SOME FLUCTUATIONS "CUMULATIVE"?

As we noted earlier, neither recessions nor inflations follow a uniform pattern. Some recessions are deeper than others; some last longer than others. Similarly, an inflation may develop slowly, or it may become a "runaway." The recession of 1960–61 was less severe than the recession of 1937–38 or the depression that followed 1929. The inflation that followed the Second World War was more gradual than the one that followed the First World War. Severe fluctuations in business activity generally are the result of the tendency of small changes in spending to gain momentum as they are transmitted through the economy.

One aspect of the cumulative effect is what economists call the "multiplier principle." Let us say there has been a decision to build another large atomic energy plant. The payments made to the workers, to the suppliers of concrete, to the owners of the land needed, and so on, will increase income in the community nearby. Presumably private spending will be increased, too. The workers, for example, will spend more money in the grocery and clothing stores, at the local taverns and gas stations, and on renting houses and apartments. The grocery and clothing store proprietors, the tavern keepers and gas station operators, and the landlords and builders of the community can be expected to increase their spending, too, as they receive larger incomes. Thus the increase in total spending is likely to be several times the initial amount invested and to result in an expansion not only of income but also of output and employment in many communities.

The original investment sets up a chain of consumer spending, which could go on indefinitely if people always spent their entire income. But they do not. People save a portion of their income. Consequently, the multiplier is not infinite; unless new investments are made, the chain of added consumption will gradually peter out.

The multiplier can also work in reverse. It can contribute to a shrinkage in national income since a decline in investment spending will be followed by a chain of reductions in consumer spending. Without going deeper into multiplier analysis, the basic point to remember is that increases or decreases in investment or government spending may initiate relatively larger increases or decreases in income, output, and employment.

Cumulative changes in spending may also occur in accordance with the "acceleration principle." This means that changes in the rate of growth in the demand for consumer goods can lead to changes in the level of production of the capital goods needed to make the consumer items.

For example, assume that there is a steady consumer demand for 1,000 widgets per year, and that production for this level of demand requires the use of 10 machines, each of which produces 100 widgets. Assume further, as is reasonable, that one widget-making machine wears out and has to be replaced each year. As long as consumer demand stays the same, the demand for widget-making machines will be for one machine per year.

But suppose that for some reason the consumer demand for widgets increases from 1,000 to 1,100 per year, an increase in consumer demand of 10 per cent. To produce the additional 100 widgets, the manufacturer will not only have to replace one widget-making machine as scheduled for that year but will also have to buy another one as well. The demand of the manufacturer for widget-producing machines has thus doubled whereas the consumer demand for widgets has increased only 10 per cent.

Now, if consumer demand fails to increase further and stabilizes itself at 1,100, the demand for machines will actually *decrease*—to 1.1 a year. Thus capital goods industries may expand sharply when consumer demand increases, but they may also contract as a result of the failure of consumer demand to maintain a rate of increase. If consumers merely buy as much as they did before, the capital goods industry will go into a slump. It is as though we have to keep running faster and faster to stay where we are.

On the other hand, if consumer demand for widgets should fall by 10 per cent—that is, from 1,000 to 900—the producer would need only 9 machines for the coming year instead of 10. He would not need to buy any new widget-making machine at all. So a 10 per cent decline in consumer demand would have reduced the demand for machines to zero. This simple example helps explain why the capital goods industries experience the greatest fluctuations.

The acceleration principle applies also to inventories. Suppose again that consumer demand for widgets is 1,000 per year and that the retailer maintains an inventory equal to sales, that is, an inventory of 1,000. Plainly, then, he must buy 1,000 widgets a year from the manufacturer. But suppose consumer demand increases by 20 per cent (that is, from 1,000 to 1,200). In the year of that increase, the retailer would have to buy 1,400 widgets, an increase of 40 per cent in his purchasing. He would have to increase his purchasing by that much in order to satisfy the increased consumer demand (200) and to bring his inventory up to the new sales level (up, that is, by 200). Thus a small increase in consumer demand may bring about a much larger increase in production. If demand later stabilizes at 1,200, he will *cut* his orders from 1,400 to 1,200. The "acceleration principle" builds up the force of an expansion, but it also provides a cause for the downturn; thus when consumer demand is stable or growing slowly, producers of capital goods or inventory may suffer.

Because people expect a continuation of what is happening, the role of expectations is another source of cumulative economic change. Earlier we noted the effect of expectations of consumers and businessmen in periods of rising or falling incomes or prices. If, for instance, the public interprets a slight rise in unemployment as an indication that the economy is headed for a major decline, it may curtail spending for all but the essentials of life. Similarly, if bankers and other creditors interpret a small decline as an indication of worse days ahead, they may reduce their volume of loans, causing a shrinkage in the money supply and forcing sales of goods at a loss.

However, a change in the level of spending need not become cumulative. Many downturns in incomes and spending have reversed themselves without any new outside stimulus to spending. For example, if incomes fall because of a decrease in business purchasing for inventory, the decline may be "automatically self-correcting." That is, if other spending holds up fairly well, the depletion of inventories will eventually force businesses to order more goods. Or, if some production stops because prices are not moving up as rapidly as costs and some firms are losing money, employment will tend to fall. If the decline in employment leads to lower costs for such items as labor and raw materials, it may enable idle firms to resume production. In these examples, the stimulus to recovery is caused by forces that the contraction itself generates.

The key to such "automatic correction" lies in the continuation of "other" spending. As we have seen, there are reasons to suspect that a decline in one part of the economy will be transmitted to another part, but this may happen only gradually and in the meantime the contraction may come to a halt. "Minor cycles" of this sort occur repeatedly in our economic system, and they only become a matter of major public concern when the period of readjustment is unduly prolonged.

The 1957–58 recession is an instructive illustration of a "minor cycle." From prosperity to downswing to recovery took less than a year. The table below shows the changes

GROSS NATIONAL PRODUCT
THIRD QUARTER, 1957 AND FIRST QUARTER, 1958[a]
(In billions of dollars)

Item	High 1957	Low 1958	Net Change
Gross national product (total expenditures)	446	427	−19
Personal consumption	288	286	− 2
Durable goods	40	36	− 4
Nondurable goods	141	140	− 1
Services	107	110	+ 3
Gross private domestic investment	67	51	−16
New construction	37	36	− 1
Producers' durable equipment	28	23	− 5
Change in business inventories	2	−8	− 10
Net foreign investment	5	2	− 3
Government purchases	86	88	+ 2
Federal			
National security	45	44	− 1
Other	5	6	+ 1
State and local	36	39	+ 3

[a] U. S. Department of Commerce, *Survey of Current Business* (February 1959). Figures are at annual rates.

in the components of the gross national product between the high point in 1957 (July–September) and the low point in 1958 (January–March). Spending for some purposes declined as follows:

National security	−$ 1 billion
Business inventories	− 10 billion
Producers' durable equipment	− 5 billion
Consumers durable goods	− 4 billion
Net foreign investment	− 3 billion

It is apparent that the principal reasons for the reduction in aggregate demand were curtailed spending for producers' durable equipment, business inventories, and consumers' durable goods. Without these reductions in spending, the gross national product would have been the same as in 1957 (assuming the other expenditures remained the same). In a crude sense, we can say that these were the cause of the recession. But, of course, this tells us nothing about *why* they declined. Therefore, we shall try to make some interpretations and conjectures.

The principal factor affecting business spending on durable equipment was the widening gap between the supply and use of industrial capacity. In manufacturing, for example, productive capacity had been increased by one fourth in four years although production increased only 7 per cent. During 1957 it became increasingly apparent to businessmen that a pause in capital expansion was advisable to allow demand to catch up with capacity. In addition, investment was further discouraged by the rising cost of borrowed funds.

The sharp cuts in consumer purchases of durable goods, particularly automobiles, were to be expected in view of the rising unemployment. The sizeable decline in exports was due to the recession in Canada and Western Europe.

The decline in inventory spending was closely related to the reductions in demand, which have been described.

Faced with a decline in demand, it was normal for businessmen to pare their stocks on hand but this further reduced output and employment in the supplying industries.

The seriousness of the decline was lessened, however, by the fact that spending for other purposes increased as follows:

Consumer services	+$3 billion
State and local spending	+ 3 billion
"Other" federal spending	+ 1 billion

The rather substantial increase in consumer expenditures for services suggests that consumers' incomes were not seriously affected by the recession. It also reflects a long-run tendency for expenditures for consumer services to increase. Moreover, as rents, public utility rates, and the prices of personal and transportation services were still gradually moving up, expenditures for these items had a higher dollar value.

The increase in state and local expenditures was a reflection of the increasing attention that state and local governments have been giving to the improvement of road and school facilities to meet the needs of our growing population. The increase in "other" federal spending was in large part on the new highway program.

This brief survey gives an idea why the recession of 1957–58 did not develop into a full-scale depression. The spending of consumers for services and housing, the non-defense spending of the federal government, and the spending of state and local governments did not contract with business and defense spending and exports. The cumulative decline did not develop because some spending was not rigidly tied to the flow of income. Recovery was therefore easier. Various steps were taken by government to hasten this recovery. These are discussed in the next chapter.

ECONOMIC RELATIONSHIPS WITHIN
THE ECONOMY

The level of aggregate demand, important though it is, is not the only problem to be concerned about when analyzing economic fluctuations. The relations between various parts of the economy are also significant, particularly the relations between costs and prices.

The effect of cost-price relationships on economic fluctuations can perhaps best be understood by considering the role of wages. Wages are an important cost of production to the businessman as well as an income to the worker. Some people believe that one remedy for a depression is to reduce wages because producers will be able to hire more workers at lower wage rates. Others believe that widespread wage cutting would lead to a worse depression because wage cuts reduce the purchasing power of workers and thus their demand for goods. Similarly, some people believe that prices should be cut when sales are declining, but others believe that this may result in a shrinkage of profits that would tend to curtail business spending for investment.

The ultimate effect of changes in wages or prices on the economy will depend largely on how widespread they are. If most wages are rising or most wages are falling, the entire economy will feel the impact, but if only a few firms are changing wages, the cost and income effects may be scarcely noticed.

A rise in the wage level can add to inflation if producers compensate for it by increasing prices. This is sometimes referred to as "cost-push" inflation to distinguish it from inflationary pressures arising from growing demand. To make matters worse, a rise in prices can lead to a new round of wage demands to catch up with the cost of living. Supports for farm prices, "fair trade" prices, or minimum wage laws may have similar effects because they influence the incomes of some groups and the costs of others.

No one can really say what the "right level" of wages or prices is at any particular time. Wages and prices are, to a large extent, determined by private bargaining, without the direct intervention of government. The economic fluctuations that sometimes result can, perhaps, be thought of as one of the prices we pay for this system of private bargaining.

Geographic relationships are another significant aspect of economic fluctuations. We have emphasized total or aggregate demand, but this total may be spread in different ways—and the way it is spread will affect the economic condition of millions of people. When spending shifts from the products of one town to those of another, some factories may shut down while others expand, workers may lose jobs in one town while labor shortages exist in others. On the whole, the economy may be prosperous and growing, but prosperity does not spread uniformly; some areas may be left behind.

This raises a problem that has received much public attention in recent years—what to do about "pockets" of unemployment. We can explore this problem by the same steps we have used in earlier chapters.

The Problem and the Issues

The map below shows unemployment during a month when the number of jobless ranged from 1.9 per cent in the District of Columbia to 14.2 per cent in Alaska. As we have seen, the flow of income through the economy is not governed by state boundaries—production, employment, and the generation of income all take place within the national economy. But for some reasons, certain areas miss out on some of the income flow; for some areas, a serious depression may be at hand, even when the economy as a whole is relatively prosperous.

The main reasons for localized unemployment may be summarized, as follows:

VARIATIONS IN STATE UNEMPLOYMENT RATES[a]

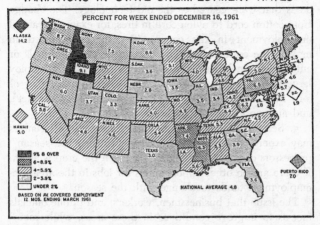

PERCENT FOR WEEK ENDED DECEMBER 16, 1961

ALASKA 14.2

HAWAII 5.0

PUERTO RICO 7.0

NATIONAL AVERAGE 4.8

9% & OVER
6-8.9%
4-5.9%
2-3.9%
UNDER 2%

BASED ON AV COVERED EMPLOYMENT
12 MOS. ENDING MARCH 1961

[a] U. S. Department of Labor, *The Labor Market and Employment Security* (January 1962). The percentage figures relate to workers covered by unemployment insurance—they *do not* show the percentage of the total work force that is unemployed.

1. Temporary cutbacks in demand for certain products. For example, unemployment rises sharply in Detroit and Pittsburgh as a result of reduced spending for automobiles and steel. When defense spending is reduced, similar cutbacks occur in areas that are geared to a large volume of defense production.

2. Long-run loss of the competitive position of an industry. For example, some textile areas of New England have lost out to textile producers in other areas. Similarly, anthracite coal mining areas have suffered employment losses because of the increased competition of other fuels, notably gas and oil.

3. Exhaustion of natural resources. Lumber, lead, zinc, and coal mining areas have frequently experienced unemployment after their most accessible sources have been depleted.

4. Technological changes. Changes to new products or methods of production have resulted in unemployment in areas that were geared to the old technology. The change from cotton cord to nylon cord in tires, for example, caused unemployment in the communities that specialized in making the cotton cord. The introduction of new tools or automated machinery into industries that usually employ large numbers of workers will tend to cut the number of jobs in those industries, as experience in the coal, steel, and automobile industries has made clear.

5. Seasonal changes in specialized areas. Resort centers may experience a large labor surplus in their "off-season"; processors of crops may be laid off when the crop is all in. If there are no other opportunities for jobs in the area, unemployment tends to change with the season.

The issue that businessmen, workers, and public officials face is to improve conditions in these areas, while maintaining prosperity in the rest of the economy. Thus it involves the relation of one part of the economy to the rest; it involves the distinction between national and local depression.

The Objectives

Removal of these pockets of unemployment is the immediate objective. The unemployed find little comfort in knowing that prosperity exists in other parts of the country. Moreover, these unemployed workers are not producing; their idleness is therefore a social loss.

Another objective may be to keep the economy as free from specific governmental controls as possible. The American people want to hold down unemployment, but they do not want their government to undertake a program of relief every time some plant shuts down operations.

Additional requirements may be that corrective measures do more than (1) merely shift income out of prosperous areas into the depressed areas, (2) subsidize uneconomic industries, or (3) hamper the ability of the economy to adjust to changes in the pattern of consumer demand.

The Alternatives

First, the federal government can take steps to increase the level of national income. By monetary and fiscal measures (see Chapter 7), the federal government might expand aggregate demand, which, in turn, might bring more prosperity to the depressed areas. The program could also lead to overstimulation in other sections of the economy. Where workers are fully employed, the additional pressure of aggregate demand could lead to wage and price increases. An over-all program might therefore correct problems of the depressed areas by turning others into inflated areas.

Second, the federal government could try a regional approach. It might undertake new projects—dams, roads, or other public works—in an effort to stimulate local production. It might also shift its pattern of spending so that it bought more in the depressed regions. If we assume that it was buying its goods from the cheapest source beforehand, a shift would result in higher governmental costs—the additional outlays would be the cost of trying to cure these spot problems. Other areas that formerly supplied the needs of the government might have to cut back on production. If other opportunities for employment arise in these localities, the shift might increase total employment. But if the shift merely changed the location of unemployment, the national economy might be no better off than before.

The federal government could also make loans to enable local governments or local businesses to spend more on public works or modernizing factories. Generally speaking, firms find it difficult to borrow when their future looks dark; thus lenders may shun the additional risk. But, as some of these spot problems arise because the local industry has not been able to keep up with production improvements, new loans for improvements might give a boost to sales and employment. Loans for improving the efficiency of firms would enable them to compete with firms in other areas, and loans for public works may modernize the community and attract new firms.

The Appalachian Program of 1965 and the earlier Area Redevelopment Act illustrate this regional approach. Focused on the needs of communities that have a chronic unemployment problem, such laws provide funds for business loans, urban renewal projects, and community facilities. They also include provision for retraining unemployed workers for new jobs in new industries.

Third, the state governments could carry the burden of the program. Some have tried to solve the problem by offering special inducements to attract new firms to move to their area. They may make special market surveys, provide loans for new plants, give tax reductions for new firms, and in other ways attempt to provide an incentive for the firms to move to their areas. State development programs have expanded in recent years, and they may have some effect on the location of firms. But as more of them develop, and they compete in their inducements, they tend to cancel the efforts of one another. States may still need such programs to hang on to the firms that they have, but as special inducements, they seem to be losing their force.

Finally, the area may be left to solve its own problem. Local business may find new ways to attract business, but if it doesn't the "unemployment pocket" will tend to remain. In this case the correction may require a number of years. If the area is declining because it specialized in production of things that are no longer wanted or if it has run out of some needed resources, the solution may be for workers and capital to move.

This may be hard on many workers—especially those who have lived in the area for years—but if the area cannot produce things that the economy wants at a price that it is willing to pay, the workers and capital may have to go elsewhere. This may be the problem confronted by some agricultural communities and some that produce coal, textiles, and shoes; it may be the same problem that was confronted earlier by the village blacksmith and vaudeville.

Appraisal

This problem combines the basic elements of the market system and the problems of economic fluctuations. The market system assumes that workers and capital will tend to move to the jobs where they will be most useful; it assumes that they will follow the flow of consumer spending. To do so, however, they must first have a reason for leaving the jobs they are in.

Low wages, unemployment, low profits, and declining sales are the marks of an industry from which workers will tend to move. They are also a depressing influence on our national economic growth. For this reason, elimination of "pockets" of unemployment can contribute to growth in our total income and production. Thus this problem illustrates the occasional conflict between the workings of the market system and economic stability. To resolve the conflict, we must be able to analyze the reasons for the unemployment, and we must determine what our objectives really are.

This chapter has stressed the following ideas:

1. Economic fluctuations do not occur at regular intervals. Their severity varies from cycle to cycle and their impact on each industry may be different each time. The causes of fluctuations are equally varied—they may begin with any series of events that causes total spending to change. Explanations of cycles that rely on psychology can help us understand why some cycles are severe and others are mild, but psychology cannot explain why cycles begin.

2. We can analyze cycles by using the breakdown of the gross national product. By these measures we can see

where spending, or aggregate demand, changed—and then we can try to find out why they changed. Consumers, businessmen, and government spend for different purposes so we must try to understand the conditions that influence all three groups.

3. Consumer spending is the largest and most stable part of aggregate demand. The relationship between outlays of consumers and their income is close, although at times consumers have upset predictions of their spending. Investment spending is more unstable and depends heavily on the expectations of businessmen for profitable investment opportunities. It is influenced by the flow of technological developments, the cost of borrowing money, and a host of other considerations involved in managing a modern business. Government spending reflects a number of social objectives: national defense, public works, aid for the underprivileged, and the needs of stabilizing aggregate demand, to mention a few.

4. Some fluctuations are cumulative. The multiplier effect of investment can increase the flow of consumption. The acceleration principle may lead to large changes in outlays for investment. But not all fluctuations need be cumulative. Some will correct themselves.

Suggested Reading

Paul A. Samuelson, *Economics: An Introductory Analysis*, Chaps. 13 and 14, pp. 222–56. George L. Bach, *Economics: An Introduction to Analysis and Policy*, Chaps. 10 and 11, pp. 138–77. Some of this reading may be a little difficult for the beginner but, if mastered, it will be highly rewarding. It deals with some of the theories used to understand business cycles—one of the most useful tools for thinking about economic affairs. See also *The Economic Report of the President*, a new issue of which appears every January. It includes a number of details about the current economic situation and business cycle developments. It is prepared by the Council of Economic Advisers and gives some of the economic reasoning behind many government proposals. The Council's report on "The Nature and Extent of Poverty" is reprinted in *Readings in Economics* (Samuelson et al., ed.), pp. 67–68.

Chapter 7

CONTROLLING BUSINESS FLUCTUATIONS

In the depression of the 1930's, the federal government borrowed money and launched a public works program in an effort to stimulate business. In the Second World War, Congress raised taxes to drain off spending power that might have been used to bid up prices for consumer goods. From time to time, the government has also influenced private spending by changing the cost of borrowing and the ease with which consumers and businesses can obtain borrowed funds. In this chapter we shall look at these and other measures that the government has used or may use to smooth out fluctuations in income and employment. We shall see that our economy has a number of methods of pursuing one of its foremost objectives—economic stability.

Economic stability generally means a rising national income under conditions that will assure steady jobs for those who want to work. In a broad sense, it means "full employment." But what does full employment mean? How full is "full"? Must there be no more than transitional unemployment among those who are able and willing to work? Or should the limit of tolerable unemployment be defined as a percentage of the labor force—such as the recently used target of 4 per cent? Will our concept of full employment differ if most unemployment is concentrated in a few industrial centers rather than spread thinly throughout the economy? In recent years the term "full employment GNP" has come into use to signify a level of output that is consistent with full use of our labor supply; and there has been growing discussion of ways to eliminate the "gap" between what the economy can produce, "potential GNP," and what it produced, "actual GNP." Clearly "full employment" is not a precise term, but in a general sense, it is undoubtedly one of our objectives.

Economic stability also means that the average price level changes slowly or not at all. Certainly, we want to avoid the kind of price collapse we had in 1929–33 and the kind of inflation we had in 1946–48 and again in 1950–51. On the other hand, we do not want to introduce so many rigidities into the price structure that prices cannot perform their proper function as indicators of what goods people want produced. In general, we might say that we want flexibility in individual prices with reasonable stability in the average price level.

Let us take a look at the formal commitment the United States has assumed in this field and see what light it throws on our objective of economic stability. The Employment Act of 1946, Section 2 of which is entitled "Declaration of Policy," states:

> The Congress declares that it is the continuing policy and responsibility of the Federal Government to use all practicable means consistent with its needs and obligations and other essential considerations of national policy, with the assistance and cooperation of industry, agriculture, labor, and state and local government, to coordinate and utilize all its plans, functions, and resources for the purposes of creating and maintaining, in a manner calculated to foster and promote free competitive enterprise and the general welfare, conditions under which there will be afforded useful employment opportunities, including self-employment, for those able, willing, and seeking to work, and to promote maximum employment, production, and purchasing power.

In less formal language, the meaning of the Employment Act can be stated as follows:

The United States Government will co-operate with private industry and labor to promote maximum employment and production and to avoid serious depression. The act has also been interpreted to mean that the government should use its power to prevent disruptive changes in the price level. These objectives are to be achieved within the framework of a system of competitive private enterprise.

There are many ways in which the government can promote a steady rise in income and employment. But we are concerned here only with those that operate through their effect on total spending in the economy. The foremost of these controls involve the monetary and fiscal powers of our government.

Most of the following discussion of economic policy concerns monetary and fiscal policy because the most influential economic powers of the government are its power to control the money system and its power to collect money from the public and to spend it. Sometimes, the government takes more drastic action, such as rationing goods, fixing prices, allocating raw materials and labor. But in a free economy, these compulsory measures are generally measures of desperation. Thus in wartime, when the nation is fighting for its existence, the public may surrender its normal rights and permit the use of direct controls to govern the economy. But except in such emergencies, the government discards direct controls and relies mainly on indirect instruments of regulation.

MONETARY POLICY

Monetary policy involves control over the sources of our money supply. Monetary policy deals mainly with the commercial banking system, for historically it has been considered a major source of instability. In the past, banks have tended to share in the optimism of booms, creating more credit and more spending power. They also have shared in the pessimism of depressions by calling in loans and destroying purchasing power. Thus they have tended to aggravate the severity of cycles in business.

The Federal Reserve System has primary authority for monetary policy because it exercises the major control over the credit-creating activities of commercial banks. As stated in Chapter 5, the Federal Reserve System, consisting of 12 banks located around the country, is under the central direction of a Board of Governors. This board has the primary responsibility for determining what monetary controls to use and when to impose them. Although not all commercial banks are members of the Federal Reserve System, member banks hold over four-fifths of our checking accounts; therefore the Federal Reserve System is in a strong position to influence the entire money and banking system of the United States.

All member banks have deposits at the Federal Reserve Banks. These deposits, or "reserves," must equal a designated percentage of deposits held by the public at the member bank. The portion of the reserve account of the member bank with the Federal Reserve that exceeds the required minimum is called "excess reserves" and may be used as a basis for the expansion of bank loans or the purchase of securities. Without excess reserves, a commercial bank cannot create credit.

The crucial power of the monetary authorities is their control over total reserves. When a Federal Reserve Bank buys something, a bond or some other type of IOU, it gives the seller a claim on the Federal Reserve Bank. When these claims are held by commercial banks, in the form of deposits in the Federal Reserve Bank, they are called bank reserves. Total reserves change, therefore, because the total deposits (debts) *owed* by the Federal Reserve Banks and *held* by the commercial banks change. Let us see how some of these changes take place.

Total reserves change when commercial banks withdraw or deposit cash at the Federal Reserve Banks. At Christmastime, for example, consumers and business firms may want to have more cash in hand than usual. To meet such demands for currency, banks probably will turn to their Federal Reserve Banks, which will give them the currency, deducting the amount from the reserve accounts of the member banks. The total reserves of the commercial banking system are reduced by the amount of currency withdrawn by the public. When the currency finds its way back into the banks after Christmas, it is deposited in the Reserve Banks, and reserves will be increased again. Thus changes in the amount of currency in circulation change total reserves of commercial banks.

Total bank reserves frequently change when the public sends money to the United States Treasury or receives money from it. The change occurs when the money is deposited by the government or withdrawn from the deposit of the government in one of the Federal Reserve Banks. The procedure is as follows. An individual sends a check to the Treasury in payment of taxes. The Treasury deposits it in its account at the Federal Reserve Bank. Then the Reserve Bank will deduct the amount of the check from the account of the bank of the individual and credit it to the account of the Treasury. The individual's bank will, in turn, deduct the amount of the check from the individual's account. But the important effect is that the amount of the check has been withdrawn from the total reserves of the commercial banking system. Later, if the Treasury should write a check payable to an individual, the reverse process would occur. The account of his bank at the Federal Reserve Bank would be increased, the account of the Treasury reduced, and the total reserves of the commercial banking system enlarged.

Commercial banks can also borrow reserves from the Federal Reserve Bank. When they do so, they increase the total reserves of the whole banking system. When member banks borrow from the Federal Reserve, deposits to their credit are created—by the same process that private deposits are created when individuals borrow at commercial banks. Banks borrow by putting up collateral, as do private citizens. As a matter of fact, among the securities that they might pledge are the notes that firms have given when they borrowed from the commercial banks. Most of the time, however, the banks use government securities as collateral.

The volume of bank reserves, therefore, is dependent on a number of things. We have seen that the public, the United States Treasury, the banks themselves, and the Federal Reserve Banks all influence the amount of bank reserves. However, as the Federal Reserve System has the duty to control the volume of commercial bank credit, its effects on reserves are deliberate and planned. Its tools for controlling commercial bank reserves are called "quantitative controls."

The most flexible quantitative tool is called open-market operations.[1] When a Federal Reserve Bank sells some of its holdings of government securities on the open market, it reduces total bank reserves. The reduction comes about in the following way. The purchaser of the securities pays the Federal Reserve Bank by writing a check on his bank. The Federal Reserve Bank collects the payment from the bank of the purchaser by reducing its reserve account. The bank, in turn, reduces the purchaser's account. Thus at the end of the transaction, the purchaser has the bond formerly held by the Federal Reserve Bank and his bank account is lower. But most important, the account of his bank—or reserve—at the Federal Reserve Bank is lower. A lower reserve reduces the volume of deposits that the bank can have.

The process is reversed when the Federal Reserve au-

[1] Here the "open market" means simply the place where United States government securities are regularly bought and sold. The Open Market Committee, consisting of members of the Board of Governors and representatives of the Federal Reserve Banks, has primary control over open market operations.

thorities want to increase total bank reserves. The Reserve Banks buy government securities on the market, giving their checks, which ultimately are deposited by commercial banks in their reserve accounts. If the Federal Reserve buys $1 million of government bonds, it creates a like amount of reserves for commercial banks. Such an increase in reserves is capable of supporting an expansion of commercial bank credit.

The Federal Reserve Banks can also influence the amount of reserves by controlling the conditions under which they will lend to commercial banks. Commercial banks can build up their reserves at the Federal Reserve Banks by "rediscounting" loans—that is, by borrowing from the Reserve Bank and putting up some of the assets they own as collateral. An obvious means of control, then, is to change the *rediscount* rate, the rate of interest that the Federal Reserve Bank charges the commercial bank that wants to borrow money. The Federal Reserve authorities can raise the rediscount rate and thereby discourage member banks from borrowing to build up their reserve accounts, or can reduce the rediscount rate and make it cheaper for banks to borrow reserves.

Because moderate changes in interest rates are seldom enough to encourage or discourage banks from borrowing reserves to make loans, such changes in the rediscount rate are only a mild means of control compared with open market operations. However, when they are combined with open market sales, the rates can be raised to put "the squeeze" on banks that need to borrow reserves. Changing the rediscount rate also has psychological value. When bankers encounter higher rediscount rates, they know that the monetary authorities believe that credit is expanding too rapidly. They will expect other, more stringent steps if the expansion continues.

Within a range set by Congress, the Federal Reserve System also has the power to set the legal ratio of bank reserves to deposits. This power gives the Federal Reserve System a third quantitative control: a control over the amount of credit that a given amount of reserves will support. When the Federal Reserve authorities want to restrain credit creation, they can raise requirements, say, from 18 to 20 per cent of commercial bank deposits. This action changes "excess" reserves into "required" reserves, leaving less room for credit expansion. In order to contract credit, the authorities could even increase reserve requirements beyond the point where banks have excess reserves, forcing them to reduce their deposits to bring their reserve ratios back into line.

As frequent changes in reserve requirements would complicate the banking business, the Reserve System does not readily use this method of contracting credit. It is used mainly when the Federal Reserve wishes to have a prompt, over-all effect on reserves. For the most part, it raises reserve requirements to "sop up" excess reserves and make the banks more sensitive to other controls. When credit expansion is desired, it is, of course, a quick way to give the commercial banks excess reserves.

Other tools of monetary policy are the so-called "selective controls." Selective controls, unlike quantitative controls, apply to particular types of commercial bank credit and do not affect bank reserves. Selective controls affect some sort of down-payment arrangement. They say, in effect, that if a person is going to buy something on credit, he cannot borrow more than a certain portion of the total price—he must pay cash for the rest. Regulation "U" gives the Federal Reserve System the power to say how much down-payment, or margin, must be made in order to borrow money to buy stocks. Regulations "W" and "X" were two other selective controls that were authorized by Congress for short inflationary periods. Although the authority to use them has now expired, they may be re-enacted when needed again. Regulation "W" stated the down-payment necessary in order to borrow money for consumers' durables, and Regulation "X" did the same thing for houses. Regulations "W" and "X" also gave the Reserve System the right to determine how much time will be granted the borrower to pay off his loan. These selective controls were not designed to attack monetary problems by changing the reserves of banks. Their purpose was to make credit more or less available for the customers of the banks.

A further tool of the Federal Reserve System has been called "moral suasion." This is the power of the Federal Reserve System to make suggestions to bankers. Such suggestions are given some force by the fact that the Reserve authorities can restrict certain privileges that members ordinarily enjoy at Reserve Banks, and in extreme cases, the Federal Reserve can expel member banks from the system. The Voluntary Credit Restraint Program used during the Korean War illustrates one application of moral suasion. In this program, the Federal Reserve System joined the American Bankers Association and other lending institutions to restrain credit that might add to inflation. The Reserve Banks and lending institutions got together and decided what types of loans would be most appropriate in the tight wartime situation, and everyone agreed to do his part to see that only the proper financing was done. The same thing might have been accomplished by the more convincing means of taking away the reserves of the banks, but the voluntary approach was tried so that banks might curtail some unnecessary borrowing at the same time as they were permitting war industries to borrow.

The Federal Reserve System can use its controls one at a time or in unison. From time to time, it has combined open market operations and rediscount rate changes in a "scissors operation." When it felt banks were expanding credit too rapidly, it sold government securities in the open market and raised its rediscount rate at the same time. Thus as bank reserves were drawn down by the open market operations, the banks were forced to borrow new reserves at the higher discount rate. Then when bank expansion was desired, the Federal Reserve reversed these two tools; it bought government securities and lowered the rediscount rate.

In general, economists are rather optimistic about the use of monetary policy to correct a moderate business decline. Without the virtual paralysis of a major crisis, they believe that expanding bank reserves and easier credit terms can help to reverse a decline. Monetary policy, especially when it is coupled with other stabilizing programs, may therefore prevent a deep collapse. It can also help to sustain economic activity, as was shown by the expansive monetary policy of 1962–65.

We should recognize, however, that monetary policy cannot invent new products or new technology. Alone, it cannot make people borrow and spend when they are in the midst of a major depression and strongly pessimistic about the prospects for the future. It may, however, create a monetary environment that encourages business. This in turn may help hasten recovery.

How can monetary policy encourage recovery? First, excess reserves encourage commercial banks to search for good loans. Excess reserves are "idle funds"; they do not earn interest and to make a profit with them new loans must be made. Excess reserves can therefore heighten competition among banks for the better (less risky) loans and thus can lead to a decline in interest rates on these loans.

Lower interest rates are a stimulus to greater production and employment. A businessman may have an opportunity to produce and sell a product, but he may not be willing to do so because the profit is too small to compensate for the time and the risk. However, if he can reduce his interest payments to the bank, he may go ahead. For example, a $50,000 inventory loan would cost $2,000 per year if the interest rate is 4 per cent, but if the interest rate falls to 2 per cent, his interest costs will be cut in half —the saving of $1,000 may be enough to persuade him to borrow and expand production.

During a recession many individuals and businesses want to convert assets into cash—in time of uncertainty they would rather be holding money than holding goods or the IOU's of other people. Monetary policy, by increasing the supply of money, can help to satisfy this desire for liquidity. By increasing banks' excess reserves and the cash holdings of the public, an expansive monetary policy will hasten the day when people would rather use (spend or lend) money than merely hold it.

Economists are also generally agreed that the Federal Reserve has the power to pull the economy up short during inflation. It can do this by using its existing tools to contract the supply of bank reserves. To combat inflation, the Federal Reserve authorities need to contract the supply of reserves enough to raise interest rates; they need to contract credit until spending shrinks enough to stabilize the price level. But, as the following historical illustration indicates, the Federal Reserve does not always choose to intervene when a price rise seems imminent.

To contract the deposits held by the public after the Second World War, authorities would have had to reduce commercial bank reserves but, instead, reserves were allowed to grow. In other words, the controls over reserves were not really used to prevent inflation. Monetary policy might have been used to stabilize prices, but the Federal Reserve authorities considered other problems more important. Why?

In the first place, the possible return of prewar depression conditions was considered quite likely. Past experience indicated that the postwar boom would not last—a sharp drop had always come after our other major wars. Knowing that their effort to pull us out of the prewar depression had not been wholly successful, the Federal Reserve authorities were therefore reluctant to curtail the boom. They were, in other words, aware that a restrictive policy could be too successful—it might move us from inflation into depression!

In the second place, the Federal Reserve authorities did not contract bank credit because they were concerned over government securities prices. The Federal Reserve System bought government bonds whenever their prices threatened to fall below par. By doing this, it fostered further credit creation.

With the Federal Reserve System standing ready to buy government securities from any one who wanted to sell them, the effect on the economy was similar to an expansionist open-market operation. Nor did it do any good when the Board of Governors increased reserve requirements. Banks simply sold more government securities in order to meet the new requirements; and, of course, raising the rediscount rate had almost no effect because banks did not need to borrow at the Federal Reserve Bank.

The Federal Reserve System was concerned about postwar government security prices because large shares of the financial resources of banks, insurance companies, businesses, and individuals were government securities. It felt that in a period of uncertainty, it was important to prevent a drop in the value of these assets. Also, it was feared that a decline in security prices might panic some holders of government debt into selling their securities rapidly. That had happened after the First World War, and the Federal Reserve authorities did not want to risk the possibility of setting off another wave of panic selling. Pressure from the Treasury also persuaded the Federal Reserve authorities to support the prices of government bonds.

This episode illustrates a point that has been stressed in this volume: economic policy involves decisions over *alternatives*. We must be careful therefore in evaluating the results of the measures used. As we have seen, we cannot say on the basis of the postwar episode that monetary policy cannot stop an inflation—it was not really tried. Since that time, it has been used several times to curtail what appeared to be inflationary situations—and although we cannot be absolutely sure, it appears that these steps helped to stabilize the levels of income and prices.

Monetary policy is a useful tool in spite of its limitations. In the first place, it is indirect and impersonal. In using monetary controls, the government does not directly intrude into individual transactions, incentives, or goals.

Instead it changes the economic environment in which people transact their business. It creates an environment in which credit is easier or more difficult to obtain.

In the second place, monetary policy is useful because it can be changed quickly. It is controlled mainly by an administrative group, the Board of Governors of the Federal Reserve System, and is therefore more flexible than controls that are imposed by congressional action. Because a business decline can spread quickly, the rapidity with which controls can be applied is extremely important. Mild action early in a business decline may be far more effective than drastic action later on. In the mild recession that occurred in 1953 and 1954, Federal Reserve policy changed abruptly at the first sign of a decline in spending and employment. Other stabilization policies, which were being considered by Congress, were still in the discussion stage months after the recession began.

FISCAL POLICY

Fiscal policy involves the use of federal taxing and spending powers to change the level of income and employment. When the federal government was small and accounted for only a minor part of the total spending of the economy, its ability to influence national income was limited. Today, however, it purchases over 10 per cent of our gross national product, and consequently can exercise a substantial influence over national income and employment. It may use its fiscal powers to moderate inflation or recession, as explained below, or to influence the rate of economic growth.

Fiscal policy affects the volume of spending. When the federal government taxes more heavily than it spends, it may reduce aggregate demand. When it spends more than it receives in taxes, it may increase aggregate demand. And to some extent, the government may stimulate or depress national income by merely altering its rate of taxing and spending, even though the budget is kept in balance.

There are two types of fiscal stabilizers: the *automatic* and the *discretionary*. Of the automatic or "built-in" stabilizers, the federal corporation income tax and the individual income tax are most important. Without any change in their rates, they draw in more revenue as national income rises and less when income falls. On the spending side, social security payments, unemployment compensation, farm subsidies, and payments on the many types of loan insurance sponsored by the federal government, have automatic stabilizing effects. Such payments decrease in times of prosperity and increase during depression without any changes in the laws. Taken together, the various programs tend to increase government spending and reduce government receipts as national income falls; they tend to do the opposite as national income rises.

Because automatic stabilizers operate without any new action by Congress, they quietly go to work as soon as income and employment change. Even if a depression becomes so severe that the government must pass additional laws to stabilize national income, the task is easier because the automatic stabilizers are operating while the lawmakers debate the issues.

Discretionary fiscal action occurs when Congress changes tax and spending laws. Thus during a period of declining income, the government can stimulate the economy not only by spending money on existing programs (automatic), but also by spending more money on new programs (discretionary). It can further stimulate the economy by reducing tax rates or eliminating some taxes altogether. But changing taxes and spending presents many difficulties. The process is not a simple one of pumping money in and out of the economy at will. First of all, policy makers must decide which of three alternative approaches to use.

The government can hold spending constant and change taxes, hold taxes constant and change spending, or change both taxes and spending. Considerable difference of opinion has existed among economists over which of these methods is most desirable. However, most will agree that in any serious decline, the program probably should involve changes in both taxing *and* spending.

A *reduction in taxes tends to increase private spending and an increase in taxes tends to contract private spending.* The relationship between consumption and "after tax income" is fairly stable although not constant. Hence an increase in taxes that cuts disposable income will have a depressing effect on the volume of consumer spending. A decrease in taxes will tend to stimulate consumption. The effect of tax changes on investment is less certain. Lower taxes, like lower interest rates, encourage investment, but they will not bring it forth unless other conditions and expectations of businessmen are favorable. Yet, there are usually some investment opportunities that will attract investment if the returns are less heavily taxed. In other words, tax reduction tends to stimulate investment, although the degree to which it does is less predictable than it is for consumption.

Of course, all taxes do not affect income in the same way. Sales or excise taxes fall heavily on those who spend their money for consumption. Progressive income taxes or estate taxes fall more heavily on the higher-income groups that tend to save or invest a larger portion of their income. Corporation income taxes, special tax exemptions and deductions, social security taxes, and excess profits taxes affect spending in different ways. The following discussion deals with taxes as a whole, but it is important to remember that the final effect of tax changes depends partly on which taxes are changed.

Tax reduction leaves more income in the hands of spenders, therefore it stimulates demand. But it has limitations in a stabilization program. In the first place, it is generally difficult to determine when a recession has started. Second, an administration may delay action because it fears that recognition of a recession may undermine confidence. Third, changing taxes is generally a slow process. Therefore a recession may be well under way before tax reduction can offer help. In 1962, the President requested

Congress to approve a measure that would shorten the time-lag for tax reduction to combat recession. His request for standby authority to make temporary across-the-board tax cuts reflected growing awareness among economists of the need for more timely action if this anti-recession tool is to be fully effective. However, the political obstacles to this idea are numerous, and a search has continued for acceptable alternatives.

The effectiveness of tax reduction may be reduced, critics point out, because a portion of the cut will not be spent.

A dollar of tax reduction may result in, say, only 90 cents of new spending, whereas an extra dollar of government spending will add a dollar to aggregate demand. Supporters of tax changes argue, however, that tax reduction has a great effect on investment incentives and therefore may foster additional spending for investment. The potency of tax reduction as a fiscal tool was amply demonstrated by the Revenue Act of 1964. Congress cut taxes by approximately $11 billion in an effort to reduce the gap between what the country could produce and what it was producing. An increase in private spending followed that led to a reduction in unemployment from 5.7 per cent in 1963 to 4.5 per cent in mid-1965. (By the end of the year unemployment had fallen further to 4.1 per cent as a result of the increasing expenditures for the Vietnam conflict.)

If the government decides to alter expenditures rather than taxes to correct cycles in income and employment, it must decide how to spend varying amounts of money. During the 1930's, the government spent large sums for relief payments and so-called make-work projects. But now these are not generally considered a basic part of a fiscal program for economic recovery. Relief spending is an emergency program designed to alleviate the acute suffering of the unemployed and to get the economy moving again. Although it reduced distress, the fabled "leaf-raking" of the 1930's was a slow way to restore public confidence in the ability of the nation to regain prosperity. The necessity for this "stop-gap" spending has been reduced by our present-day programs of unemployment compensation, farm subsidies, and aids to other groups.

Most people prefer that the government produce useful facilities and services by its spending. A great deal can be done to build schools, roads, dams, and other public works while combating depression. But it is well to recognize that when the nation is threatened with an economic breakdown, it is important to encourage *spending* in general. In such a crisis, the most important goal may be to put funds into the hands of those who will revive spending and thereby generate normal production and employment.

Some economists have pointed out that if the government wants to stimulate the economy, it could even build "pyramids" as a way of putting funds into the hands of those who will spend. They say this to point out that the income effect of government spending should not be confused with the usefulness of the things it buys. Even building a pyramid is useful if it is the only way to put people back to work on farms and factories.

Most economists agree that in any severe decline the government must spend on public works, such as roads, schools, hydroelectric facilities, parks, post offices, and river development. As timing is important in such spending, it is necessary that plans be available for public works projects. Herbert Hoover, when he was Secretary of Commerce, suggested a "shelf" of public works plans for possible depression emergencies. Similar suggestions have been made by succeeding administrations.

Two major objections have been raised to the use of spending for public works to smooth out cycles. One objection is that it is difficult to turn some spending programs off when the depression emergency has come to an end. A dam started in the midst of a depression cannot be left unfinished. Thus some of the projects begun in the 1930's continued over into the 1940's, when the depression was far behind us. A comprehensive program of public works for the future should therefore have some short-range and some long-range projects. Of course, the difficulty is that the government may be unable to determine whether a short-range or a long-range program is needed. The second objection is that public spending might discourage some private spending. If, in building a dam, the government gives the impression that it wants to build all hydroelectric facilities, it may retard private spending for power development. Public spending for recovery should clearly raise the level of total spending, and not merely take the place of private investment.

In certain circumstances the level of income and employment might be changed by programs of taxing and spending, even though the total budget is balanced. For instance, if the government starts with a balanced budget and then increases *both* its taxes and spending by, say, $10 billion, gross national product will rise by some amount up to $10 billion, since total private spending may not decline, or may decline by less than $10 billion. On the other hand, if the government cuts both its taxes and spending by an equal amount, total spending may fall. The actual effect, of course, would depend on what happens to private spending for consumption and investment.

Fiscal policies designed to stabilize the economy require surpluses in some years and deficits in others. Some economists suggest that our goal should be to balance the budget over the whole business cycle, so that the surpluses accumulated during the boom would offset the deficits of the depression. But even a cyclically balanced budget may be difficult to obtain. New emergencies and new requirements for public services arise at all stages of the cycle. Moreover, there is no assurance that the cycles that fiscal policy seeks to correct will be neatly balanced cycles of inflation and deflation.

Continued deficits could result from political maneuvering, continued high defense requirements, a chronic tendency for the nation to slide into depression, or simply the growing need for public services required by an expanding population. Whatever the cause, a continuous rise in the national debt must be considered a possibility.

Much has been learned about the national debt in recent years. The economic effects of debt are now better understood, and the national debt is not regarded with the horror that it once was. Today, a major depression is seldom thought to be preferable to an increase in the public debt. Moreover, public debt management is now considered a tool for stabilizing income and employment.

Public debt management is a meeting ground for fiscal and monetary policy. The debt, which results from an excess of expenditures over taxes, exerts strong influences on our credit system. When the government redeems securities held by the public, it puts money in the hands of the public. When the government borrows from people, it takes money away from them—as it does when it taxes. But government borrowing is not as strong a restraint as taxation, because people acquire bonds, which are income-bearing assets. An increase in the debt, then, is only a partial substitute for an increase in taxes when the desire is to restrain public spending.

An increase in the national debt is a restraint on total spending as long as the government only takes money away from people. But if the government spends what it borrows, the effect is to increase expenditures. In other words, to determine the impact of a debt increase, it is necessary to know what the government does with the borrowed funds.

Moreover, it is necessary to know where the government borrowed the money. Government borrowing from the commercial banks is often more inflationary than borrowing from people. This is because the Federal Reserve Banks often supply the banks with excess reserves so they can loan to the government without curtailing their loans to private borrowers. When this is done, the government can spend without drawing funds from private spending. If the government spends $50 billion, which it obtains through an "easy money" policy of the Federal Reserve, the effect will be inflationary—more inflationary, of course, than taxing for the whole $50 billion, and generally more inflationary than borrowing only from individuals and businesses.

HOW EFFECTIVE ARE MONETARY AND FISCAL POLICIES?

Experiences to date do not tell us conclusively how effective these policies have been. The evidence that must be used to prove or disprove the validity of monetary and fiscal theories is inadequate. Because the effects of monetary and fiscal actions cannot be isolated from the influence of other factors in the economy, it is always difficult to determine what a given policy may have accomplished.

What can be said of these devices is that they appear to work reasonably well *when they are properly applied*. The effective use of monetary and fiscal policies depends on: (1) a prompt recognition of the need for corrective action, (2) an understanding of the consequences of various monetary and fiscal measures, and (3) the political feasibility of carrying them out.

We do not have precise indicators of danger points in the changing flow of income. Therefore, it is frequently difficult for public officials to decide when to use new policies. Without clear-cut indicators of future conditions, the use of public policy must depend on discretion based on an accumulation of incomplete evidence. Perhaps it is only when enough indicators of economic activity show signs of a harmful trend that policy changes can be justified; and by then some damage may have been done. However, our statistical data have improved, and our forecasting skills have become better over the years. Thus even though the timing of fiscal action cannot always be unerringly correct, it has been improved. Nevertheless, the choice of proper timing and the choice of proper methods will always be major problems in economic stabilization.

Our limited knowledge of the full effects of particular policies also hampers our ability to control business fluctuations. Economists are not completely certain about the effects of different programs on private spending. As a result, the selection and timing of various monetary and fiscal policies cannot be precisely scheduled. For instance, we do not know how much stabilizing action is derived from the automatic fiscal devices, and therefore we cannot be sure how far inflation or deflation should be permitted to continue before new tax and spending programs are inaugurated. Similarly, if the monetary authorities are not entirely clear on how well monetary policy can bring about an upturn in business, they may be reluctant to use their powers to curtail and possibly reverse a developing boom. However, these limitations are most apparent in the selection and timing of action for moderate fluctuations; in the event of major economic fluctuations, precise measures of the effects of particular policies are less necessary.

A major characteristic of monetary and fiscal programs is that they tend to be over-all or aggregate controls. Thus they tend to influence the total volume of spending instead of a particular situation that may be causing trouble. But improvements have been made in controlling specific problems. The government has, from time to time, increased its purchases in areas in which unemployment has developed; it has also fostered crop restrictions and marketing programs to bolster farm prices; on occasion, the federal housing authorities have dealt with housing credit by altering their requirements for down payments and interest rates on insured mortgage loans; and, as noted earlier, Congress has several times given the Federal Reserve authorities the power to impose restraints on specific types of credit—stock market loans and consumer and housing loans.

These are steps that tend to improve the precision of our stabilization program. Further power of a similar nature would enable the government to approach the problem in a *selective* manner by correcting specific danger spots, rather than waiting until the *over-all* weapons of monetary and fiscal policy can be brought into play.

Political considerations also limit the application of monetary and fiscal controls. American economic policy is generally responsive to popular demands. If, for various reasons, the people are opposed to a change in public policy, the government tends to reflect their wishes. The government generally cannot raise taxes during inflation if the public strongly disapproves of higher taxes. Similarly, if the public fears larger government spending or a growing public debt more than it fears a decline in income and employment, then various anti-depression policies cannot be used. These limitations on the use of monetary and fiscal controls diminish, however, as the need for stabilization grows. When conditions get bad enough, the public usually demands action.

In spite of these limitations, monetary and fiscal policy combined can contribute greatly to stability of income and employment. Monetary policy, we have seen, may operate quickly in a mild dip, but it may be handicapped in a period of deep depression. Expanding bank reserves and declining interest rates can stimulate private spending under most conditions; but in a depression crisis, the response may be slow. Fiscal policy, however, can probably provide a more definite boost in either a major or a minor decline. By facilitating new spending, fiscal policy can act directly as the prime mover. Then if the upturn occurs, monetary policy can make a major contribution to the revival.

In curtailing inflationary pressures, the two can also be co-ordinated. Generally, monetary policy can act quickly and unobtrusively without creating fears of a subsequent collapse. The automatic fiscal devices also move quietly into action as spending rises. Finally, if a major inflation appears to be under way, Congress may undertake major changes in taxing and spending programs to shrink private spending.

As noted in Chapter 6, the American economy experienced a mild recession from the summer of 1957 to the winter of 1958. We may use the figures on page 160 to illustrate the problems of selecting the weapons for economic stabilization. We shall follow the outline used in the preceding chapters.

The Problem

From the summer of 1957 to the winter of 1958, the total output of goods and services (GNP) declined 4 per cent. Consumers spent less on durables, but more on services. Businessmen reduced the rate of their investment in inventory and were actually using up their inventories faster than they were purchasing new stocks of goods and materials. Businessmen also cut back their investments in new capital equipment. Construction of new homes and commercial structures decreased slightly.

Federal government expenditures remained unchanged but there was a small increase in spending by state and local governments. Federal taxes also declined, leaving the government with a slight cash deficit for the year. The number of jobless doubled during the period, from 2.5 million in 1957 to over 5 millions in 1958.

Let us assume that we are asked to devise a program that will halt the decline. More specifically, the issue is what can be done with monetary and fiscal policy.

The Objectives

The immediate objective is to bring the decline to an end. When that is done, we shall want to put the economy back on the path to economic growth. However, we do not want to overstimulate the economy and bring on a price inflation.

There are a number of additional requirements that we might have for a stabilization program. Perhaps we object very strongly to an expansion of the national debt; perhaps we do not want to increase the scope of government spending; perhaps we want the benefits of tax reduction to go to some specific group. These objectives and requirements may be in conflict, hence choices or compromises may have to be made.

The Alternatives

First, what can be achieved by monetary policy? Suppose reserve requirements are reduced, rediscount rates are reduced, and purchases of government securities by the Federal Reserve Banks are increased. These steps will tend to increase commercial bank reserves. On the basis of the new reserves, the banks could create more credit.

But will there be a demand for this additional credit? Is spending likely to increase simply because banks make borrowing easier? Easier terms may stimulate consumer installment purchases of "big" durables, such as automobiles or electrical appliances. Business borrowing for inventory may not respond until more inventories have been "sold off." Lower interest rates resulting from the easier money policy may induce some state and local governments to borrow. Easing payment terms on home mortgages would also have a tendency to increase housing sales, because the demand for housing is apparently high.

Altogether, it appears that monetary policy could help to bring the decline to an end. Moreover, it would prepare the economy to take advantage of any forces that may tend to stimulate it. For example, liquidation of inventories may soon cease because the stock of goods may become too low to meet the current level of consumption. When businesses are ready to reorder, the availability of bank credit can stimulate new spending for inventory. However, if conditions should improve quickly, the new credit could also lead to a price inflation. If this is possible, the monetary authorities would have to move with caution.

Second, what techniques of fiscal policy might be used? A higher level of government spending is one possibility. Most of the decline in GNP came, as we have seen, as a result of decreased spending for private investment. If that deficiency were offset by increased spending for public investment or other types of government spending, GNP would probably increase. New government spending would be more likely to lead to an increase in GNP if taxes were not raised as much as expenditures—in other words, if the government had a deficit.

If federal spending is to be increased the question is: What type of spending? Should the government build roads and schools? Increase employment benefits or veterans' payments for schooling? Give grants to our allies? Stockpile military goods or pay subsidies to farmers and other producers? Obviously, some of our reasons for any of these expenditures will be noneconomic; nevertheless, each must be evaluated in terms of its effect on private spending.

It may be politically easier to create a deficit by cutting taxes, leaving expenditures unchanged. This decision raises the question: Which taxes are to be cut? We cannot explore the alternatives in detail, but we can note the problem involved. A reduction in the corporate income tax will tend to have more effect on business spending than a reduction in the federal excise taxes; a cut in tax rates for lower-income groups will have more effect on consumption than cuts for higher-income groups. Should the government give income-tax relief by increasing the tax exemption per dependent, by cutting taxes across the board, or by reducing the rate of taxation on dividends? Any of these methods could be used in such a way that the loss in revenue to the government would be about the same, but the effect on private spending would be different.

The choice of a fiscal program must be based in part on an expectation of how private spending will react. If government spending increases, will people offset it by cutting their own spending? Will reduced taxation result in more idle funds in the hands of the public? Even though we cannot say with certainty what the public will do, the evidence of spending by the public during the recession (more for consumption and housing) suggests that it will tend to respond to fiscal stimulation. Therefore, the long-run problem may be to devise a fiscal program that will stimulate but not overstimulate.

Appraise the Alternatives

In choosing among these alternative programs, we must keep in mind the fact that each alternative has effects that are somewhat different from the others. We must be careful, therefore, to examine both the stabilizing tools and our goals to get an effective program. The policies that were actually used are described in *The Economic Report of the President, 1959.*[2]

This chapter has stressed these basic ideas:

1. The federal government has assumed the responsibility for smoothing out the fluctuations in income, employment, and the average price level that occur in our economy. Its goal is not to prevent change; rather it is to provide a steady and stable growth of spending and jobs.

2. Monetary policy is one of the tools that may be used for this purpose. By working primarily through the commercial banking system, the Federal Reserve System influences the level of interest rates and the volume of lending in the whole economy. Fiscal policy is another tool that can be used by the federal government. By changing the flow of taxes and spending, the government can influence the flow of private spending.

3. These policies are not precise instruments of control that can eliminate every ripple in the level of income or employment. To some extent, all of them require decisions based on the judgment of government officials, and these decisions must sometimes be based on inadequate information. There are a number of administrative problems in using monetary and fiscal controls—nevertheless, they offer a means of positive action to curb harmful fluctuations in economic activity.

[2] Pp. 33-44.

Suggested Reading

Paul A. Samuelson, *Economics: An Introductory Analysis*, Chaps. 18 and 19, pp. 316–58. George L. Bach, *Economics: An Introduction to Analysis and Policy*, Chaps. 12–14, pp. 178–209. These readings will provide a fuller understanding of the theory and practice of monetary and fiscal stabilizers. Several selections in *Readings in Economics* (Samuelson et al., ed.) show an interesting contrast in views on government stabilizing action. They appear under the headings "Fiscal Policy and Income," "Inflation," and "Monetary Policy." Two recent Brookings books provide a layman's guide to many issues in stabilization policy. See *Federal Budget Policy*, by David J. and Attiat F. Ott, and *Federal Tax Policy*, by Joseph A. Pechman.

Chapter 8

ECONOMIC GROWTH

The United States has a growing economy: population is increasing and living conditions are improving. In prosperous times, this expansion is taken for granted, as something natural and inevitable. But as studies of living conditions in many other nations indicate, the expanding production of the United States is not typical of the entire world. Nor has it been constant throughout our history. Looking back on our past, we are reminded that just three decades ago the outlook for economic progress was dark indeed. The economic catchword of the 1930's was "stagnation." Then there seemed to be no new frontiers to develop; unemployment was high, investment in new equipment was negligible, and we seemed more preoccupied with just "hanging on" than with visions of great economic advances.

Let us now take a "long-run" view of our economy. Let us see why the 1930's now appear as a temporary interruption in economic growth rather than as a turning point. We shall explore the sources of economic growth and try to identify the reasons for our expanding production. With this background, we shall then try to show what conditions are most likely to influence our future growth.

MEASURING OUR GROWTH

One common measure of economic growth is the increase in real gross national product. This is the figure that economists usually have in mind when discussing the question: How fast should the economy grow and what can be done to foster a better growth rate for our kind of economic system? Real gross national product measures the economy's total output in dollars of the same purchasing power—thus it is not affected by changes in the price level.

Historically, the average annual rate of growth, by this yardstick, has been just under 3 per cent for the period 1909–60. In the five years following 1960, real GNP increased at an annual rate of 4.5 per cent. From year to year during this century the rate has varied with changes in the business cycle. It also has varied geographically: areas of the United States have not grown at a uniform rate. And, in addition, it has varied by sector. In the 1960–65 period, the fastest growing markets were consumer durables and private investment. State and local government spending also went up sharply, rising 5 per cent a year, while federal spending was rising less than 2.5 per cent a year. The chart on p. 203 shows the trend of the nation's growth rate and how widely it has varied over the past half century.

An important measure of our advancing level of living is the growth of real income per capita. As we noted in Chapter 2, this measurement is useful because if is not distorted by changes in the price level or by changes in population. Before using it, however, we must recognize that it is not a complete measure of economic welfare. It does not tell us about the many improvements in the quality of living conditions, such as the improved health of the American people, better recreational and cultural facilities, or the greater leisure for enjoying them.

Per-capita income is an *average* figure computed by dividing the total income of the nation by the total population. Thus it obscures regional differences, occupational differences, and individual differences in income. Furthermore, it does not show what products were produced, and how these products were distributed.

AGGREGATE OUTPUT, 1910–65

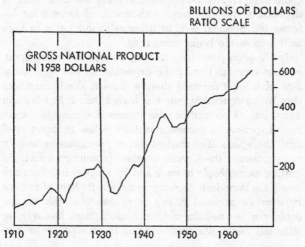

BILLIONS OF DOLLARS
RATIO SCALE

GROSS NATIONAL PRODUCT
IN 1958 DOLLARS

a Source: *Long-Term Economic Growth, 1860–1965*, U. S. Department of Commerce, Bureau of the Census (1966), p. 14. This data is shown on a "ratio scale" chart that shows at a glance what the growth *rate* is at any time. On this type chart an increase of $5 billion in a year when GNP is $50 billion would show the same slope as an increase of $50 billion when GNP is $500 billion. The slope would be the same because each of these is a 10 per cent increase.

The level of living is particularly difficult to measure in a growing economy in which new products are constantly being introduced and old ones improved. Today our level of living includes television, airplane transportation, synthetic fibers, and life-saving antibiotic drugs—none of which could have been purchased by a millionaire in 1900. If we recognize these limitations, we can use changes in real income per capita as an approximate measure of the trend in our level of economic life.

The chart on page 204 shows the growth in the income per capita after payment of taxes. The figures cover the period 1929–65, during which the government's share of income has grown sharply, yet per-capita disposable income has increased 80 per cent. In other words, in spite of depression, war, and large withdrawals of income for defense, our personal level of living is almost twice as high as it was in the boom year, 1929.

In the years from 1929 to 1965 per-capita income grew, but not steadily. During the depression of the 1930's, the flow of income declined sharply; then it slowly began to rise. By 1939, total income was higher than it had been in 1929, but as population also increased during the same period, per-capita income remained below its 1929 level until the 1940's. The marked rise in per-capita income by 1944 reflected the intense wartime production effort. By putting more people to work and by lengthening the work week, the American economy increased its flow of income by over 40 per cent in five years. Much of this income could not be used for civilian consumption, however, so although per-capita income rose, there was not a cor-

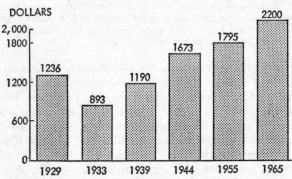

REAL PER CAPITA DISPOSABLE INCOME [a]

(SELECTED YEARS IN 1958 DOLLARS)

[a] *Economic Report of the President, 1966,* p. 227. Disposable income excludes not only taxes but also the income retained by corporations.

responding increase in the level of consumption. Instead there was a sharp increase in personal saving. After the Second World War, production declined during reconversion, and then resumed a gradual growth. This growth was accompanied by a rapid increase in our population so that per-capita income rose more slowly.

The advance in the level of living has been even greater than these income figures show because the work week has been shortened. That is, people have preferred to take some of the benefits of economic growth in the form of leisure rather than in income. The accompanying table illustrates the trend of the average hours worked for the last century. In the early 1960's, the average work week in private employment was still about 40 hours.

AVERAGE WEEKLY HOURS WORKED, 1850–1950[a]

Year	Nonagriculture	Agriculture	All Private Employment
1850	66	72	70
1900	56	67	60
1920	45	60	50
1930	43	55	46
1940	41	55	44
1950	39	47	40

[a] J. Frederic Dewhurst and Associates, *America's Needs and Resources* (1955), p. 1073. Figures are rounded.

Thus at the same time that per-capita income has risen, the number of hours worked has decreased. Furthermore, as shown in Chapter 2, this growth in income and leisure has been distributed widely among our population.

THE INGREDIENTS OF OUR GROWTH

The United States has been blessed with an ample supply of natural resources. It has fertile fields, vast forests, and extensive grazing land. It has been able to draw on rich deposits of coal, petroleum, iron, copper, and other minerals. Rivers crisscross the land, offering potentials for navigation, irrigation, and generation of power. The climate is predominantly temperate yet varied enough to nurture the growth of many kinds of useful plants.

But natural resources offer only the raw material for economic activity. Many nations with abundant resources have failed to develop them effectively. The potential usefulness of resources must be recognized; techniques for developing them must be devised. In short, putting resources to work productively requires manpower, knowledge, research, managerial talents, tools, and capital.

In the United States, the labor to develop resources has been provided by a continually increasing population. Immigration has brought millions of people to our shores. The birth rate has varied considerably, but always has been large enough to bring about an annual net increase in population. The life span has lengthened. As a result, the population of the United States increased by about one third every decade from 1700 to 1860. Since the turn of the century, the population growth rate has varied considerably, as the following table indicates:

Year	Total Population (in millions)	Percentage Increase Over Preceding Decade
1900	76	26
1910	92	21
1920	106	15
1930	123	16
1940	132	7
1950	152	15
1960	181	19
1970 (est.)	208	15

These population figures tell us that the nation had a growing supply of labor and more mouths to feed, but they do not explain the growth in the level of living. If population were the only requirement for a high level of living, people in areas such as China, India, or Puerto Rico would be living much better than they do.

An expanding population can help raise the level of living only if the additional people deliver a *more than proportionate* increase in production. Thus if population increases 10 per cent, the total production of the society must increase by 10 per cent merely to stay even. If the level of living is to grow, production must increase faster than population. Over the years, that is what the American economy has done. It has provided an increasing population with a rising level of living. In brief, the keys to economic growth are the conditions that enable the nation to produce goods and services faster than it produces new consumers.

The task of producing goods and services for a growing population is complicated by the fact that not everyone works. The civilian labor force, for example, does not include children, students, the incapacitated, the aged, or members of the armed forces. It includes a much smaller number of women than of men, as most women are occupied with domestic chores. Thus the ratio of men to women, the age composition of the population, the drain on manpower for military service, and the traditions of the people—such as their attitude toward child labor and retirement—help determine the size of the labor force. In the United States, the civilian labor force in 1965 was about 40 per cent of the population—76 millions out of a population of about 195 millions. For per-capita income to grow, this 40 per cent must produce more—not only for themselves, but for the rest of the population as well.

Since 1929, the nation's work force has grown from about 49 millions to 76 millions—an increase of 50 per cent. But this overstates the growth in the nation's labor effort. As we have seen, over the long run, as the nation has become more wealthy, the average number of hours that each person worked has been reduced. Because of this trend, the growth in man-hours worked has not kept up with the growth in the number of people able to work.

The major reason for our increased level of living has been the growth in the productivity of our work force.

In 1929, the American people worked about 116 billion hours. In 1965 their annual work time amounted to about 144 billion hours—about 25 per cent more than in 1929—yet the economy produced about three times as much income as it produced in 1929. This shows clearly the main source of our growth. The reason that the economy produced so much more goods and services is that productivity more than doubled.

The most common measure of productivity is *output per man-hour*. A growth in output per man-hour indicates the growing efficiency with which labor is used. Let us take an example to see how we measure the growth of productivity by output per man-hour. Suppose an appliance factory with 10 men working an eight-hour shift can produce 160 washing machines a day, with the help of a mechanized production line. In this case, the input of labor is 80 man-hours (10 men × 8 hours), and the output is 2 washing machines per man-hour (160 machines ÷ 80 man-hours). Now let us assume that the engineering department of the factory develops and installs a faster punch press to form the tubs and installs new handling equipment that enables the men to keep up with the new punch press with ease. The 10 men are now able to produce 200 washing machines each day. Output is now 2.5 washing machines per man-hour (200 washing machines ÷ 80 man-hours). Productivity in this factory has increased 25 per cent.

Although it is easy enough to figure productivity in a factory that produces just washing machines, it becomes quite difficult to figure productivity in a plant that produces half a dozen different products with the same men and machines. It becomes even more complicated when statisticians attempt to measure output per man-hour for manufacturing as a whole or for the economy as a whole. In general, economists believe that productivity figures are more reliable for measuring long-term trends than for measuring short-term improvements from year to year.

Recent estimates, covering the period since 1900, indicate that output per man-hour has increased at a long-run rate of about 2.2 per cent per year for the private economy as a whole.[1] At this rate of increase in productivity, our total private production of goods and services would *double* every 32 years, even if the number of man-hours worked remains unchanged.

This 2.2 per cent increase in output per man-hour is an average over a long period, and it may vary considerably from year to year. The evidence suggests, for instance, that in the period immediately following the Second World War, output per man-hour fell. The decline in productivity was probably due to the fact that old equipment was used to supply the unusually high demand for consumer goods and because rather poorly trained wartime workers were being shifted into new jobs. During other periods, such as the late 1920's and recently, the increase in productivity was apparently higher than 3 per cent per year, probably because firms were investing in a great deal of new and improved equipment, and the work force was becoming more skilled.

Not only is there a good deal of variation in growth of productivity from one year to the next, depending on economic conditions, but there is also a great deal of difference among industries. Agriculture, for instance, probably lagged behind nonagricultural industries before the Second World War, but in recent years the use of mechanization, improved fertilizers, and insecticides has caused output per hour of farm work to increase faster than the long-run trend. On the other hand, manufacturing productivity has apparently grown faster than the trend for the nation as a whole. Some estimates place the long-run

[1] Joint Economic Committee, *Productivity, Prices, and Incomes*, 85th Cong., 1st Sess., 1957, p. 18. Productivity estimates for man-hours of government work involve special problems, and they are not included in these figures. See also U. S. Department of Commerce, Bureau of the Census, *Long-Term Economic Growth, 1860–1965* (1966).

rate for manufacturing at about 3 per cent per year—and in recent years the average increase may have been closer to 5 per cent per year.

As the accompanying chart shows, in some industries, productivity soars. In others, little or no progress is made. Even within a single industry, changes in the productivity of labor vary from firm to firm. However, for our inquiry the important fact is that the measurements show a long-run growth in productivity for the economy as a whole.

CHANGES IN OUTPUT PER MAN-HOUR
PRODUCTION WORKERS IN SELECTED INDUSTRIES, 1947-60[a]

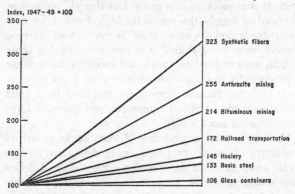

a Data from U. S. Bureau of Labor Statistics.

SOURCES OF INCREASED PRODUCTIVITY

Output per man-hour depends in part on the quality of the labor force—its age distribution and its level of skills and education. The quality of the American labor force is partly a reflection of the fact that most workers are between the ages of 20 and 65. To produce our food and man our factories and stores, it has not been necessary to put children or the aged to work. More importantly, the quality of the labor force has been improved by free public education and vocational training, and the consequent ease of learning an occupation. One study attributed a fifth of our growth in the period 1929–57 to education.[2]

Beyond these factors, which determine what the labor force *can* do, is the pattern of work incentives that determine what the labor force *wants* to do. Work in this country is not considered degrading or unworthy, but is accepted as a normal activity. The desire for complete idleness is rare; a disposition to work is a traditional characteristic of our people. Another characteristic has been their "mobility"—their willingness to shift to new jobs, adjust to new techniques, and seek new opportunities. Unlike the people of some societies, Americans have tended to welcome change, hence efficient workers are more able to get to positions where their efficiency will count.

Advances in technology have contributed immeasurably to the rising productivity of our growing labor force. These advances—represented by better equipment and greater generation of power—are the fruits of research. They are the results of the unceasing efforts of science and business to learn more about the universe and to find better ways of doing things. Millions of man-hours have been spent, not only on applied research, which draws on theoretical knowledge to solve practical problems, but also on basic research. Underlying these technological discoveries, of course, is the teaching of accumulated knowledge and of the tools of thinking. Each generation builds on the knowledge it inherits, and applies this knowledge to the improvement of production. This unbroken chain of education, research, and new technology has fostered our economic growth.

Our technology embraces an expanding volume of knowledge, tools, and techniques for improving production. In a larger sense, it has also included such diverse elements of our economy as the development of industrial engineering and labor unions and fiscal policy and ac-

[2] Edward F. Denison, *The Sources of Economic Growth in the United States and the Alternatives Before Us* (1962).

counting techniques—these "new ways" have all had an impact on the performance of the economy. However, we shall concentrate here on the role of technology as it is generally understood. In this sense, technology refers to the industrial "arts"—the processes by which we produce our material goods and services.

Technological innovation has its main impact on productivity through the building of new plants and machinery. As we pointed out in Chapter 1, "capital" is the economist's name for productive equipment, and "capital formation" is the name for the process of creating capital. The following chart shows an estimate of the stock of business capital—plant and equipment. In general, the periods of rapid growth were periods when improved technology had its greatest effect. We should realize, however, that the rate of capital growth does not always show how fast we are introducing technological innovations. Even in

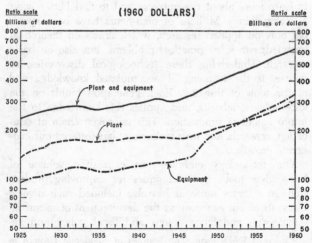

INVESTMENT IN THE STOCKS OF BUSINESS
PLANT AND EQUIPMENT[a]
(1960 DOLLARS)

[a] Data supplied by Machinery and Allied Products Institute.

years when the total stock of capital goods remained the same, its *quality* improved as old facilities were discarded and new ones took their place.

It is apparent that over a long period, productivity and the stock of capital have both increased. Logically, we expect some causal relationship between the amount of capital and the increase in output per man-hour of work. But actually, for an increase in capital to bring greater productivity, it must bring either an increase in capital *per worker* or an improvement in the quality of the capital.

Over the years the total plant and equipment *per worker* has grown. As the accompanying chart shows, the growth has been irregular, and the sharpest increases since 1925 have occurred since the Second World War. In a sense, the chart shows we have become more "capital-istic"—we are now using more capital per worker.

PLANT AND EQUIPMENT PER WORKER, 1925-60
(1960 DOLLARS)

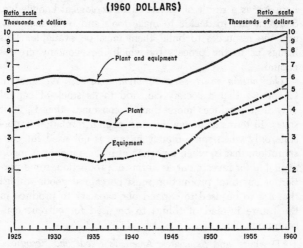

Data supplied by Machinery and Allied Products Institute.

We cannot catalogue all the types of capital equipment of the nation, but it will be useful to stress the importance of power facilities. All of the productive equipment of the nation requires the use of energy. The leading sources of energy used in the United States are petroleum, coal, natural gas, and water power, and a new source with great potentialities is being introduced, atomic energy. In 1850, about two thirds of the work in this country was done by animal power and human power; little more than 10 per cent was done by fuel combustion. In 1950, the situation was reversed; about 90 per cent of the work was done by fuel combustion and less than 2 per cent by human beings and animals.[3] In 1950, the United States used more electric power in one week than it produced during the entire year 1902. The development of the techniques and equipment to substitute a growing volume of more efficient sources of power for manpower, animal power, wood or wind power is a basic requirement for an expanding industrial economy.

Capital formation is not automatic, something that just happens as a result of increased technological knowledge. Someone has to decide to make tools and build factories, and the resources to build them must be available. This brings us to the process by which the economy creates capital.

The nation must save to create capital. We saw in Chapter 2 that a society can add to its stock of capital only if it produces more than it consumes—that is, if it saves. In terms of money income, capital formation is possible only when some money income is not used for consumption, that is, when a portion of income money is made available for investment. In terms of production, some portion of our total production must be capital goods—things that are to be used to expand our capacity to produce in the future instead of things to be used for current consumption.

[3] Dewhurst and Associates, *America's Needs and Resources,* p. 1116.

The rate of saving from income varies from one society to another, and within any society, it varies from one time to another. In some societies, most of the national income must be used to keep the people fed and sheltered; consumption is high and saving low. In more productive societies, the rate of saving can be higher. Wealthy nations therefore may set aside a larger part of their national income for investment—which further increases their wealth.

In the United States the customs and traditions of the people, the personal distribution of income, and the institutions of our economy have encouraged saving and investment. An attitude of self-reliance requires individuals to save in preparation for possible future "rainy days." The determination of parents to give their children a better start in life also requires saving. These typical American attitudes can be contrasted with those in cultures in which parents regard their children as a source of economic security.

Another reason for our willingness to save is that the rewards for saving and investing in the undeveloped potential of the nation have been large enough to induce people to forego current consumption in order to share in these rewards. For years our nation had vast unused land resources, but the labor to develop them was scarce. Labor was therefore the relatively expensive resource. Tools and equipment that could increase the work that men could do cut this expense by reducing the labor time necessary to produce a given product. The desire to save was therefore partly a result of the desire to get tools to reduce labor costs and expand production.

The unequal distribution of income is another reason for the high rate of saving in this country. More has been saved by the wealthy few who have received a larger share of national income than would have been saved if income had been distributed more equally. More equal distribution would have led to higher consumption and lower saving. Of course, some other countries that have unequal distributions of income have not saved as large a share of their income. In any society, the wealthy people at the top of the income scale have the capacity to save—in our society they have been rewarded for doing so.

Another important reason for the relatively high share of income being used for investment is that businesses save and invest a major portion of their earnings instead of distributing their entire net profit to their owners. Since the Second World War, for example, retained business earnings financed about two thirds of new plant and equipment purchased by American industry. The corporation has proved to be an especially large saver. Because corporation executives may want to expand the operations of their companies, they may save and invest, even though some of the owners prefer to receive dividends they could use for consumption. When this happens, the corporation functions as a device to induce the group to save more than they would as individuals.

Banks and other financial institutions have also played a part in the saving-investing process. As we noted in Chapter 5, financial institutions make saving more attractive to many people by providing them with liquid assets to hold (insurance policies, savings accounts, or demand deposits). For the many people who do not want to own a direct share of the capital of industry, these assets provide another method to accumulate savings. If many of these people could not hold an insurance policy or a savings account, they would save less, or perhaps they would save nothing at all.

But the role of financial institutions in the saving-investing process goes deeper than this. Banks can help force the economy to invest. If business wants to borrow and spend a greater proportion of national income than savers want to lend, the banks can meet the needs of business by creating demand deposits. And if businessmen can borrow enough, they can bid the necessary labor and resources away from consumers. The banks can, in other words, generate a process that is similar to saving—they can cause some of our production to be used for investment instead of consumption. Thus even the "wild-cat" banks of the 1800's aided the growth of capital for a while. Although many such banks were on shaky financial footing and later failed, the money they created and loaned to businessmen kept men at work building factories and railroads rather than working on consumption goods.

The main catalyst that turns savings into investment is the businessman working under the profit motive. Although consumers and governments are users of savings, it is the businessman who makes most of the decisions to put the savings of the economy to work. His willingness to try new methods and to expand production is an intangible but crucial aspect of our process of capital formation. He must make his investment decision in the face of many uncertainties—uncertainties about government tax and monetary policies, uncertainties about the supply of labor, uncertainties about consumer tastes, and uncertainties about what his competitors will do. Because of these uncertainties, the decision to invest involves risk. That is the reason risk taking is said to be a key factor in our economic growth.

The American economy has generally encouraged risk taking. As a result, there has usually been a strong demand by business for funds to invest. Although from time to time we hear the view that the government or unions have destroyed risk taking in our economy, the fact that business continues to invest record sums of money indicates that investment motives remain strong and active. In a sense, the economy forces investment by business. Because the economy is largely competitive, each firm must expand and improve with the others in its industry. Like a squirrel in a wheel, the business firm in a competitive economy must run to keep up; as long as someone tries to get ahead, there is pressure on everyone to invest and improve.

An expanding market for the increased production of the economy is a requirement of economic growth. If the economy is to continue to pour out goods, there must be a demand for the products—people must be willing to buy them at a price that covers the cost of their production. Over the broad sweep of our history, there has been an adequate demand. The same population that supplied the growing labor force has also expanded the market for the things produced; and the same characteristics that have caused Americans to look for new ways to improve their ability to produce have also caused them to seek higher and higher levels of economic welfare.

But the demand for goods has not always paralleled the growth in our productive capacity. From time to time, the demand for goods and services has fallen behind or moved ahead of our ability to produce. These fluctuations in purchases have made our rate of growth unstable and occasionally have brought severe hardship to some people. They were discussed in Chapter 6, on "Prosperity and Depression," so we will not go into further detail here.

Before examining the outlook for future economic growth, let us summarize briefly the basic factors that have been responsible for the past growth of the American economy:

First, the United States has had abundant resources—land, raw materials, and sources of power.

Second, its growing population has supplied the labor force needed to put these resources to use.

Third, the labor force has been mobile and willing to work for greater output.

Fourth, the productivity of labor has increased because education, research, and technological improvements have fostered the development of new productive equipment.

Fifth, the capacity and willingness of the American people to save and invest has provided the funds for new machines and factories.

Sixth, the prospect of profits and the pressures of competition have induced businessmen to take risks in order to improve and expand their output.

Seventh, a gradual, although unsteady, growth in the demand for goods and services has encouraged producers and workers to continue to expand production.

THE POTENTIALS FOR FUTURE GROWTH

The prevailing view in the 1960's is that the United States has a vast capacity for continued economic expansion. Projections of per-capita income in 1970 and beyond are typically optimistic. Let us now take stock of our capacity to grow during the period 1965–80—a period long enough to establish a trend with allowances for short-run fluctuations, yet short enough to be of practical concern to all of us. The period is also short enough to justify the assumption that there will be no serious shortage of natural resources to support the growth.

Population has increased much more rapidly than the forecasts of demographers led us to expect after the Second World War. Back in 1946, the Bureau of the Census and other population studies estimated that the population of the United States would reach about 165 millions in 1990 and then level off. But by 1955—thirty-five years ahead of time—the population of the nation reached about 165 millions. The rate of population growth has slowed since the 1950's, but projections point to a population of almost 245 millions in 1980.

Past experience with projections cautions us, however, against placing absolute faith in any single estimate. In fact, the Bureau of the Census now issues several projections, each based on a different assumption. During the next decade, the birth rate and mortality rate could change considerably and therefore change the rate of population growth. But changes in the next ten years would not have an appreciable effect on the capacity of the nation to produce, because those who will enter the work force during the next decade are already in school.

By assuming (1) normal mortality rates, (2) the tendency for a given portion of the nation's youth to continue to go to school after reaching an age when they could go to work, and (3) continuation of present retirement habits for older persons, it is possible to estimate that the labor force in 1980 will be 100 millions—nearly 40 per cent more manpower than was available in 1965.

Continued reduction in the average hours worked is probable. The reduction may take the form of a shorter work day, longer rest and recreation periods, or extended vacations and holidays. Of course, the tendency for average hours of work to decline is not likely to continue as rapidly as in the past, but it is quite possible that the hours worked by a full-time worker without "overtime" could drop from the 40 hours average during the 1940's to about 36 or 37 hours in 1980. Any decline in average hours worked would partly offset the increase in the size of the labor force.

How much technology will change during the years ahead is even more difficult to estimate, but seemingly the tempo of innovation is quickening. Factory production has been undergoing what has been called "the second industrial revolution." Large producers are substituting mechanical, electronic, and other devices for human observation, decision, and effort; and a few have moved close to the fully automatic factory. Computer technology has provided powerful new tools for research and management. Farms, too, are becoming more and more mechanized, continuing the trend of the 1940's when the number of tractors on American farms doubled. The depredations of insects and plant parasites, like the wheat rusts, are being combated by the development of insecticides and new varieties of plants. Fertilizers, too, are being improved to help swell the output per acre of American farms.

In addition to the rising productivity being achieved with the technological developments already on hand, new ones seem on the way. More than 3 per cent of national income is spent on research and development. Business firms, universities, and government agencies are engaged in research aimed at discovering fundamental principles and improved techniques of production. About 65 per cent of the nation's R & D is being financed by the government mainly for military purposes—nearly 90 per cent of it in recent years being concentrated in six industries (aircraft and missiles, electrical equipment, chemicals, machinery, motor vehicles, and professional and scientific instruments). The effects of this effort on civilian production are uncertain, but in some areas, such as the peacetime application of atomic energy, the combined efforts of government and industry promise a direct contribution to our level of living.

The growth of incomes, the increase in pension plans, the rising sales of life insurance, and so on, suggest that there will be large personal savings to finance business investment. In making their projections, some economists predict an average rate of saving of about 6 to 7 per cent of personal disposable income. A rate of 6 per cent for personal savings, together with the savings of business, is expected to be sufficient to sustain continued expansion.

Conversion of a large volume of these savings into investment in new plants and equipment would enable output per man-hour to increase at an estimated rate of 2.5 per cent per year, or about one third in ten years. If businessmen continue to perform the risk-taking function as they have in the past, and the nation continues to provide an environment that encourages innovation, productivity could increase faster than the long-run trend. In terms of actual figures, the table below indicates one way this variety of economic conditions and assumptions might be added together to show our potential economic growth for the period 1965–80.

The next question is: Will the nation need or want these additional goods and services? If we concede that the economy has this capacity to boost its total production, can we also conclude that there will be a demand for these goods and services? The addition of about 50 million people to the population by 1980 suggests that there will be. These millions must be fed, clothed, housed, trans-

ECONOMIC GROWTH, 1965–80[a]

Item	1965	1980
Population (in millions)	195	245
Employment (in millions)	72	95
Annual man-hours of work (in billions)	144	175
Gross national product per man-hour (in 1965 dollars)	$4.65	$6.98
Gross national product (in billions of 1965 dollars)	670	1223
Gross national product per capita (in 1965 dollars)	$3,435	$4,990

[a] Figures are from "The American Economy, Prospects for Growth Through 1980; A Report of the McGraw-Hill Publications Department of Economics" (1965). The 1980 projection assumes a 4.1 per cent rate of growth of GNP. A change in working hours, population growth, investment, saving, or any of the other specified conditions would naturally change the figures for 1980. Alternative assumptions and their effects on this sort of projection are discussed in James W. Knowles, *The Potential Economic Growth in the United States*, Joint Economic Committee, 86th Cong. 2nd Sess., Chap. IV. Among these assumptions, those relating to the way the nation will choose to use its productive capacity are the most difficult to forecast.

ported, equipped with tools, and provided with opportunities for recreation. The children must be sent to school; the ill provided with medical care and hospital facilities. To provide these added millions with a level of living comparable to that which we enjoyed in 1965 is a staggering challenge in comparison with the past. And if the urge for a higher level of living remains a strong incentive, there will be no lack of demand for the goods and services that the work force can offer.

Moreover, there is a backlog of demand for many products. In spite of the housing boom in recent years, a fifth of our housing is still substandard. The nation has also failed to keep pace with the demand for more and better highways. Cities have failed to meet the need for urban renewal. The construction of new schoolrooms, too, has lagged far behind the need, partly because school construction was postponed during the Second World War and partly because of the rising birth rate. Further investment in conservation of our resources is needed. Overseas, our commitments to our allies and to the emerging nations will require funds for military support and for assistance in combating poverty, ignorance, and disease. Over-all, there should be no lack of private and public demand for the full output of our growing productive capacity.

Bringing together the demand potentials for the next decade, the accompanying table compares an illustrative projection of some major outlays in 1980 with expenditures in 1965.

POTENTIAL GROWTH IN DEMAND FOR
GROSS NATIONAL PRODUCT, 1965–80[a]
(IN BILLIONS)

Item	1965	1980
Consumer expenditures		
Durable goods	$ 66	$124
Nondurable goods	190	324
Services	175	340
	$431	$788
Business expenditures		
New construction	$ 53	$ 85
Producers' durable equipment	45	81
Inventory and foreign investment	16	21
	$114	$187
Government expenditures		
National security	$ 50	$ 48
Other federal programs	17	44
State and local	69	156
	$136	$248
Total expenditures	$681	$1,223

[a] Source: See footnote to table on p. 222. The projection assumes that state and local government spending will account for a larger share of total spending in 1980 than in 1965.

Two things should be noted about the foregoing discussion on potentials for economic growth in the coming years. First, the projection is not intended as a forecast that the United States gross national product will rise to $1,223 billion, but only as an indication that this level is feasible and attainable within the assumed conditions. Second, this figure is not a reflection of our full potential. It is based on the assumptions of a gradual decline in the average hours worked per week and a 4 per cent unemployment rate in the civilian labor force. A reserve potential remains that could be called upon in an emergency.

In projecting our potentials for economic expansion to 1980, we assumed that there would not be any serious shortage in the availability of natural resources. But what about the supply of resources in 1985 or in 2000? Can we justifiably assume that there will be enough to go around indefinitely?

WILL OUR RESOURCES HOLD OUT?

The drain on the nation's natural resources has been severe. Timber, metals, petroleum, and other resources have been consumed at an accelerated pace to meet wartime demands, cold war demands, and the demand for better living conditions. Taking stock in 1952, the President's Materials Policy Commission estimated that the amount of copper, lead, zinc, and oil taken from the ground during the previous 50 years exceeded the known reserves. Forests have been cut over recklessly in some areas, and intensive cultivation of the land in some areas has reduced the fertility of the soil. Even fresh water has run short in many communities.

Rising demand has made the nation increasingly dependent on foreign supplies of essential minerals and many vegetable and animal products. For example, in 1950, we were producing 51 per cent and consuming 63 per cent of world production of aluminum; we were producing only 4 per cent and consuming 63 per cent of the world's cobalt; we were producing 29 per cent and consuming 64 per cent of the lead; and we were using 65 per cent of the world's production of tin and not producing any of it. For our supplies of copper, manganese ore, nickel, tungsten, zinc, rubber, wool, and newsprint, we were also coming to rely more and more on foreign sources of supply.

Not only do we have to contend with the possible gradual exhaustion of our own resources, we also have to consider the possible exhaustion of the resources of nations with which we trade. Even more significant is the likelihood of greater competition for the available resources of friendly nations. Many of these nations are a generation or several generations behind us industrially—living conditions in some have virtually been unchanged for centuries. Now they are awakening to their potentials for economic growth. Their demands on their own resources are likely to increase, thereby reducing their ability to satisfy our needs.

We began our story of economic growth with natural resources, and all that followed was based on the assumption that our resource base would last. But if we are not careful, limited natural resources will mark the end of our growth. Continued economic expansion requires that we turn more of our attention to this problem. By conservation, exploration, substitution, and innovation we can prevent "resource starvation." But to do so, we must use some of our present energies to provide for the future.

The attempts made to avert a possible shortage of iron ore illustrate the many-sided approach that is essential if we are to keep the supply of resources plentiful. For years the major source of the iron ore of the world has been the deposits of the Mesabi, Vermillion, and Cayuna ranges of northern Minnesota. So intensively have these ranges been mined that it seemed that they would be exhausted before the end of the century. Consequently, geologists began making aerial magnetic surveys to locate areas that warranted further surface exploration. At the same time, after twenty-five years of research, metallurgists developed ways to make profitable use of taconite, the abundant low-grade ore formerly considered virtually worthless; as a result, a new industry was born in northern Minnesota. Meanwhile, in Venezuela and Labrador, the development of new, rich deposits has provided other sources of supply. Another approach to the problem has been the rapid development of substitutes for iron and steel, such as the expanded production of aluminum, magnesium, and other materials.

The implications of these facts are clear: our geologists must find new deposits; our engineers must devise ways to use resources more efficiently and to make economical use of low-grade deposits; our public policies must foster efficient use and proper conservation of resources; our scientists must discover an increasing number of synthetic substitutes; our businessmen must continue to risk funds in new techniques for the use and development of resources.

OTHER POSSIBLE OBSTACLES TO GROWTH

An all-out war could completely upset our calculations for economic expansion. Even minor conflicts could increase the drains enough to slow down the expansion of consumer goods production and the growth of public services. Moreover, war would tend to cut us off from many foreign supplies of raw materials and other products we need for continued growth.

Economic instability could cause serious dislocations. Inflation, recessions, and depressions are constant hazards to expansion, though as pointed out in Chapter 7, tools have been developed to help minimize fluctuations in business activity. Mild fluctuations are to be expected in a changing economy, but severe fluctuations resulting in widespread unemployment and stagnation of investment are not consistent with continued economic development. Moreover, economic growth itself may be disruptive. As old obstacles are overcome, new ones emerge. For example, technological changes, while increasing productivity, may displace workers and even render industries obsolete.

Less tangible and more difficult to assess is the possibility of a long-run change in the attitude and temper of the American people. Perhaps the incentive for greater economic advancement will diminish. We may succeed so well in satisfying wants that the philosophy of the nation will change. Will the wage earner who works so hard today to give his family a new house, a new car, and the latest appliances continue to strive as hard after he has provided these goods? This is a great imponderable.

Conceivably, the preoccupation with economic growth may diminish and preoccupation with spiritual, intellectual, and leisure pursuits increase. Certainly, there will be an opportunity to choose among alternative uses of time and effort. It is not within the scope of this book to examine the psychological, religious, and philosophical issues underlying our assumptions that economic growth is desirable, but the fact that we have made this assumption needs to be reiterated. If a major change in popular attitudes does take place gradually, it will require a major change in the assumptions on which much economic reasoning rests. Such a change, however, is not yet in prospect for the foreseeable future.

Because the objective of economic expansion is a part of our national culture, we frequently hear proposals advocated for their possible effect on our long-run economic growth. The arguments often stress one or two aspects of the problem, although, as we have seen, economic growth has many ingredients. One of the functions of economic reasoning is to help us keep track of a many-sided problem of this sort so that we can understand the problem as a whole. The problem on tax policy discussed below will illustrate some of the complexities in tracing the effect of governmental policy on economic expansion.

227

The Problem

As we know, our known reserves of petroleum, coal, and natural gas will not last forever. New techniques of extraction, new discoveries, and more efficient combustion techniques can extend the life of our fuel reserves but, in time, the costs of drawing on less accessible and lower-grade supplies will rise. With this prospect, the development of atomic energy and energy from the sun would be an important contribution to economic expansion.

In order to accelerate this development, suppose the federal government undertakes a costly program of research and experimentation. Suppose, further, that two alternative tax changes are proposed to cover the cost of this program: A *decrease in the amount of the income tax exemption* allowed to each taxpayer for each member of his family; or an *increase in the tax rate on incomes over $10,000.* The problem is to determine which of the two modes of taxation would best serve the interests of economic growth. The question of expanded federal activity is *not* an issue for this problem, although it could be explored separately. For purposes of analysis the issues have been limited here to taxation and economic growth.

Reducing the amount of the personal exemption will increase the taxable income of all taxpayers. And the proportionate tax increase will be larger for those in the lower-income brackets. Addition of $200 to the taxable income of a person receiving $5,000 will have a larger percentage effect on his taxes than it would for a person with $10,000 of taxable income. The reduction in the exemption will also mean that many more people in the low-income brackets will pay taxes. When the exemption is $600 per person, a family of four must have a taxable income of $2,400 before it starts paying income taxes. If the exemption is reduced to $500, the family may have to pay taxes if its taxable income exceeds $2,000. The exemption method thus has a heavier impact on the low-income groups. Increasing the rates for those with incomes over

$10,000 will, of course, place the major burden on those in the upper-income groups.

The issue then appears to be the following: What are the effects of taxation on economic growth? More specifically, how do taxes on high income and taxes on low income affect economic expansion?

The Objective

In the broadest sense, the long-run economic objective of the American people may be said to be to improve the health, education, and material well-being of society. More specifically, if we want to continue our economic growth while we meet the day-to-day problems of a modern economy, we will want:

To encourage expansion of our reserve of natural resources;

To foster conditions that will encourage the growth of an efficient labor force;

To foster education, research, and technology;

To encourage investment;

To preserve the competition and incentives that will make initiative and risk-taking attractive;

To encourage an increasing level of consumption.

The Alternatives

First, increasing tax revenue by raising tax rates for the high-income brackets.

The tax increase would not tend to have an appreciable direct effect on consumption. We cannot be certain, of course, but it appears likely that the taxpayers would attempt to maintain their level of consumption and allow the burden of taxation to fall on their savings. If this should occur, the market for consumption goods would tend to remain strong.

The direct impact of this method would be on the volume of personal savings and the incentive to invest. Personal savings would tend to be cut because the tax increase falls most heavily on the groups that do much of the nation's saving. The incentive to invest would tend to be diminished because the rewards for successful risk-taking would be reduced. This does not mean that all of the profit of investment would be eliminated but, as long as some of the profit is taken by taxation, certain risky projects will not be as attractive to investors.

It is also possible that some business executives, doctors, and others with high incomes will be less inclined to work. As their level of income is already high enough to provide many comforts, they may decide to take more leisure if the reward for additional work is cut sharply. On the other hand, many of those in the upper-income brackets may actually work harder in an effort to maintain their level of living. They may try to earn more income in order to offset the effect of the tax increase.

Investment plans would also be influenced by the impact of the tax change on the expectations of business. If the tax change is considered a temporary change to bring faster results in energy research, business expectations will be optimistic. On the other hand, if the tax change is interpreted as a shift in general tax policy, the prospects for future investment may seem less bright.

Some other effects of the tax increase on high incomes might be: upward pressure on prices as business owners attempt to regain the lost income; greater effort to resist the pressure of unions to raise wages; lower private grants for education and research. We cannot attempt here to measure the likelihood of these possibilities—but they show that a variety of effects must be considered.

Second, increasing tax revenue by reducing exemptions. Inasmuch as those in the very lowest-income brackets use most of their income for consumption, a tax increase by this method will retard spending by consumers. In terms of the requirements for economic growth, it will tend to have the initial effect of curtailing the private demand for production.

Business expenditures for capital are based on the expectation that consumption will be adequate to buy the things produced at a price that will cover the costs of production and leave a profit. The tax change may, therefore, have a depressing effect on the investment plans of some businesses. But the governmental research program may tend to improve expectations.

It is possible that the reduced tax exemption could cause an increase in the labor force. In order to maintain their level of income, some families might urge their children to start to work earlier; more wives might enter the labor force, and older people might continue to work longer before they retire. We cannot say exactly what this would do to the quality of the labor force, but it is possible that the use of untrained or older workers and curtailment of education would lower the average quality.

If total income and taxes remain reasonably stable, private saving should not be seriously affected. As the exemption method of raising taxes places a smaller share of the tax burden on the high income or saving groups, their saving habits may be virtually undisturbed. Some of these savings may be borrowed by those in the lower-income groups in order to bolster their consumption, but in general there should be a small effect on the supply of savings available for investment.

The impact of taxes might cause unions to intensify their demands for higher wages. If they were successful, union workers might succeed in shifting a portion of the taxes to the costs of production. This, in turn, might increase the incentive of producers to invest—in the hope that with better equipment, they could escape the additional labor costs. Or it may discourage the investment plans of those producers who are uncertain about their ability to cope with higher wage costs.

The Decision

Quite clearly there are a number of aspects of the tax-growth problem that we have not explored. But we are not interested here in a complete analysis of the issues— we merely want to illustrate the kinds of considerations that are involved. Simplified statements such as "high bracket taxes (or low bracket taxes) curtail economic growth" are clearly not adequate—their direct and indirect effects must be analyzed carefully. The ultimate choice of governmental policy will be more reasoned if we pursue this analysis and then judge the results in terms of our own pattern of goals.

This chapter has stressed these basic ideas:

1. Economic growth can be measured roughly by the growth of per-capita income. Although this measure does not take into account the many changes in the quality of the things produced in our society, it does show that the average level of living of the American people has tended to rise from decade to decade. We now tend to take this trend for granted, but a look at our depression experience and at many other societies shows that economic growth does not always occur.

2. The essence of economic growth is the expansion of production faster than the increase of population. A number of diverse ingredients must be brought together to bring this about; natural resources, skilled labor, knowledge, tools, managerial ability, and a desire for a higher level of living.

3. At the present time, it appears that the basic ingredients for continued economic growth are present in the American economy. But a variety of circumstances can prevent us from attaining the growth of which we are capable. As citizens we can help to minimize these obstacles by carefully analyzing public policy and encouraging those measures that appear, on balance, to meet the specific requirements of expansion.

Suggested Reading

Paul A. Samuelson: *Economics: An Introductory Analysis,* Chap. 37, pp. 705–24. George L. Bach, *Economics: An Introduction to Analysis and Policy,* Chaps. 15–17, pp. 228–73. For a systematic analysis of the factors responsible for our past growth and a summary of the choices available to increase the rate of growth, see Edward F. Denison, *The Sources of Economic Growth in the United States and the Alternatives Before Us,* Supplementary Paper No. 13, Committee for Economic Development, 1962. Denison's projections cover the period 1960–80. He reviews the potential contributions to growth from one-time actions that would remove obstacles to effective use of resources and changes that make a gradual contribution over a longer time span, such as improvement in education. Denison's approach is illustrated in the article, "Why Growth?," which he wrote with Herbert Stein for *Goals for Americans.* It is reprinted in *Readings in Economics* (Samuelson et al., ed.) pp. 362–67. Robert M. Solow's article, "Sources and Outlook for Growth," which also is reprinted in the *Readings,* discusses the expansion of the economy's capacity to produce. See pp. 367–75.

Chapter 9

INTERNATIONAL ECONOMIC POLICY

Three familiar issues keep recurring as we consider the economic problems of the United States. These are economic stability, economic growth, and the workings of the market system. Up to now, we have examined them within a national context. They are equally important, however, in an international setting. One might wonder, therefore, why there should be a special field called international economics. The answer is that certain features of international economic relations are distinctive. They stem from the political fact that the world is divided into a large number of independent nation-states, each of which is capable of autonomous economic action.

In the first place, governments can and do erect a number of obstacles to the free flow of goods and services between countries. In contrast to the generally unrestricted flow of American products from state to state, the international flow of goods is obstructed by tariffs, quotas, and administrative restrictions of various kinds. There are restrictions, too, on the free movement of labor between nations. For example, in contrast to the great migration of Americans to the West-Coast states in recent years, there are immigration regulations that restrict the movement of Japanese workers into Australia, and of foreign workers into the United States. There are also barriers to the flow of savings between countries. For a variety of reasons, American savings do not flow into the growing economies of Egypt or Indonesia as easily as they do into the growing economies of Texas or Tennessee. These trade barriers are reinforced, of course, by differences in language, commercial customs, laws, and trading practices.

Another complicating factor is that each country has its own monetary system and pursues its own independent monetary policy. This frequently obstructs international payments and creates a barrier to international trade and investment. There is a striking contrast between the smoothness with which we are able to make contracts and pay for goods and services within the United States, and the instability and uncertainty encountered in making contracts and payments abroad.

Finally, special mention should be made of an important noneconomic factor that strongly influences international economic relations. That is the use of war as an instrument of national policy, and the subordination of economic goals to the needs of national defense. Thus many countries support, by subsidies or other means, uneconomic industries that are regarded as vital to national defense.

This chapter will consider several aspects of international economics: why international trade is important, how it is organized, and how it is financed, what the consequences are of barriers to international trade, and how the problem of economic growth and the business cycle are related to international economics.

WHY IS INTERNATIONAL TRADE IMPORTANT?

A nation gains by producing what it is best fitted to produce, and exchanging its products for those of other nations. The economic reason for trade between nations is, therefore, no different from that for trade between different parts of the same country.

What a region is best fitted to produce depends on its relative supply and quality of the factors of production—natural resources, labor, capital, and entrepreneurial skills. For example, location, the relative abundance of skilled labor and capital equipment, and the relative scarcity of land, make Rhode Island unsuitable for ranching but most suitable for manufacturing. Similarly, Wyoming—with its abundance of land, its relative scarcity of labor, and its remoteness from heavily populated areas—is unsuitable for heavy industry but most suitable for sheep raising. Florida has a special advantage in oranges, Iowa in corn, the Pittsburgh area in steel, and Oregon in lumber. These special advantages provide the bases of trade among cities, states, and regions.

Similarly, the United States is notably efficient in producing automobiles and in growing tobacco, Brazil in growing coffee, Australia in raising sheep, and Switzerland in making watches. The way to maximize real income internationally would therefore seem to be to specialize and to trade.

Price differences arise from these differences in productive resources. Therefore prices are a basis of trade. When new sources of raw materials are discovered, when skilled labor becomes available, or when new modes of production are developed, these changes will be reflected in changing prices and in a different pattern of trade. Thus the price mechanism works internationally to decide what shall be produced, how it shall be produced, and who shall get it, in a manner similar to the way it works within a country.

International (or interregional) trade is beneficial because it helps us to use scarce resources efficiently, to maximize output, and to satisfy wants on a larger scale. The reasoning behind this statement is contained in what economists call the theories of absolute and comparative advantage. These theories hold that a country (or region) will do better to concentrate on producing those things in which it has the greatest cost advantage over other areas, or those in which its competitive disadvantage is least.

The term "comparative advantage" may be unfamiliar, but the principle it describes is not. We all recognize that a busy executive finds it advantageous to hire a stenographer even though he is a better typist than she. It is advantageous because it permits him to specialize in business affairs in which his administrative skill is much more scarce and more valuable than his typing skill. Such specialization helps maximize output within the limits set by the available resources. Similarly, in a larger sense, the United States is better off if it specializes and trades than if it tries to produce every commodity in which it has a competitive advantage.

International trade not only provides goods at lower costs, it also widens the range of available products. There are many things, such as tin and nickel, which we need but do not have within our boundaries. We have copper, newsprint, petroleum, and bauxite (for aluminum), but not in sufficient quantities. We also import many highly specialized products because their quality is superior or their prices cheaper—for example, Scotch whiskey, Belgian lace, Swiss watches, Japanese cameras.

Specialization has been carried to such lengths that we export and import different qualities of the same product —we export American Fords and import British Fords. These imports help contribute to our high living standards, and, in addition, they help make our exports possible. In the long run, trade is a two-way proposition, for a nation cannot continue to sell unless it is also willing to buy.

International trade helps sustain high levels of income and employment. In agriculture and in the mass production industries, foreign markets are of particular importance. In some years, we have exported as much as 40 per cent of our total annual production of cotton, tobacco, and wheat; indeed the prosperity of farmers has been linked with foreign trade since colonial days. Many manufacturing industries also rely on foreign demand for machinery, trucks, tractors, and electrical equipment. A decline in foreign sales of farm or manufactured products can lead to a decline in income and employment for the entire economy. Thus aside from its effect on long-run economic efficiency, international trade also affects our short-run stability.

Benefits are maximized when international trade is multilateral. Exports and imports of any two countries do not need to be in balance. For example, we normally buy more from Malaysia than we sell to Malaysia, and we usually sell more to Britain than we buy from it. Britain, for its part, sells more to Malaysia than it buys from Malaysia. In this simplified triangular example, we can think of Malaysia's surplus earnings from exports to the United States as being spent on British goods, and of Britain financing some of its imports from the United States with the proceeds of its exports to Malaysia. Each country is buying its imports from the cheapest source and selling its exports in the most profitable market, with the result that trade is multilateral and all nations benefit.

BARRIERS TO INTERNATIONAL TRADE

If international trade is beneficial, why are tariffs, quotas, embargoes, licensing systems, exchange controls, and other protective devices used by almost all nations? Why is the argument over "protectionism" a perennial one in the United States? In order to find the answers to these questions, we must examine the arguments and the assumptions involved in the issue of free trade versus protectionism.

Traditionally, free traders have not paid much attention to particular situations and to problems of adjustment in the short run, although they are beginning to do so more today. They have presented an *economic* argument, which assumes that the most efficient use of resources and maximization of real income are the primary objectives of society. The argument for the maximum freedom of trade considers the world or the nation as a whole and the benefits to be derived in the long run by all nations and all people. The arguments for protectionism are usually special or local in nature, are based on short-run considerations, and often are noneconomic in nature.

A strong noneconomic argument for the use of controls

over international trade is based on military need. The prospect of armed conflict intermittently fosters trade restrictions and embargoes among many nations. The purpose is to withhold strategically important goods from others and to protect industries that may be militarily important.

A further argument that has always carried great weight in the world, and still does today, concerns economic development or, to use the old-fashioned term, "infant industries." Industrialized countries tend to favor more liberal trade policies because they wish to buy raw materials and foodstuffs from the cheapest sources and sell their manufactured products in the most profitable markets without restriction. This was the position of Great Britain in the nineteenth century. In advocating free trade, the great economists of the "Classical School"—Adam Smith, David Ricardo, John Stuart Mill, and others—were reflecting the interests of Great Britain as an advanced industrial nation.

People in less developed countries, however, were often less enthusiastic about the free trade doctrine. They saw themselves doomed by it to remain specialists in agriculture and raw materials, dependent on Great Britain for manufactures. They therefore advocated protectionism in order to enable their "infant industries" to get established or, as we say today, to promote economic development. Alexander Hamilton was one of the earliest advocates of this point of view in the United States.

Today, the arguments are similar, but the cast is different. It is the United States that now, as the most advanced industrial nation of the world, tends to advocate a relaxation of trade barriers in the free world as Great Britain did 100 years ago. And as 100 years ago we practiced protectionism to promote our economic development, so today India, Egypt, Brazil, Mexico, Indonesia, Spain, and many other countries seek to promote their economic development by protectionism. They believe that in the long run this policy will foster economic growth as it did in the United States in the nineteenth century.

This argument has much validity, but it also has limitations. It is difficult to know in advance what industries will be able to stand on their own feet eventually and, in view of the vested interests that tend to grow up, it is even more difficult to remove the protection when the "infants" have become "adults." Thus underdeveloped countries run the risk of developing uneconomic industries that can never survive in competitive markets. The gains of specialization and trade are still available to most nations; hence it may be highly wasteful for many of them to attempt to imitate the industrial pattern of the United States.

Some American protectionists also argue that imports made by cheap foreign labor represent unfair competition. They contend that the jobs and high wage scales of American workers will be undermined unless they are protected. One might ask, then: If low wages mean low costs and high wages high costs, how can the United States export anything? Actually, our mass production industries such as the automobile industry, pay the highest wages in the world and yet undersell the whole world. And Great Britain, whose auto workers receive considerably less than is paid in Detroit, levies a high duty on "cheap" American cars in order to preserve the home market for Hillmans and Rovers.

It is not wage rates alone, but wage rates in combination with labor productivity that determine labor costs. If, for example, an Italian pencil maker getting 50 cents an hour and using hand methods turns out 5 pencils, the labor cost per pencil is 10 cents. If an American worker getting $1.50 an hour and using modern machinery turns out 50 pencils, the labor cost per pencil is 3 cents. As we have seen in earlier chapters, labor is only one factor of production, so we cannot determine production costs by looking at wages alone.

Some foreign countries tend to have an advantage over the United States in the production of goods that require relatively large amounts of skilled labor, of which they have plenty, and relatively small amounts of capital, in which they are deficient. This is simply the counterpart of our specialization in goods that require large amounts of capital, of which we have plenty and which is relatively cheap, and small amounts of labor, which is relatively high-priced. Trade takes place largely because of this difference in productive resources.

Protectionists have also argued that a reduction in tariffs will create unemployment and that an increase in tariffs will diminish unemployment. Obviously, if an industry is exposed to increased competition from cheaper imports, the result may be an immediate increase in unemployment in that industry. Certainly, if the American tariff were abolished overnight, chaotic conditions would result in particular industries. But there are few today who believe that "free trade" is an immediate practical objective. What is advocated by a large number of persons is *"freer* trade." Their argument calls for a gradual, selective, and moderate program of reducing trade barriers, so that attention can be given to the short-run problems of adjustment that arise in particular industries. This is the process being followed by the six member countries of the European Economic Community, and the seven members of the European Free Trade Association (EFTA). A similar approach to tariff reduction is being undertaken by the Latin American Free Trade Association (LAFTA) established in 1960.

It is difficult to defend the argument that raising the tariff is a satisfactory cure for unemployment. A higher tariff will not appreciably reduce unemployment that is due to technological or cyclical causes. Raising the tariff will not alleviate unemployment in such export industries as automobiles, machinery, or wheat; indeed, it will tend to harm export industries. And the harm will be even greater if foreign countries retaliate with additional barriers against our exports. Actually, keeping out imports may increase employment in a protected industry, but it may lead to layoffs in other industries. When the United States excluded Danish cheese, Denmark switched its coal purchases to Poland. What may have been gained in Wisconsin, therefore, was probably lost in Pennsylvania and West Virginia. Even if, in such cases, total employment should be increased, there would still tend to be a loss because labor would have moved out of areas where it was more productive into areas where it was less productive.

There are, of course, other arguments for and against protectionism. Some are naive; some are sophisticated. The most important requirement in examining any of them is this: to set forth carefully the assumptions on which the argument is based and to consider their broad, long-run consequences as well as their narrow, immediate effects.

The tariff has traditionally been an important problem of public policy in the United States. Before the Civil War, northern manufacturing interests used the "infant industry" argument to demand a high tariff, while the South, whose interests lay in exporting agricultural products to world markets and importing manufactured goods from the cheapest sources, favored more liberal trade policies. After the Civil War, the protectionist influences triumphed and gradually the tariff was raised. By 1930, when the Hawley-Smoot Tariff Act was passed, American trade policy was one of the most restrictive in the world.

In the last thirty years a reversal has taken place. The Reciprocal Trade Agreements Act, originally passed in 1934 and extended periodically since then, gave the President the power to negotiate trade agreements with foreign countries. These agreements provided that the United States would lower the tariff on selected imports in return for reciprocal concessions from the other country. Between 1934 and 1947, numerous trade agreements were concluded. Since 1947, the process has been broadened under the General Agreement on Tariffs and Trade (known as GATT) to cover multilateral negotiations by a large group of nations, all of which reduce duties on one another's imports. In addition, the general rise in prices during the last twenty years has reduced the protective effect of many so-called "specific duties,"—those expressed as a specific amount of money per unit of quantity. As a result of these two developments, the United States tariff is now in general a relatively moderate one, although some individual duties are still very high. The Trade Expansion Act of 1962 gave the President renewed powers to lower the U.S. tariff in return for reciprocal concessions by other nations.

Many other trade practices are more restrictive than the tariff. For example, the United States imposes quantitative restrictions (quotas) and even embargoes on many agricultural imports. When procuring supplies for itself, the United States Government, under the "Buy American" legislation, sometimes gives preference to domestic goods over foreign goods even when foreign goods are cheaper. A great deal of red tape is involved in importing goods into this country, and the process of classifying imports for duty purposes, valuation procedures, sanitary regulations, and so on all hamper the free flow of goods. In addition, the "escape clause" in our trade agreements with other countries permits the United States to cancel concessions already granted if the imports of such commodities harm or threaten to harm domestic industries. It is sometimes argued that this hardly makes it worth while for foreign producers to attempt to build up a market for their goods in the United States.

The question of trade barriers continues to be a major problem of American foreign economic policy. Those who favor removing or scaling down many of the restrictions on imports argue as follows: (1) The United States can more easily sell if it also buys; international trade, therefore, can help maintain high levels of employment and income. When the nation is running a deficit in its Balance of Payments, it is particularly important to stimulate our efficient export industries in order to increase our international receipts. (2) Both the government and private firms have made large investments abroad; the logic of our creditor position requires that we permit other countries to earn the dollars to service and repay these debts by selling goods to us. (3) The Soviet economic challenge to the West requires that we do everything possible to promote the economic strength and unity of the free world; this means working with friendly nations to strengthen trade ties, rather than creating divisions among them by maintaining trade barriers. (4) The United States lives in an increasingly competitive world. Its exports can have access to such expanding markets as those of the European Economic Community only if it is prepared to co-operate with other nations in measures to promote mutual trade.

The arguments against liberalizing import restrictions stem mostly from concern over the problems of such industries as textiles, watches, glass, pottery, and dairy products, which would be confronted by the need for painful and serious adjustments if subjected to the competition of more imports.

An interesting change in political orientation has occurred in the field of the tariff over the years. As already stated, it used to be the northern industrialists who wanted a high tariff, and the farmers of the South who wanted a low one. But today the liberal trade group is spearheaded by many of the leading businessmen of the nation, representing such industries as automobiles, business machines, and petroleum. Their interest in more liberal trade policies is, of course, related to their interest as exporters in expanding world markets and as importers in getting cheap foreign raw materials. In this respect, the wheel has turned full cycle, and the United States is using an argument put forward by British industrialists 100 years ago. On the other hand, certain agricultural groups—producers of sugar, dairy products, and certain fruits—have turned protectionists.

One of the most important single issues faced by the United States in the field of trade policy concerns its relationship to the European Economic Community (EEC), popularly known as the Common Market.

The EEC, which came into being on January 1, 1958,

is an association of six countries—France, West Germany, Italy, Belgium, the Netherlands, and Luxembourg—which is designed to gradually merge the six individual economies into an integrated market. The members are abolishing all trade barriers on each other's goods and are establishing one common external tariff with respect to the rest of the world. They are establishing free movement of labor and capital, common agricultural policies, a common anti-trust policy, and certain supra-national governmental institutions including a parliament, an executive, and a court of justice.

The significance of this development is that there is now emerging in Europe a new economic power, comparable to the United States in population and resources. Its per capita income is the highest in the world after the United States and Canada and its rate of economic growth is rapid. As the world's largest trader, the EEC will play a major role in determining whether the world will become more protectionist or more liberal in trade policies.

The Common Market constitutes both a challenge and an opportunity to the United States. It constitutes a challenge because its rapidly growing and increasingly efficient industries are providing increasing competition for American firms not only in Europe and in areas such as Latin America and Asia, but even here at home. It constitutes an opportunity because the expanding purchasing power and rising living standards of the West Europeans make them important customers for our exports and create new opportunities for profitable investment by American business. The greatest volume of trade in the world is between nations with high national incomes.

THE BALANCE OF PAYMENTS

A nation's total exports of goods do not usually balance its total imports. The United States, for example, has exported more goods than it has imported in every year since

1873; Britain, on the other hand, has had an import surplus about as long. But although imports and exports of goods need not be equal, a nation's total international debits and credits must be equal in an accounting sense. International transactions are all listed in a statistical table called the Balance of Payments, which includes not only exports and imports of goods but also the expenditures of tourists, government foreign aid grants, private international capital flows, payments for shipping services, and other items, including gold movements and other flows of funds to settle outstanding balances. These items are usually listed as either international payments or international receipts. The following page shows an abbreviated version of the Balance of Payments of the United States for 1965, as published by the Department of Commerce.

This table shows that total international payments by the people, businesses, and government of the United States totaled $40.8 billion in 1965, while the international receipts of the nation were $40.2 billion. The international payments of the nation included payments for imports of merchandise, the overseas military expenditures and foreign aid program of the federal government, investment abroad by business firms, the spending by American tourists abroad, payments by American traders to foreign shippers, and charitable funds or pension payments sent to Americans living abroad. The international receipts of the nation included the proceeds of our export sales, the income derived from our foreign investments, the spending of foreign tourists in the United States and of foreign traders on United States shipping, the repayment by foreigners of money owed the United States Government, and the investment made by foreigners in the United States.

When the item entitled "unrecorded transactions" (which consists mainly of statistical errors and omissions) is included, the total Balance of Payments deficit of the United States in 1965 was $1.3 billion—even though exports of goods and services exceeded imports of goods and services. Putting this another way, the United States in 1965

BALANCE OF PAYMENTS OF THE UNITED STATES, 1965[a]
(BILLIONS OF DOLLARS)

Item		Amount
U.S. International Payments		
Imports of Goods and Services		$32.0
Merchandise	$21.5	
Overseas Military Expenditures	2.8	
Income on Investments	1.6	
Other (Tourists, Shipping, etc.)	6.1	
Remittances and Pensions		1.0
U.S. Government Foreign Aid		4.3
Private Investment Abroad		3.5
Total International Payments:		40.8
U.S. International Receipts		
Exports of Goods and Services		$39.0
Merchandise	$26.3	
Military Sales	0.8	
Income from Foreign Investments	6.0	
Other (Tourists, Shipping, etc.)	5.9	
Repayment of U.S.Government Loans		0.9
Foreign Investment in U.S.		0.3
Total International Receipts:		40.2
Deficit from Above Items		−0.6
Deficit from Unrecorded Transactions		−0.7
Total Balance of Payments Deficit:		$−1.3
How the U.S. Deficit Was Met:		
Loss of Gold by the U.S.		$−1.7
Decrease in Short-Term Liabilities of U.S.		+0.4
		$−1.3

[a] Source: U. S. Department of Commerce, *Survey of Current Business*, (March 1966), p. 22. The table shows only the arithmetic of the nation's international economic transactions. To find out *why* a given item is what it is—and larger or smaller than in previous years—requires further analysis.

earned a surplus of $7 billion from trade in goods and services alone. But this "trade surplus," together with the repayment of loans and new investment by foreigners, was not enough to cover our payments for foreign aid, overseas military expenditures, and overseas investment by American business.

How was this deficit met? In 1965, it was met by the transfer of gold from the United States to foreign governments and central banks. Gold is still a basic means of settling international accounts between nations even though such transactions are now only handled by central banks and national treasuries instead of by private persons and commercial banks as was the case under the old gold standard. The 1965 gold outflow was unusual in that it exceeded the payments deficit. Typically in recent years, part of the deficit has been made up by a transfer of gold and part by an increase of foreigners' deposits in United States banks, that is, by an increase in United States liabilities (or indebtedness) to foreigners. But in 1965, the gold outflow totaled $1.7, though the deficit was only $1.3 billion; and foreign deposits were reduced accordingly.

The deficit was lower in 1965 than it had been in several previous years, but it was still a matter of serious concern. The outflow of gold ($7 billion since 1958) had alarmed many observers, and even though the dollar continued to be the world's strongest currency, fears persisted in banking circles that the dollar was in jeopardy.

In dealing with the balance of payments problem during the 1958–65 period the government had faced a dilemma. Since the economy was operating at less than full employment, some of the steps proposed to reduce the deficit were undesirable because they would have aggravated unemployment. For example, if interest rates were raised to dissuade foreign investors from transferring their funds to other countries, borrowing would have been more costly to American producers. Investment would have been discouraged and output depressed.

To cope with this problem of achieving adjustment in the international financial market without sacrificing domestic economic objectives, a number of policy measures have been introduced since the late 1950's.

A National Export Expansion Program was started to encourage businessmen to export more and to acquaint them with export opportunities. A new export insurance scheme was authorized by the Export-Import Bank. Tourist purchases abroad were discouraged by reducing (from $500 at wholesale to $100 at retail) the value of goods that could be brought back to the United States duty free. Some tax reforms and limited monetary adjustments were also undertaken.

The need for stronger steps became apparent in early 1963, however, when the gold outflow increased sharply. The government chose to enact a selective tax that would help the balance of payments without making money tighter within the United States. This *interest equalization tax* required Americans who purchased foreign securities to pay a tax equal to 1 per cent interest. Thus, in effect, it raised the interest rates foreign borrowers had to pay to United States lenders. (These provisions were made to exclude the less developed countries and Canada.)

When further action seemed required in 1965, a voluntary program was stressed. Banks were advised to limit their loans of all types to foreigners to a 5 per cent increase over the level of loans outstanding at the end of 1964. Large business firms were also asked to take balance of payments factors into consideration in their operations. The voluntary program was given much of the credit for reducing private capital outflows in 1965.

Through these short-run measures the United States was able to strengthen its balance of payments position without crippling its aid program (although there have been some cutbacks in foreign aid), and without restricting imports by tariffs and quotas, though it did not succeed in assuring a long-run solution to the problem. Moreover, the maintenance of long-term restrictions on the outflow of private American capital could reduce both the income from foreign investments and the exports which this capital flow finances. In addition, such restrictions could interfere with our long-run goal of promoting economic growth around the world.

Some observers have argued that the underlying difficulty was not the United States balance of payments, but rather the inadequacy of the international monetary system. Since the Second World War the United States deficits had provided much of the liquid assets needed to facilitate international payments. If the United States achieved a payments surplus, other nations would incur a deficit and might be forced to take steps that would hamper their economic growth. What the world needed was an additional source of reserves that would enable nations to finance deficits in their balance of payments without injuring their economies. A full-scale examination of international monetary problems is now under way in the leading financial nations and the International Monetary Fund.

Monetary problems are especially difficult to cope with in the international arena because each country has its own currency and pursues its own monetary and fiscal policies independently. Those engaged in international trade and finance must thus convert their money into the money of other countries. Generally, they do this by buying "foreign exchange"; they buy claims for foreign money. These claims are usually obtained from people who sell goods abroad and want to convert the payment into the money of their own country. Thus an American exporter might sell the British pounds he has earned to an American importer who wants to buy goods from Great Britain. The exporter will end with dollars and the importer will get the pounds he needs to buy in Great Britain. Both the importer and the exporter are therefore concerned with the rate of exchange, the price at which dollars can be converted to pounds.

The principal objective of an international monetary system is to establish reasonably stable exchange rates while maintaining a reasonably free foreign exchange market. "Stability" in exchange rates does not mean that rates cannot change slightly from day to day. It means only that rates will not fluctuate so widely that foreign buyers and sellers cannot make plans for the future. If rates change rapidly from day to day, trade is harmed, for it is like buying or selling a product without knowing the delivery price. Stable exchange rates encourage international trade by providing more certainty in the terms of trade.

Before the First World War, this objective was achieved fairly well by the international gold standard. Under the gold standard, the nations defined their currency units as equal to so much gold. Different currencies were thus all related to one another in a network of exchange rates established by reference to this common gold content and known as the "mint pars of exchange." For example, as a British pound contained the same amount of gold as 4.8665 American dollars, the "mint par" between them was $4.8665 = £1. Citizens had complete freedom to convert their cash or bank accounts into gold and to send this gold to foreign countries if they wished. There were thus two alternatives for settling a debt in a foreign country—to buy the currency of that country in the foreign exchange market at the current rate of exchange, or to obtain gold and ship it abroad. The existence of the alternative of shipping gold abroad meant that the market rate did not change materially from the mint par of exchange.

The reasons for the successful operation of the gold standard in the nineteenth century cannot be explored here, but we should realize that the system was based on a set of circumstances that were in many respects quite unique in history and that most certainly have vanished today. They included relatively free trade, flexible prices and wages, a peaceful capitalistic world living in an atmosphere of confidence and believing in the inevitability of progress, and the dominance of Great Britain in world trade and finance.

The breakdown of the gold standard began with the First World War. Since that time, international monetary affairs have been unsettled. Following the war, exchange rates fluctuated widely, and although many nations later returned to the gold standard, prewar conditions were not restored. The twenty years between the First and Second World Wars was a period of recuperation from the dislocations of the First World War. It was also a period of economic instability and political uncertainty, with recurring threats of a renewed outbreak of war. In this setting, the gold standard system of international monetary cooperation was discarded. By 1939, international monetary relations had been put into a strait jacket of government controls over the prices and uses of foreign exchange (exchange control).

After the Second World War, most countries found themselves short of the one currency they needed most to buy the goods needed for the reconstruction of their war-ravaged economies—the dollar. Thus the term "dollar shortage" became a part of our language. This "dollar shortage" was alleviated in part by Marshall Plan grants and by other schemes, and the recipients rationed their scarce supplies of foreign exchange by means of strict exchange controls.

By the 1960's the countries of Western Europe were fully recovered from the effects of the Second World War and growing rapidly. Countries such as Germany, France, and Italy now have free, or virtually free, foreign exchange markets. Their currencies are as acceptable in world trade as the dollar; their "dollar shortage" has vanished.

However, many economically underdeveloped countries in Latin America, Asia, and Africa, are still seriously short of foreign exchange and still impose exchange control. The needs of these countries for imports to promote economic growth are great and their capacity to earn foreign exchange is limited. As a result, they have balance of payments problems and their governments have to ration out their scarce supply of foreign exchange, giving priority to essential imports.

In recent years, the International Monetary Fund, a spe-

cialized agency of the United Nations has assumed increasing importance.

The Fund is a pool of foreign currencies and gold contributed by more than a hundred nations, which can be drawn on by a member who is temporarily short of a particular foreign currency needed to buy imports or to meet debts. A member can "borrow" from the Fund only under certain conditions, and not indefinitely. As a short-run aid in stabilizing foreign exchange rates, the Fund is very useful. In any event, it is the principal medium for dealing with some of the international monetary problems in existence today.

INTERNATIONAL TRADE AND ECONOMIC GROWTH

The desire for economic development is now worldwide. It is characteristic of almost all countries today. It is much in evidence, for example, in the Soviet Union and China, where the communist authorities are bending every effort to promote increased output and industrial development. It is particularly intense in the countries of Latin America, Southeast Asia, and the Middle East. The basic needs of such countries as India, Brazil, and Turkey are capital, the development of technical and managerial skills among the population, and the development of stable political and economic institutions that will facilitate growth.

One way to acquire productive capital for economic development is to encourage domestic saving. The processes of domestic saving and investing can be helped by modern financial institutions, particularly a sound system of banking and credit. Most underdeveloped countries lack these. A more serious obstacle to domestic saving is poverty. The millions of people in India, for example, who are already living at the margin of subsistence can hardly abstain from consumption in order to save. The irony of the situation is that countries are poor because they lack capital, and they are unable to accumulate much capital because they are poor. A rich country like the United States, on the other hand, can devote a sizable part of its annual production to capital accumulation without any hardship.

Another way to acquire capital is to borrow it from more advanced countries. During the nineteenth century, the United States borrowed large amounts of capital from Great Britain. The *money capital* borrowed by selling bonds and stock to British investors was used in part to buy *capital goods*, such as railroad equipment and machinery, from abroad. Later, in the twentieth century, the United States not only became independent of foreign capital, but became able to lend capital to others.

What is the nature of the problem today? Why does not capital flow from the United States to the underdeveloped countries of Asia, the Middle East, and Latin America in the same adequate quantities that it once flowed from Europe to this country?

First, the political and social upheavals of the world today stand in the way of international investment. The world is torn by ideological conflict. Capitalism and property are subjected to the twin attacks of socialism and communism on the one hand, and nationalism on the other. Both present the threat of property expropriation or nationalization or, at the very least, rigid controls over its use. Second, there is no smoothly functioning mechanism for international payments comparable to the gold standard. Investors are reluctant to risk their money in a country with exchange control because they fear they may be unable to convert their earnings into the currency of their own country, or will suffer losses in doing so. It is hardly surprising, therefore, that capital does not flow freely. Most American capital investment abroad today goes either to countries like Venezuela or Saudi Arabia, where American firms are making direct investments in oil, or raw materials such as iron ore and bauxite, or to countries which are already well developed, such as England, the Common Market, and Canada. At the beginning of 1966, 31 per cent of the direct investments overseas of United States business were in Canada and 28 per cent in Western Europe. Only 7 per cent were in Asia.

The principal international investment institution is the International Bank for Reconstruction and Development, known as the World Bank. As one of the specialized agencies of the United Nations, the World Bank has a capital fund of $22.4 billion subscribed by more than 100 members. It makes loans out of this capital and also out of the proceeds from the sale of its bonds. These loans are designed to promote the long-run economic growth of the borrowing country. They are usually obtained for such purposes as improving transportation and communication, power facilities, and industrial equipment.

Several international investment institutions have been formed to accomplish specific development objectives. The International Finance Corporation, for example, was established in 1956 to channel "risk capital" into medium-sized manufacturing firms in the less developed countries.

The International Development Association (IDA) was started in 1960 to make long-term loans to the less developed countries on more liberal terms than the World Bank. Its loans have been interest-free and repayable over fifty years with no payments at all for the first ten years. The IDA was established as an affiliate of the World Bank to meet the criticism that the World Bank was too conservative in its lending policies.

The Inter-American Development Bank was established in 1960 by the Organization of American States to finance developmental projects in Latin America. Its members at present are the United States and all the Latin American republics except Cuba. In addition to its lending activities, the Inter-American Development Bank manages the Social Progress Trust Fund established by the United States in 1960 to channel funds into the development of housing and health and education facilities in Latin America. In 1966, an Asian Development Bank was established to help finance the economic development of that continent.

A foremost example of government lending abroad is the Export-Import Bank, which was established by the United States in 1934. Its original purpose was to make loans to finance American exports during the depression, but it has since become the principal medium for foreign lending by the United States Government to promote the national interest.

The United States has also concluded a number of "investment treaties" with foreign countries. It has tried to persuade those who need capital of the importance of creating an atmosphere favorable to private enterprise. The United States Government has encouraged foreign governments to guarantee that foreign property will not be expropriated, that the earnings of foreign investors will be convertible into the currency of their country, that foreign technicians will be allowed access to the country and so on. Turkey is an example of a country that has done this and has benefited accordingly. For its part, the United States is willing, under certain circumstances, to insure prospective American investors against loss of their property through expropriation and against loss of their earnings through inability to convert them into dollars.

Underdeveloped countries also seek the accumulation of technical skills that have been acquired in advanced countries over the years. It is useless to provide complicated pieces of capital equipment to people who lack the technical skill to operate them efficiently. Consequently, one of the most significant developments of recent years has been the initiation of programs to give technical assistance to underdeveloped areas. These programs are now being carried out by the United Nations, by the United States Government, and by several other countries.

The United Nations Development Program (UNDP) is a joint venture participated in by most of the UN's member nations. Under this program, experts of all nationalities in agriculture, public health, elementary education, public administration, and industrial development are sent to underdeveloped areas to survey local problems and to help the local people deal with them. Fellowships are provided so that persons from underdeveloped areas may go abroad and study to acquire the skills their homelands need. The United States program of technical assistance is carried out through agreements with the countries concerned. The Colombo Plan is a co-operative program involving the British Commonwealth and including such other countries as Indonesia, Burma, and Japan. It involves, among other things, a mutual exchange of technical services in Southeast Asia.

These investment and technical assistance programs can benefit both the underdeveloped countries and the advanced countries. In the underdeveloped country, resources can be developed, production increased, national income increased, and the inhabitants can enjoy rising living standards. An advanced country such as the United States—which provides the capital and technical assistance—may obtain new sources of supply for needed raw materials, and the creation of a more prosperous market for exports. For example, United States investments in Venezuela are opening iron ore mines the output of which is increasingly needed for our steel industry; the rising Venezuelan national income means not only a better life for the Venezuelan people but also a growing demand for American exports.

It is sometimes suggested that the United States will be harmed if its investments help create competitive industries in foreign countries. If the United States helps establish a textile industry in Iran, for example, the Iranians may stop buying American textiles. In the short run, of course, such problems of adjustment will arise. Usually the first industries to become established are those producing light consumer goods such as processed food, clothing, and furniture. As these become established, the immediate market for American food and clothing may be temporarily reduced. But the market for textile machinery, tools, and other American-made capital equipment will increase and, ultimately, economic development will lead to a growth in the total volume of trade. The greatest volume of trade and the most profitable economic relations today are between advanced countries with highly specialized production and high levels of income. For example, Canada with 19 million people is a far more important trading partner than Mexico with 40 millions.

Economic development abroad will require adjustments in the structure of production in the country that is exporting capital. But these adjustments cannot necessarily be considered "harmful". They are similar to the adjustments that must constantly be made as economic change occurs *inside* the United States. The railroads have had to adjust to the competition of automobiles, truck lines, and air lines; the motion picture industry to television; the silk manufacturers to nylon; the downtown department stores to suburban shopping centers; New England to the textile mills in the South; and hotels to motels. Economic growth and expansion are characterized by continual change and, as a result, adjustments of all kinds are constantly needed both in the United States and in the world economy. The long-run benefits are apparent; it is the day-to-day problems that are difficult.

"Economic development," strictly defined, means the development of the resources of a nation in a way that will contribute to a rising real income and expanding output and trade. For instance, in many countries, the first step should logically be the development of a more efficient agriculture. In the United States in 1965, only 6 per cent of the civilian labor force was engaged in agriculture; yet, because of the use of capital and scientific methods, this relatively small number of persons was able to produce more than enough food and fiber for the entire population. In most underdeveloped countries, however, virtually the whole population labors on the land to try to keep itself alive. A more efficient agriculture would release labor for use in industrial and commercial pursuits.

In many countries, however, development is thought of primarily in terms of factories. They want to industrialize rapidly because they feel that industrialization will bring not merely more goods but also military power, an advanced urban society, modern technology, and social institutions in keeping with nationalistic desires for recognition and status in the world. The mixture of economic and noneconomic considerations results in economic programs that are not always in the best interests of greater productivity and trade. Nevertheless, nationalism and the desire for industrial development and military power are the major facts of life today in most of Asia, Latin America, and the Middle East and seemingly are considered more important objectives than the most efficient use of resources.

WORLD TRADE AND ECONOMIC STABILITY

During the last thirty years, it has become clear that there is a close relationship between world trade and domestic stability. By virtue of its tremendous economic power, the United States may be a center of cyclical disturbance, transmitting depression or prosperity to the rest of the world.

If, for example, the United States has a depression, consumers reduce their demand for goods, and industry reduces its demand for raw materials. This decline in demand and production is likely to affect imports as well as domestic production. Thus the impact of an American depression will be felt by the foreign producers of these imports. As they will be selling less to the United States, they will have to curtail production, too. Inasmuch as they will be earning fewer dollars from exports to the United States, they will probably reduce their purchases of American goods.

On the other hand, if the American economy is booming, our rising national income will increase the demand of consumers and producers for both domestic goods and imports. Thus foreigners will be able to sell more goods to the United States; larger sales will stimulate income and employment abroad; and this higher income will tend to create a new demand for American products.

The United States exerts a greater influence on the world economy than any other country. American industries and households were responsible for the buying by the United States of about $33 billion worth of imported goods and services during 1965—more than one sixth of total world imports. The United States is, in other words, the greatest market in the world for exports of other countries. Indeed, Canada, Venezuela, the Philippines, and Brazil ship one quarter, one third, and even one half of their total exports to the United States. The prosperity of these and many other countries depends on their ability to sell in the American market—and on our ability and willingness to buy. As prosperity and political stability go together in some underdeveloped countries, the burden of responsibility resting on the United States is particularly great.

A decrease in national income and employment in the United States is often transmitted quickly to other countries. In 1949, for example, many other countries not only experienced recessions of their own, but also developed "dollar shortages," which forced them to restrict their imports. Even relatively mild and brief recessions in the United States, like that of 1954, can have a serious effect on the economies of other countries, because the "income elasticity of demand" for imports into the United States tends to be fairly high. This means that a small change in the national income will result in a rather large change in imports.

The countries that are most affected today by these declines in income and employment in the United States are the less developed ones which sell us raw materials. The experiences of the American recessions of 1957–58 and 1960–61 suggest that the industrialized countries of Western Europe can continue to enjoy prosperity and growth even though the United States does have a recession. But the less developed countries suffer a decline in their export earnings not only as a result of selling less to us but also because they sell at lower prices.

On the other hand, the great increase in American defense production following the outbreak of the Korean War caused an upsurge in our demand for raw materials all over the world. This demand forced up the prices of commodities and induced inflationary pressures in many other countries. Thus fluctuations in the level of income and employment in the United States are a matter of world-wide concern. A program for stabilizing American economic activity at a high and rising level is therefore important to both the United States and the world economy.

Let us now analyze a specific policy issue that has been of great concern to the American people for over ten years —foreign aid. We shall once again use the procedure outlined in Chapter 1 and seek in this way to gain more skill in dealing with economic problems.

Identify the Problem and the Issues

From the end of the Second World War through 1965, the United States supplied over $115 billion worth of foreign aid to other nations. This has been added to approximately $40 billion granted during the Second World War. Aid has gone to almost all countries except the major communist nations and has been given for a variety of military and economic purposes and in various forms. In recent years, the foreign aid programs have involved almost $4 to $5 billion per year.

Let us summarize the background for our present-day program. In the early postwar period, the bulk of American aid went to the countries of Western Europe. In 1949, for example, almost 80 per cent of our aid went to Western Europe. Great Britain, Germany, France, and Italy received the greatest share.

In recent years, however, such countries, having recovered their economic health, have themselves become donors of aid. The bulk of U.S. foreign aid today is going to the less developed countries of Asia and Latin America. Military aid has gone in substantial amounts to South Vietnam, Taiwan, Turkey, Pakistan, and others. The largest recipient of economic aid has been India but almost every noncommunist Asian country is receiving some help. And a substantial amount of economic aid has also gone to Latin America under the "Alliance for Progress" program.

The purpose for which the aid is given has also changed. In the years immediately following the Second World War, foreign aid was primarily economic—designed to alleviate the dollar shortage and to help reconstruct war-damaged economies. American contributions to the United Nations Relief and Rehabilitation Administration, the Treasury loan to Great Britain in 1946, and the European Recovery Program (Marshall Plan) grants were of this nature. During the 1945–48 period, foreign aid was conceived as a temporary program, which would come to an end as soon as the recipients recovered their economic health.

Gradually, however, the objectives of the United States foreign aid program became increasingly political and military in nature. The communist seizure of Czechoslovakia, the Berlin blockade, and above all the Korean War accelerated a military build-up of which foreign aid was a part. The Greek-Turkish Aid Program (Truman Doctrine) and the shipments of arms and other supplies to our allies in NATO and Southeast Asia, as well as to Spain, Yugoslavia, and Pakistan, illustrated the growing emphasis on political and military objectives. By the mid-1950's foreign aid was ceasing to be thought of as a temporary expedient; it was becoming an established part of our foreign policy.

In the early 1960's, although the emphasis on military aid was still strong, there was also an expansion of economic and technical assistance to underdeveloped areas. The purpose of such aid is to help such countries make a breakthrough into sustained economic growth. This, in turn, it is claimed, will contribute to expanding world trade and also to political stability in such areas.

The background and origin of these vast programs over a twenty-year period can be summarized simply. They stem first from the physical devastation and economic dislocation caused by the Second World War, second from efforts by the Communist Bloc to destroy, by one means or another, our type of society and to replace it with a communist society. American foreign aid has been regarded as one of our principal instruments for combating the threats of poverty and communist aggression, and it has played an extensive role in expediting development in many emerging nations.

Many Americans, however, are critical of the size of the foreign aid program and the way in which it is administered. They point out that the money comes from the pockets of American taxpayers, and they argue that the sums now involved could be reduced. Some also have grave doubts that the desired objectives will be achieved, and they believe that more attention should be paid to the impact of the program on such domestic matters as the level of federal spending and the national debt.

For example, it is argued that our aid does not win friends—that, on the contrary, we are arousing resentment and alienating those who dislike dependence on a "rich uncle." When aid is given, this question always arises: Should strings be attached? Should the United States seek to control its use and attach conditions to its receipt? One viewpoint is that attaching strings builds up a tremendous resentment among proud and sensitive people abroad. An opposite viewpoint says that strings are necessary to prevent waste and to ensure that the aid is used for the right purposes. Finally, some people feel the aid may defeat its own purpose; they believe that other countries are under insufficient pressure to exert themselves in their own interest so long as our aid is forthcoming.

The basic issues of foreign aid have changed over time, and they also are different from country to country. They are not only economic issues; they involve considerations of social, military, and political affairs as well. But we are concerned with a way to study the issues involved—therefore we must break the problem down to manageable size. One issue that stands out in much of the public debate is the question of taxes and foreign aid. This is the issue considered below.

Identify the Objectives

When the foreign aid program is analyzed, it becomes clear that a number of economic and foreign policy objectives of the American people come into conflict. Internationally, the United States wants to resist the spread of communism and, to this end, wants to have strong allies. In addition, the United States wants other countries to have strong economies so that they can co-operate in expanding world trade and investment.

Americans, however, also would like some relief from their tax burdens. In addition, many people are disturbed by the succession of unbalanced federal budgets in prosperous times. The key to these domestic objectives is a reduction in federal spending—and foreign aid is one area where some claim that cuts could be made.

The Alternatives

We shall explore only two of the alternative courses of action: (1) cut foreign aid and reduce taxes or (2) continue the program as it now exists. There are other alternatives, but these will illustrate some of the considerations in international economic policy.

What are the probable consequences of reducing the aid program and cutting taxes? Let us assume that the tax cut is equal to the cut in federal expenditures. Those who would cut the aid program and reduce taxes argue that a tax cut will boost our domestic economy and might help us achieve our international objectives. They point out that a tax cut can stimulate private investment—a strong program of domestic investment will help us to grow and maintain our economic lead over the rapidly growing economy of the Soviet Union. Furthermore, a prosperous domestic economy will be a market for foreign goods and therefore, other nations can obtain capital equipment from us by selling us what we need. In a word, they can grow via trade—not aid. Lastly, it is argued that private investments are more likely to be made overseas if investment incentives are not harmed by continued high taxation. They argue, therefore, that it is possible that the tax reduction might contribute greatly to continued international economic growth.

Those who support the second alternative—continuing the foreign aid program—point out that the foreign aid program is actually a type of insurance policy. If it helps to prevent war or an intense arms race, it will, in the long run save taxpayers' money. If we cease our aid program and lose some of our allies, the long-run costs of a direct defense system may be far more expensive.

Supporters of the foreign aid program point out that we cannot rely on tax cuts to provide domestic and international economic growth. It is true that tax cuts leave more funds in the hands of the public, but as this program also calls for a decline in federal spending, the level of national income may fall. Moreover, as some of our agricultural and manufacturing industries depend on foreign markets, they may have to curtail production. By cutting taxes and foreign aid, the problems of farm surpluses and unemployment may be aggravated.

The supporters of the present program note that if we tax for $5 billion and allow foreign governments to spend this on American goods and services, we are providing a full $5 billion of foreign assistance. But if we cut taxes, so that American citizens can spend the money, far less will be made available for other nations. American spending for foreign products will be a small part of the $5 billion. The supporters of foreign aid argue, therefore, that the tax cut might result in slower domestic economic growth and an inadequate flow of dollars for the use of other nations.

A continued foreign aid program can provide new skills

and capital to the nations abroad. The supporters of the present program argue that under present conditions, it is more effective than relying on private investment abroad. They agree that lower taxes will provide *some* stimulation to private investment, but they argue that the effect will be slight. The main barriers to private investment abroad by American firms are foreign controls over profits, possible foreign government seizure, exchange controls, and many red tape problems. A domestic tax reduction will not eliminate these barriers, but they might be reduced by a foreign aid program that brought nations together in co-operative ventures.

As we noted earlier, taxation is but one of the issues in the foreign aid question. Other issues such as the various types of aid, the place of foreign assistance in our worldwide foreign policy, the timing of cuts in federal spending and taxing, or the military aspects of foreign assistance cannot be explored here. What we have shown is that the problem cannot be viewed merely as a "give-away" program, nor can it be considered merely as a way of "advertising" the American economic system.

Appraise the Alternatives

There seems to be rather widespread agreement on the over-all objectives of foreign assistance. But important differences of opinion arise over the means of achieving the objectives. For this reason, it is highly important to carefully analyze the effects of different programs. It is especially important because the stakes are high and, in the long run, foreign economic policy may determine whether our economic and political system will survive.

This chapter has stressed these basic ideas:

1. International trade is an extension of the principle of specialization that exists within national boundaries. Specialization permits resources to be used in the production of goods and services where they will be comparatively most efficient. But specialization requires trade.

2. There are a number of political, economic, and social

barriers to international trade. These barriers hamper the growth of the level of living for the world as a whole. They may, however, contribute to specific national objectives of military security or the development of desired industries. The arguments for higher barriers to international trade emphasize specialized, short-run, or noneconomic objectives; those favoring freer trade are more general, long-run, and stress economic issues.

3. Our policy toward international trade has an effect on the economic growth and stability of nations abroad. Many of the conditions that have contributed to our economic development do not exist in other countries, but some of them can be transplanted. Because the economic development of other nations contributes to our own economic development, the measures we take to increase the technological equipment and skills of other peoples, are in the long run helping our own economic growth. Similarly, the efforts we make to stabilize our economy will help stabilize the economies of other nations.

Suggested Reading

Paul A. Samuelson, *Economics: An Introductory Analysis*, Chaps. 33–36, pp. 621–702. George L. Bach, *Economics: An Introduction to Analysis and Policy*, Chaps. 39–42, pp. 613–66. These selections examine the economic basis for international trade and some current problems in international economics.

A clear and nontechnical account of how foreign currencies are bought and sold is provided by the Federal Reserve Bank of Philadelphia in "The Foreign Exchange Market," reprinted in *Readings in Economics* (Samuelson et al., ed.), pp. 299–303. Other useful readings in the same volume include: "The Balance of Payments in Perspective," by the Federal Reserve Bank of St. Louis, pp. 303–9; "The Dollar and World Liquidity—A Minority View," by Emile Despres, C. P. Kindleberger, and Walter S. Salant, pp. 330–34; and "Foreign Aid: Strategy or Stopgap," by Barbara Ward Jackson, pp. 348–57.

Chapter 10

GOVERNMENT AND THE AMERICAN ECONOMY

Earlier chapters have shown that government has established such devices as money and the law of contracts to facilitate the free market exchange of goods and services—also, that government has set up tariffs and regulations to restrain or control free exchange.

We have seen that antimonopoly measures have been instituted to make competition a more effective regulatory force in the market—and that other measures, such as tariffs and agricultural price supports, have been instituted to restrain or alleviate the effects of competition.

It was shown in Chapter 6 that taxes and credit controls may be used to maintain the employment of our resources at a high level, and in Chapter 2 that taxes and public expenditures may be used to modify the pattern of income distribution. The purpose of this chapter is to explore the role of these and other governmental influences in the American economy.

THE SCOPE OF THE PUBLIC ECONOMY

The public economy (the government share of economic activity) has grown at an accelerated rate since 1900. In 1900, the *percentage* of the labor force working for governments was less than one third as large as it is today. About 1 worker out of 24 was employed by federal, state, or local governments in 1900; by 1965, about one out of seven workers was on a government payroll. Similarly, the share of the government in total production is estimated to be about four times as large today as it was in 1900. Total federal, state, and local government debts have grown even more rapidly in relation to private debts; in 1900, they were about 6 per cent of the total public and private debt, and in 1965, they were about one third of the total.

The increase in government expenditures shown in the accompanying chart is not a wholly accurate indication of the growth in governmental functions. Inflation accounts for part of the rise, because over the period since 1900 the price level has more than tripled. Moreover, spending does not indicate the significance of many governmental services. For example, the antitrust program involves very little spending yet has a great impact on the

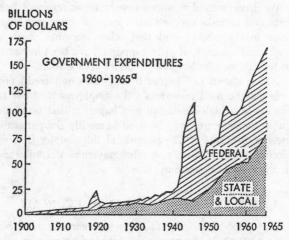

a Data from: U. S. Department of Commerce, *Government Finances in the United States, 1902 to 1957* (1959), annual issues of *Governmental Finances* (Bureau of the Census), and *Statistical Abstract of the United States, 1966* (Bureau of the Census), p. 418. Figures for some of the early years are estimated.

economy. With these limitations, however, we can get a general idea of the role of government by looking at its spending.

In 1965, the total payroll of governments (federal, state, and local) in the United States amounted to $67.8 billion. These payments may be compared with the payroll for private business in 1965 of $309.1 billion. In other words, *more than one fifth of the nation's payroll payments were made by governments.*

In the same year, the governments in the United States also purchased $68.4 billion worth of goods from private producers. These expenditures, combined with the payroll payments, brought the total government purchases of goods and services to $136.2 billion. As the gross national product in 1965 was $681.2 billion, *governments had purchased about 20 per cent of all the goods and services produced that year.*

In 1965, federal, state, and local governments made transfer payments (relief, social security, veterans' allowances, and so forth) and interest payments on government debt totaling $49.6 billion. Altogether, then, the *expenditures of national, state, and local governments amounted to $185.8 billion for the year.*

These expenditures were for a wide variety of services. A complete list of government operations that affect the economic system would require more pages than this chapter offers. A broad listing prepared by the Municipal Finance Officers Association reveals, however, a staggering array of governmental services (federal, state, county, city, and special district), classified under fifteen major headings:[1]

    I. Overhead Activities
   II. Protection to Persons and Property
  III. Highway Construction and Maintenance

[1] C. H. Chatters and M. L. Hoover, *An Inventory of Governmental Activities in the United States,* Municipal Officers Finance Association (1947), pp. 5–15.

IV. Development and Conservation of Natural Resources
V. Sanitation and Waste Removal
VI. Health
VII. Hospital
VIII. Public Assistance and Social Services
IX. Corrections
X. Social Insurance
XI. Housing and Home Ownership
XII. Educational Activities
XIII. Library Facilities
XIV. Public Recreation and Cultural Facilities
XV. Public Service Industries

For the range of governmental activities, let us look at a breakdown of just one of these classifications as presented by this survey. Class II, "Protection to Persons and Property," is further divided into eight headings, as follows:

A. National Defense
B. Police Protection and Law Enforcement
C. Fire Protection and Fire Fighting
D. Protective Inspectors
E. Regulation of Business and Industry
F. Insurance of Life, Money and Property
G. Other Protection Activities
H. Protection of Industrial Workers

Each of these items, in turn, embraces a long list of subordinate activities. Under the heading "E. Regulation of Business and Industry" are listed, for example:

1. Prevention or elimination of monopolies or trusts
2. Regulation of competitive practice
3. Banks and Banking
   a. Granting bank charters
   b. Conducting bank examinations
4. Credit institutions

5. Securities
   a. Regulation of sale
   b. Regulation of security exchanges
   c. Licensing security dealers
6. Insurance
   a. Establishment of insurance rates
   b. Inspection of financial status
   c. Granting right to do business
   d. Licensing of insurance agents
7. Transportation
   a. Railroads
   b. Interurban railroads
   c. Street railways
   d. Motor bus and truck companies
   e. Water carriers
   f. Air carriers
8. Transmission and sale of electricity and gas
9. Communications
   a. Telephone, telegraph, cable companies
   b. Radio broadcasting
10. Petroleum industry
11. Employment bureaus—private
12. Agriculture
    a. Inspecting and regulating warehouses
    b. Regulating commodity exchanges and futures
    c. Regulating and inspecting commission merchants

Each of these classifications, of course, covers a governmental activity the cost and effect of which are not even remotely suggested by the modest listing in the survey. As we shall see, they all influence, directly or indirectly, the operation of the economy—whether these effects are intended or not.

The scope of federal economic activities is indicated by the major economic legislation and administrative action taken in recent years. In 1965, for example, the federal government created a Department of Housing and Urban

Development; authorized federal aid for the economically depressed 11-state Appalachian region; authorized a program of grants to school districts with low-income families; expanded the Manpower Development and Training Program; authorized a 25 per cent increase in United States contributions to the International Monetary Fund; authorized reduction of the silver content in half dollars and the production of quarters and dimes without silver content; enacted a health care insurance program for persons 65 and over and a 7 per cent increase in social security benefits; established a program of rent supplements for low-income families; created a new Water Pollution Administration and provided for control of air pollution from automotive exhausts; provided for removal of billboards and junkyards from interstate highway systems; extended existing farm programs covering wheat, wool, and feed grains and provided new programs for dairy products and cotton; authorized a national Teacher Corps to improve education in slums and provided scholarships and guaranteed loans for college students; and revised and extended through 1971 the quotas on domestic and imported sugar.

WHY HAVE THE ACTIVITIES OF GOVERNMENT GROWN?

Defense needs, the cold war, and a variety of international commitments have greatly enlarged the economic impact of the federal government. When a society has been confronted by the problem of national survival, its efforts have turned to the production of the things needed to win a war—the services of soldiers for the battlefront must be supported by vast quantities of goods and services. Moreover, as wars have become more technical, dependent on greater industrial resources and scientific research, the economic burden placed on society has increased. All this activity is funneled through the national government—the only instrument that society has for coordinating individual efforts in a major national emergency. In recent years, defense and defense-related expenditures have amounted to over 70 per cent of total federal outlays. In the fiscal year 1965, for instance, federal expenditures were allocated as follows:

FEDERAL BUDGET EXPENDITURES, FISCAL 1965[a]

Item		Percentage of Total Expenditure
Expenditures resulting from past wars and defense		72.9
Defense Dept. and atomic energy	52.0	
International affairs and mutual security	4.5	
Veterans' Administration	5.7	
Interest on the war debt	10.7	
Other expenditures		27.1
Space research and technology	5.3	
Health, labor and welfare	6.1	
Agriculture and natural resources	7.9	
Commerce and transportation	3.6	
Others	4.2	
Total federal expenditures		100.0

[a] *Statistical Abstract of the United States, 1966*, p. 391.

The portion of the budget spent for "other" includes all of the so-called "normal" activities and "welfare" activities of the federal government. These, too, have grown over the years, but not steadily. In the postwar period of 1946–48, for instance, these "other" activities cost less than in 1940—primarily because depression relief and agricultural surpluses were less of a problem.

Population growth has led to a long-run expansion of governmental activities. The population of the United States in 1965 was more than double what it was in 1900, and nearly 60 per cent larger than it was in 1930. As a result, many areas that were formerly sparsely populated have been turned into urban and suburban communities that need all the services usually provided by government.

This growth has required government to build more schools, roadways, and sewer lines, to dispose of more garbage, to put out more fires, and to build more jails and hospitals.

A rising level of living for consumers has prompted a rising level of governmental services. Bigger and faster automobiles have required the replacement of two-lane highways by four- and six-lane freeways with cloverleaf intersections. As more people plan to send their children to college, they require larger and better equipped state colleges and universities. As the well-being of the society has grown, more attention has been given to health, sanitation, libraries, and a host of other ingredients of a high level of living. As many of these services are best provided by government, its economic role has expanded.

Governmental activities have expanded as a result of efforts to resolve group conflicts. As noted in earlier chapters, a breakdown in any part of a highly specialized economy may be of vital concern to the entire society. Conflicts between groups, such as the conflict between labor and management and between the agricultural and industrial sectors of the economy, have led to broad governmental programs. These programs have attempted to settle disputes and also to change the relative economic power of the groups involved. Child labor laws, bankruptcy laws, factory inspection, and workmen's compensation are some of the ways that governments have attempted to protect the economically weak from the strong. Protection of society from the conflict of interests between society and particular groups has led to monopoly laws and the regulation of public utilities. As society has become more complex and more specialized, governmental intervention to resolve such conflicts has tended to grow.

The expansion of governmental functions has been furthered by a changing attitude of the public toward the use of government to provide security against many economic risks. One of these risks is the risk of depression. Some reasons for the reaction of society to depressions have been suggested in earlier chapters and need only be mentioned here. Ours is a complex urban society. When people move to cities, they are dependent upon a vast system of production and exchange for the necessities of life. In earlier days, when a large share of the population lived on farms, most people could at least produce for themselves in a period of declining economic activity. The conveniences of life might not be forthcoming, but life could go on. In an urban, specialized, industrial society, a large part of the working population has no way to produce for itself—in depression, an unemployed factory worker may be completely without means of livelihood. Thus economic decline is regarded as a social problem—a problem that the individual cannot, by himself, solve. The primary instrument we have today for dealing with this social problem is government.

Depression results in a contraction in the flow of income. Therefore, in order to maintain the level of national income, the government now uses a variety of monetary and fiscal controls. But the flow of a man's income can also be stopped by accident or old age. Therefore various levels of government attempt to diminish this personal risk by workmen's compensation, unemployment compensation, and old-age payments.

There is scarcely a group in the United States that has not shifted some of its economic risks to the government. Depositors in banks and savings associations have deposit insurance, farmers have crop insurance, lenders have housing mortgage insurance, veterans have life insurance, some businesses have obtained fair trade laws protecting them from some of the risks of competition, others have obtained tariffs, others have tax privileges that reduce the risks of investment, and so on. The very length of the list suggests that the American people as a whole place great value on economic security. In doing so, they have contributed to the growth in governmental activities.

As governmental activities expanded, there was also a shift of many state and local responsibilities to the national government. Most of what is called "social legislation"—care for the aged, unemployment relief, aids to agriculture, regulation of monopolies, regulation of financial institutions, and so on—first appeared at the state or local level of government. But as the country grew and became more closely knit, affairs in Kansas or Louisiana affected the welfare of the people of New Jersey or Oregon; hence, they were no longer left to the exclusive discretion of the states. Furthermore, some of the problems became too large for state or local resources—unemployment relief during the depression, for example. In many of these instances, the conflict between "states rights" and "federal power" was resolved in favor of the level of government that was willing and able to assume the economic costs of the program—the federal government.

Nevertheless, state and local governments still provide most of the funds for education and other nondefense purposes. The demand for these services has increased greatly in recent years, placing major stresses on the taxing systems of these governments. As a consequence, problems of tax reform and tax co-ordination are attracting increasing attention. One novel proposal provides for returning a portion of federal tax revenues to the states in the form of unrestricted federal grants.

To summarize, the growth of governmental activities has been due to a variety of factors, but mainly to:

War and Defense. This requires a mobilization of an important part of the national economy, the continuation of services for veterans, and the maintenance of allied nations as strong political, military, and economic powers.

Economic fluctuations. This brings about the development of programs of unemployment relief and the use of governmental controls to limit the range of economic fluctuations.

Economic growth. This has caused an expansion of governmental services not only for a wider area and a larger number of people, but also for improvements in the quality and variety of governmental services to keep pace with the improvements in our over-all level of living.

Resolving conflicts within the economy. This has resulted in the government influencing the economic power of conflicting groups and, in some instances, determining the characteristics of their operations.

The quest for economic security. This has been reflected in a variety of programs designed to diminish many of the risks of economic activity in a modern industrial society.

HOW DOES THE GOVERNMENT INFLUENCE THE OPERATION OF THE ECONOMY?

Government provides the necessary framework for private economic activity. Without certain basic institutions and practices, an elaborate system of production and exchange like ours could not develop. Vital to our economy are the institution of private property, enforceable contracts, a regulated money system, individual rights, and a system of justice.

The institution of private property is established and maintained by government. Without government, a man's property rights would generally be only as strong as his ability to keep others from taking his possessions. Federal, state, and local governments enforce property rights (even against themselves and against each other) and, in doing so, they maintain a source of economic incentive for many of the productive activities of the people.

Government provides the economy with the legal basis for free contracts. This basic feature of the economy sanctions agreements among individuals, permitting them to join together for collective production and to enter into transactions with one another. They may, however, receive support from the law only if their contractual agreements do not harm the public interest (they cannot band together for the purpose of monopolizing the market, for instance). As co-operation among individuals is a necessary part of an economy based on the division of labor, the contract laws that facilitate co-operation are major requirements for our type of system. Together with governmental sanction for the corporate form of business, the law of contracts, which requires people to perform contracts as agreed to, is a fundamental requirement for countless business transactions.

The federal government has established a monetary system. Money provides a standard unit by which individuals may compare the value of commodities. It is a medium of exchange that permits trading without the hindrances of bartering. To protect the usefulness of money, the government defines its characteristics and establishes the conditions under which it is issued. As the government has granted commercial banks the authority to create deposits, which constitute the major part of the nation's money supply, governmental control of commercial banks is essential for an orderly monetary system.

The freedoms enumerated in the Bill of Rights, a system of administering justice, equal protection under the law, "due process" (prohibiting government from depriving any person of "life, liberty, or property" without recourse to the standard protections of the legal system), have all helped to determine the basic characteristics of the American economic system. They have facilitated the growth of organized production and exchange in an environment of individual freedom.

Government promotes and aids various types of economic activities. Public policy is used regularly to encourage and discourage various lines of development. In addition, private activities are facilitated by governmental agencies that gather and supply essential information and that foster the health and economic capabilities of the people.

Encouragement to specific kinds of production shifts the allocation of the nation's economic resources. For years the federal government has used tariffs to encourage the production of certain goods that might be supplied by foreign competitors. Many state and local governments have used their powers and public monies to support the construction of roadways, canals, and railroads. The federal government also contributed, by its land grants, to the development of a railroad system. Governments have issued franchises, assuring freedom from competition to producers of various services. Loans and direct subsidies have been made to farmers, airlines, electric power companies, shipping companies, and metal producers. In recent years, state governments, interested in economic development, have offered tax advantages and a variety of other benefits to new industries.

In addition to these promotional activities, governments also provide a vast number of continuing aids to the economy. The results of governmental research are made available to the public through publications provided by government. The commerce departments of the federal and state governments provide statistics on incomes, shipping, sales, and a variety of other data needed for business planning. Agriculture departments supply information on crops, insecticides, erosion control, farm management, and many other productive aids to farmers. Governments maintain port facilities and highways, provide weather bulletins, job training assistance, health information, education, and poor relief—the list of such governmental aids to the economy is almost inexhaustible. In supplying these aids, the government not only influences the use of the nation's economic resources but it also contributes to the growth of the national income.

Control or regulation of certain economic activities is undertaken to foster social objectives. Government at times intervenes in behalf of the public to outlaw undesirable practices or to impose restrictions on private conduct. It regulates monopolies and establishes many of the standards for private economic operations. Producers may not advertise falsely, refuse to bargain with their employees' representatives, issue fraudulent securities, or produce certain products considered to be dangerous to the health, safety, or morals of the public.

281

The government, through regulation, has established a wide range of so-called "welfare activities." Inasmuch as the government establishes the conditions under which the economy will operate, those conditions must change as social objectives change. Thus employers may no longer hire child labor or pay wages below the minimum established by the government. Producers must pay some of the costs of protecting their workers from loss of income due to accidents, unemployment, or old age. Factories must be inspected for safety; doctors, pharmacists, and many other producers must be licensed by the state; and home construction must meet certain standards.

Regulation sometimes leads to detailed direction of economic activity. The Interstate Commerce Commission, the Federal Power Commission, and state public utility commissions, to mention a few, have strong powers to determine the prices, service, and production of the activities they control. As described in Chapter 3, these regulatory bodies are generally set up when the free market is unable to provide a check on the activities of the producers. Similarly, the Federal Trade Commission investigates and regulates for the purpose of maintaining a competitive economy.

Economy-wide regulation has also been applied from time to time—generally during emergencies. The National Recovery Administration of the 1930's, the Office of Price Administration of the 1940's and the Office of Price Stabilization of the 1950's are examples of governmental regulation of prices for the whole economy. Similarly, other controls, such as wage ceilings, output quotas for farmers, and regulations over bank loans, have been used by government to compel economic activity to meet certain social objectives.

Government takes over the ownership of some forms of economic activity. When private operation or regulated operation does not yield the results desired, government sometimes engages directly in the production of the needed goods and services.

There are many reasons for governmental enterprises such as municipal water systems, schools, transportation systems, state liquor monopolies, insurance programs, federal credit agencies and electric power installations. In some instances, these government-owned enterprises have involved activities that were provided by private enterprise until they became unprofitable. In others, the government has entered the field in order to regulate the consumption of the product or because it is a good source of revenue. Private producers have sometimes been displaced because it was felt that they were attempting to "gouge the public." On occasion, the government has undertaken such operations because the magnitude of the task to be performed was beyond the resources of private producers. And some governmental enterprises came into being partly to provide the government with a "yardstick" to measure the performance of private producers.

The lending activities of the federal government furnish a useful illustration of governmental operation to provide needed services and to facilitate economic development. By establishing a number of agencies, the government has entered the business of banking and finance. Its loans increased from $4.2 billion in 1946 to more than $30 billion by 1964. Principal lending agencies include:

Export-Import Bank
Federal National Mortgage Association
Farmers Home Administration
Public Housing Administration
Rural Electrification Administration
Area Redevelopment Administration
Small Business Administration
Department of Health, Education, and Welfare
Agency for International Development
Housing and Home Finance Agency
Veteran's Administration

Not all of federal credit agencies lend money—some of them merely guarantee loans or deposits made by private lenders. Each is designed to reduce the difficulty of obtaining credit in a particular field—by placing the credit of the government behind that of the borrower. What is important is that each is also part of a larger program designed to increase the attractiveness of some type of economic activity.

Government also pursues policies intended to influence the over-all level of economic activity. For this purpose, it may use many of the programs described above, although its major instruments are those that tend to have a broad impact on every aspect of the economy—taxes, expenditures, and controls over important categories of private economic activity.

The stabilization of the level of income and employment has become an accepted economic activity of the federal government. Its major tools for this purpose are the fiscal and monetary controls discussed in Chapter 7. During war, however, the government may expand its controls and adapt many of its existing regulations, aids, and other programs to the larger purposes of expanding and directing nation-wide production and to controlling prices. Price and wage controls, rationing, and priorities are frequently used to meet such emergencies. Furthermore, monopoly controls may be relaxed, credit regulations may be changed, taxes on investments may be reduced, and governmental operation of enterprises may be expanded to meet the immediate necessities of war. Over-all control of the economy in wartime generally results in setting aside temporarily many of the basic features of our economic system.

In summary, governmental activity affects the operation of the economy by:

Providing some of the necessary framework for private economy activity;

Promoting and aiding various kinds of private activity;

Controlling and regulating certain types of private economic activity;

Owning and operating some forms of economic activity;
Influencing the level of income and employment.

These governmental activities have determined some of
the basic characteristics of the American economic system.
In earlier chapters, the basic functions of an economic
system were outlined as follows: the system must provide
a way to decide what shall be produced, how it will be
produced, and who shall get the resulting production. In
this country, these decisions are made largely by the day-
to-day operations of the free market, which, in principle,
allows each individual to choose what he wants for himself within the limitations of his ability to produce and to
compete with others.

If such a system operates in a society, with only a few
basic rules supplied by government, it will in a given period yield a certain level of national income, a certain
distribution of national income, and a certain allocation of
national resources to various types of production. The primary significance of governmental economic activity is
that *it will change these results*—and the objective of public policy is that these changes will improve the results.

Whatever the government does will, directly or indirectly, affect national income and production. The following are some of the ways this influence might be felt if, for
instance, the government should decide to spend $5 bil-
lion for schools:

1. *The allocation of resources will be different from
what it would have been without the governmental program.* Unless there are unemployed resources (natural resources, labor, capital, and skills) available, there will first
be a shift of resources into the production of goods for
schools. If the government obtains the $5 billion by taxing
or borrowing from the public, resources will not go into
producing those things that people would have bought if
they had kept their money. For instance, somewhat fewer
houses and home furnishings and more schools, desks, and
blackboards will be produced. The national income will
be produced differently and will consist of different items.

2. *The program of the government will influence the way the national income is distributed.* This changed allocation of resources will probably occur as a result of changing prices (if all the resources are fully employed). For the government to get the materials for its building program, it will have to bid them away from present uses; it will have to pay enough to cause workers and other resources to shift into the production of things for schools. If the level of national income remains the same, those who receive incomes from producing school goods will tend to receive a larger share, and those in the other industries a smaller share of the national income.

3. *The program could change the level of resource use and the level of national income.* If there are unemployed resources available, the decision to build schools may not only shift the *allocation* of resources, but it may also change the *amount* of resources used. This might happen if the program changed aggregate demand in the economy. If the additional taxes to pay for the program are paid without a corresponding drop in private spending, total spending will rise and the level of production and employment will tend to rise. This in turn may stimulate further growth in the national income as the multiplier principle goes into action. If the funds to pay for the schools are raised by borrowing from the banking system, the stimulus will be even greater. On the other hand, if the taxes that are levied should cause a sharp cut in private spending by more than $5 billion, the governmental program could conceivably lead to a decline in the over-all level of national income and employment.

The taxes must be collected by some plan. They might be collected according to a "benefit principle" so that the people pay taxes in accordance with the benefit they would be expected to derive from the schools; or they might be taxed according to their "ability to pay" so that those who were deemed least able to afford the tax would pay less, and others would pay proportionately more. The tax might also be made an equal amount for everyone. Or it could be a sales tax so that the individual paid in relation to his purchases of taxable goods; it could be a progressive income tax or a proportional income tax; it could be a property tax (not for the federal government, however), or it could be a tax on corporation income, liquor, gasoline, or imported commodities. Whichever tax is used will have an influence on some people that it does not have on others. Whatever way the tax burden is distributed will influence the distribution of "after-tax income" and will therefore influence the way the nation's disposable income is spent. Moreover, if the tax reduces the rewards of some kinds of business, again, the allocation of resources and the composition of national income will be changed. If it seriously distorts the pattern of incentives for the whole society, it may lead to a decline in economic effort and a reduction in the level of resources used. If it increases the volume of total spending, it will raise the *level* of national income.

The indirect effects of governmental policy may be more significant than the observable direct results. In the above illustration, the direct effect may have been more schools and higher taxes, but the indirect effects on the level, composition, and distribution of national income would significantly influence the ultimate welfare of the public. Similarly, a change in the credit policy of the Federal Reserve System means much more than, say, rising reserve requirements for commercial banks. It will influence the credit terms for lenders in general. It will mean that certain things will not be produced that would otherwise have been produced, and vice versa. The distribution of income will be different and the level of employment may be changed—indeed, the whole complexion of the economy can be changed by the chain of consequences.

If the government supports subsidies for agriculture, "fair trade" laws, tariffs, or electric power plants, it will change the characteristics of the nation's income and production from what they would be if the forces of the free market were allowed to operate without the additional influence of government. Moreover, even though the government does not spend any more than is required for administering the necessary agencies, such activities as anti-monopoly laws, deposit insurance, "fair labor standards," or security regulations will change the pattern of the economy. In other words by setting the "rules of the game" the government takes some decisions away from the area of individual discretion—in doing so, it modifies the performance of the economic system.

It is because *the government can change the operation of the economy that society uses governmental processes.* As many of the chapters in this book have shown, the public does not believe that the results obtained from the free market are always the most desirable. Through the government, the public has modified the operation of the economy by a variety of controls, aids, sanctions, regulations, and other activities. The result is a "mixed economy," in which government and the free market are combined to determine the level, composition, and distribution of the nation's production.

SOME PROBLEMS OF DETERMINING GOVERNMENTAL ECONOMIC POLICIES

One of the most important problems confronted by society is to decide what governmental policies should be. What exactly is it that the American people want their government to do? As noted earlier, the answers to this question are constantly changing. Moreover, it is not sufficient to say, for example, that "full employment" is an objective; as shown in Chapter 6, there are varying degrees of full employment. Broad generalizations do not provide adequate guides for economic policy. Ultimately, governmental policy is determined on specific issues, and broad policies—such as "conservation of resources," "maintaining competition," "a fair distribution of income"—must constantly be interpreted or redefined to fit these specific issues.

Deciding what governmental policy will be is further complicated by the fact that the public has conflicting objectives. Some people want high interest rates, and others want a large volume of credit, some want a large defense program, and others want a relaxation of economic controls or lower taxes—somehow, these conflicting objectives must be resolved. Governmental economic activity, therefore, is similar to private economic activity in that it involves "economizing." The government cannot do everything it may want to do (even if people are willing to have it do so), because whenever one thing is done, another thing cannot be done. For example, if the government gets out of the electric power field, it cannot develop the power at Niagara Falls; if it uses protective tariffs, it must give up some aspects of a policy of "trade—not aid"; if it buys shoes for soldiers from producers in New England, it cannot buy as many from producers in the Midwest. A basic task of government, then, is to decide which of a variety of alternative courses will yield the greatest social benefits in relation to the social costs.

Deciding between alternatives by measuring a benefit-cost relationship is not easy. Consumers in the market place can make such benefit-cost measures when they are considering alternative purchases. They do so by comparing the benefits they expect to receive from a known purchase with those they expect to receive by spending their money for something else. But in contemplating a governmental program, the process is much more complicated. The cost of an anti-depression program, for instance, involves more than the money spent by the government; it may also involve the loss of a certain amount of economic freedom for producers, the use of some of the nation's resources in a seemingly wasteful manner, a tendency to create expectations that the government will solve economic problems, the erection of trade barriers between this and other nations, the actual destruction of some of the nation's production, or shifts in the balance of economic power among various groups in the society. How is the citizen to measure these costs to enable him to compare them with the benefits of the program? What are the benefits of the program? Precise measurement of the economic, political, and social consequences of governmental policy is virtually impossible.

Except in the very broadest terms, the citizen does not attempt to weigh costs versus benefits. When the voter is given an opportunity to vote directly on a given issue (such as a school bond issue), he can perform such a calculation. He can compare the monetary and other costs with the benefits—as he sees them from a personal or social point of view. On most issues, though, the citizen cannot do this. The costs may be unknown and the benefits highly uncertain. Moreover, he often must choose by voting for a representative who will vote on this and many other issues. The citizen, in other words, often casts his vote for a vast complex of decisions—he votes for "a package" and must take the bad with the good. It is not possible to say, therefore, that governmental policy is a reflection of the rational cost-benefit calculations of the people. The most that can be said is that governmental policy can represent, in a very general way, the broad consensus of desires of the people.

It is sometimes suggested that the problem would be simplified if the government would adopt a few basic "principles" and live by them. But government operates under constantly changing conditions, and principles that are broad enough to offer guidance for all conditions are usually too broad to offer a basis for choice in a particular situation. For example, considerable effort has been made to follow the principle of "maintaining a free competitive system." But it is sometimes argued that the way to preserve the system is to abandon the principle in particular instances. In the end, principles that cannot be uniformly followed become themselves matters of choice. No short cut to an estimate of benefits and costs exists for the public official, the legislator, or the citizen.

Public policy decisions are influenced by group or sec-

tional pressures. The activities of lobbies in securing the passage of legislation favorable to the groups they represent have become a basic part of governmental processes in this country. By being on the scene when legislation is being considered, by providing details on the issues involved (details favorable to their position), and by developing "contacts" among the administrators of governmental programs, lobbies can influence the course of governmental activities. The growing number of lobbies in the federal and state capitals indicates the importance of this type of activity—it also indicates, perhaps, that the effectiveness of any given lobby can be offset by another. Thus some legislative proposals evolve into quarrels between representatives of opposing groups, for example, between the National Association of Manufacturers and the Congress of Industrial Organizations, between milk producers and margarine producers.

Additional influence on public policy comes from governmental officials. Administrative officials in government have ideas about how a program should be carried out; they are seldom mere automatons who carry out a definite program set down by the people. In fact, the range of discretion provided by legislation leaves a vast number of decisions to the administrative branch of government. The officials, therefore, argue for the kind of program that will, in their view, be better from the standpoint of society or from that of their own agency. Moreover, conflicts between agencies frequently arise. For instance, the national park system must frequently battle with other governmental agencies that want to use the parks for other purposes, and there is a long history of conflict between the Army Corps of Engineers and the Bureau of Reclamation of the Department of the Interior over the development of the nation's rivers.

These are but a few of the problems associated with attempts of society to accomplish social objectives through the instrument of government. Several points bear emphasizing. The government is more than a collection of individuals. Decisions regarding governmental action are not made in the same way that private decisions are made. The machinery of government becomes more complicated as the role played by the government becomes larger; it is frequently too complicated to understand, in all its minute details. Nevertheless, careful analysis of particular activities can yield greater understanding of the important consequences of governmental policy. And as careful and dispassionate economic analysis is more widely employed, public policies may be more rationally chosen to promote an effective economy and the general welfare.

An Illustrative Problem

This book has noted a number of economic policies supported by government, and we have illustrated a way to examine them. Our goal has been to develop the skills needed to understand and evaluate the stream of economic proposals that always confront us. To do this, we must understand how our economy works, and we must press our economic reasoning beyond the obvious relationships.

To illustrate: Because of the mounting volume of automobile traffic the nation has embarked on a multi-billion dollar highway building program designed to meet the needs of 1975. Beyond the obvious impact on the convenience and safety of highway traffic and beyond the question of the cost of the program, there are a number of significant economic issues that can be explored.

How should money be raised for such public projects? By more progressive income taxation, by an additional gasoline tax, or by tolls paid by the users of the new roads? Should the road system be paid for on a "pay as you go" basis or should the government borrow? What effect will increased debts have on the economy? Will the financial system absorb these debts without reducing other loans, or will the increase in highway bonds lead to curtailment of other business and consumer borrowing? What will happen to the money supply and interest rates?

How will the road system and all of its implications contribute to the economic growth of the nation? How will it affect productivity? Will it increase the flow of savings to private investment? Or will it lead largely to greater consumption?

Where will the roads be built? To what extent will they bring the agricultural sector of the economy into closer contact with urban centers? Will the roads be designed to reduce congestion in the rapidly growing urban areas? Or will the road-building be done in depressed areas to provide jobs for "pockets" of unemployed workers?

To what extent will this system result in a partial subsidy to trucking firms, allowing them to compete more readily with railroads? Should construction contracts be given to the lowest bidder, or should they be distributed so that big business and small business both get a share? Will the government insist that all materials be bought in the United States even if some of them can be obtained more cheaply abroad?

What about the timing of such a program? Should the program be pushed irrespective of the level of economic activity, or should it wait until more people are looking for work? If it is to be timed to fit into an anti-depression program, how much of a slowdown in economic activity would be needed before it would be advisable to get under way?

Throughout this book, we have noted a number of economic objectives of the American people. These, too, must be considered in exploring the highway proposal. The effect of the program on these objectives may be great, or it may be slight. The effect may be direct and obvious, or it may be indirect and obscure. From one standpoint, it may advance us toward a certain objective; from another standpoint, it may retard us. To illustrate the effects of such a program, the list of objectives on pages 3–4 might be applied to the highway proposal—how might each of the objectives be affected by the program?

As we have noted before, decisions on proposals must be made. And if we want to have a role in deciding the economic conditions under which we live, we must help make these decisions. If we do not, someone else will. All of us can do a better job of establishing such policy if we undertake a careful analysis of our goals and alternative methods of attaining them.

Suggested Reading

George L. Bach, *Economics: An Introduction to Analysis and Policy*, Chap. 37, pp. 576–90. Paul A. Samuelson, *Economics: An Introductory Analysis*, Chap. 8, pp. 139–69. These selections cover three major topics: (1) the expansion of the functions of government, (2) the economic problems of war mobilization, and (3) the similarities and differences between the American economy and those economic systems in which government plays a larger role. Most of the selections in *Readings in Economics* (Samuelson et al., eds.) are related in one way or another to the issues of the economic role of government. See especially, "Best Tax System Yet," by Joseph A. Peckman, pp. 89–95; "On Improving the Economic Status of the Negro," by James Tobin, pp. 405–9; and "Planning and the Market in the U.S.S.R.," by Abram Bergson, pp. 433–36.

INDEX

Absolute advantage theory, 237

Acceleration principle, 157–58

"Actual GNP," 174

Advertising, 23, 69, 70–71

AFL-CIO, 85, 95; membership *table*, 85

Aggregate demand, 148–49, 150, 151, 156, 163, 164, 167, 185, 188

Agriculture: and the Clayton Act, 62; employment in, 36, 259; modernization of, 220, 259; output of, 209; subsidies to, 27, 146, 163, 186, 189

Alliance for Progress, 263

Aluminum Company of America, 60

American Bankers Association, 181

"The American Economy, Prospects for Growth Through 1980 . . . ," 222*n*

American Federation of Labor, 82, 85, 95

America's Needs and Resources, 205*n*, 214*n*

Antimerger Act, 59, 74, 76

Antitrust measures, 58–79

Antitrust and Monopoly Subcommittee, Senate Judiciary Committee, 65*n*, 66*n*

Appalachian Program (1965), 168, 174

Arbitration, compulsory, in labor disputes, 107, 108

Area Redevelopment Act, 168

Asian Development Bank, 256

Assets. *See* Capital

Automatic fiscal stabilizers, 186, 193, 194

Automation: and employment, 166; future of, 220; and unions, 94, 98–99

Balance of payments, 244, 249–53, *table*, 247–48

Bankruptcy, 128–29

Banks. *See* Financial institutions

Benefit-cost relationship. *See* Services

Bethlehem Steel, 73

Bill of Rights, 280

Boycotts, union, 87, 90

Brand names, 64, 69–71

Brown Shoe Company, 74

Budget, balanced, 185, 190, 265

Budgetary policy. *See* Fiscal policy

"Built-in" fiscal stabilizers, 186

Bureau. *See under* names of individual government bureaus